Middle Ages
Almanac

Middle Ages Almanac

JUDSON KNIGHT

Edited by Judy Galens

AN IMPRINT OF THE GALE GROUP

DETROIT · NEW YORK · SAN FRANCISCO
LONDON · BOSTON · WOODBRIDGE, CT

Judson Knight

Judy Galens, *Editor*

Staff

Diane Sawinski, *U•X•L Senior Editor*
Carol DeKane Nagel, *U•X•L Managing Editor*
Thomas L. Romig, *U•X•L Publisher*

Margaret Chamberlain, *Permissions Associate (Pictures)*
Maria Franklin, *Permissions Manager*

Randy Bassett, *Imaging Database Supervisor*
Daniel Newell, *Imaging Specialist*
Pamela A. Reed, *Image Coordinator*
Robyn V. Young, *Senior Image Editor*

Rita Wimberley, *Senior Buyer*
Evi Seoud, *Assistant Production Manager*
Dorothy Maki, *Manufacturing Manager*

Pamela A. E. Galbreath, *Senior Art Director*
Kenn Zorn, *Product Design Manager*

Marco Di Vita, the Graphix Group, *Typesetting*

Cover photograph of crusaders disembarking in Egypt reproduced by permission of the Corbis Corporation.

Library of Congress Cataloging-in-Publication Data

Knight, Judson
    Middle ages. Almanac / Judson Knight ; Judy Galens, editor.
        p. cm.
    Includes bibliographical references and index.
    ISBN 0-7876-4856-6
        1. Middle Ages—History. 2. World history. 3. Civilization, Medieval. I.
Galens,   Judy, 1968- II. Title.

    D117.A2 K65 2000
    909.07–dc21

                                          00-059442
                                            CIP

Printed in the United States of America
10 9 8 7 6 5 4 3 2

Contents

Reader's Guide

The Middle Ages was an era of great changes in civilization, a transition between ancient times and the modern world. Lasting roughly from A.D. 500 to 1500, the period saw the growth of the Roman Catholic Church in Western Europe and the spread of the Islamic faith in the Middle East. Around the world, empires—the Byzantine, Mongol, and Incan—rose and fell, and the first nation-states emerged in France, England, and Spain. Despite the beauty of illuminated manuscripts, soaring Gothic cathedrals, and the literary classics of Augustine and Dante, Europe's civilization lagged far behind that of the technologically advanced, administratively organized, and economically wealthy realms of the Arab world, West Africa, India, and China.

Middle Ages: Almanac offers a comprehensive overview of this period, these empires, and the societies they created. Several of its nineteen chapters are devoted to specific eras, such as the Carolingian Age (about 750–1000) and the late Middle Ages (1300–1500), while others focus on geographical regions, including China, Africa, Eastern Europe, and the Americas. Distinct ethnic and religious groups, among them the Jewish people; the Mongols; the Arabs, Turks, and other Middle Eastern peoples; the Ghanaians, Songhai, and Malians of West Africa; and the Maya and Aztecs of Central America are extensively covered as well.

Additional features

Nearly one hundred illustrations and maps and dozens of sidebar boxes exploring high-interest topics bring the text to life. Definitions of unfamiliar terms and a list of books and Web sites to consult for more information are included in each chapter. The volume also contains a timeline of events, a general glossary, research and activity ideas, and an index offering easy access to the people, places, and subjects discussed throughout *Middle Ages: Almanac.*

Dedication

To Margaret, my mother; to Deidre, my wife; and to Tyler, my daughter.

Comments and suggestions

We welcome your comments on this work as well as your suggestions for topics to be featured in future editions of *Middle Ages: Almanac.* Please write: Editors, *Middle Ages: Almanac,* U•X•L, 27500 Drake Rd., Farmington Hills, MI 48331-3535; call toll-free: 1-800-877-4253; fax: 248-699-8097; or send e-mail via www.galegroup.com.

Timeline of Events in the Middle Ages

122 Roman forces begin building Hadrian's Wall, a barrier intended to protect Roman citizens from Picts, or native Scots, on the isle of Britain. The wall is a sign that the Roman Empire has ceased to expand and will begin to shrink in coming years.

135 Banished from Jerusalem by the Romans, Jews begin to spread throughout the Mediterranean.

180 The death of Roman emperor Marcus Aurelius marks the end of the "Pax Romana," or Roman peace. Years of instability follow, and although Rome recovers numerous times, this is the beginning of Rome's three-century decline.

220 The Han dynasty of China comes to an end, plunging the country into three centuries of turmoil.

c. 300 Mayan culture enters the Classic Period, which lasts until 925, during which time the Maya undertake the vast majority of their most important building projects.

300s	Buddhism, which originated in India, begins to take hold in China.
312	Roman emperor Constantine converts to Christianity. As a result, the empire that once persecuted Christians will embrace their religion and eventually will begin to persecute other religions.
325	Constantine calls the Council of Nicaea, first of many ecumenical councils at which gatherings of bishops determine official church policy.
325	King Ezana of Aksum accepts Christianity. Eventually most of Ethiopia will become Christianized as a result.
330	Constantine establishes Byzantium as eastern capital of the Roman Empire.
372	Headed westward, the Huns cross the Volga River, displacing the Ostrogoths and setting in motion a chain reaction that ultimately leads to the downfall of the Western Roman Empire.
395	After the death of Emperor Theodosius, the Roman Empire is permanently divided in half. As time passes, the Eastern Roman Empire (later known as the Byzantine Empire) distances itself from the declining Western Roman Empire.
410	Led by Alaric, the Visigoths sack Rome, dealing the Western Roman Empire a blow from which it will never recover.
429	Having subdued Gaul (France) and Spain, the Vandals cross the Mediterranean to North Africa and conquer most Roman territories there.
Mid-400s	Angles, Saxons, and Jutes from Scandinavia invade the former Roman colony of Britain.
451	Roman troops score their last important victory, against Attila's Huns in Gaul.
455	The Vandals sack Rome.
476	The German leader Odoacer removes Emperor Romulus Augustulus and crowns himself "king of Italy." This incident marks the end of the Western Roman Empire.

481 The Merovingian Age, named for the only powerful dynasty in Western Europe during the period, begins when Clovis takes the throne in France.

500 Date commonly cited as beginning of Middle Ages.

500–1000 Era in European history often referred to as the Dark Ages, or Early Middle Ages.

529 Benedict of Nursia and his followers establish the monastery at Monte Cassino, Italy. This marks the beginning of the monastic tradition in Europe.

534–563 Belisarius and other generals under orders from Justinian recapture much of the Western Roman Empire, including parts of Italy, Spain, and North Africa. The victories are costly, however, and soon after Justinian's death these lands will fall back into the hands of barbarian tribes such as the Vandals and Lombards.

535 Justinian establishes his legal code, a model for the laws in many Western nations today.

540 The Huns, or Hunas, destroy India's Gupta Empire, plunging much of the Indian subcontinent into a state of anarchy.

541 The Byzantine Empire is hit by the first wave of a plague that will continue to strike off and on for the next two centuries. Millions of people die in these epidemics, which greatly weaken the once-powerful empire.

563 Irish monk St. Columba forms the first important monastic settlement in the British Isles, at Iona off the coast of Scotland. In years to come, with Western Europe's cultural center in Italy under attack from barbarians, monks in places such as Iona and Lindisfarne help preserve reading and writing.

568 The last wave of barbarian tribes descends on Italy as the Lombards invade. They will control the peninsula until 756.

589 More than three centuries of upheaval in China come to an end with the establishment of the Sui dynasty.

590 Pope Gregory I begins his fourteen-year reign. Also known as Gregory the Great, he ensures the survival of the church and becomes one of its greatest medieval leaders.

Late 500s Invading Europe, a tribe called the Avars introduces the stirrup, which they picked up in their migration from Central Asia. By making horsebound combat possible, the stirrup ultimately paves the way for knighthood and feudalism.

618   A revolt against the cruel Sui dynasty leads to the establishment of the highly powerful and efficient T'ang dynasty in China.

622   Arab prophet Muhammad and his followers escape the city of Mecca. This event, known as the *hegira*, marks the beginning of the Muslim calendar.

632–661 Following the death of Muhammad, the Arab Muslims are led by a series of four caliphs who greatly expand Muslim territories to include most of the Middle East.

661   The fifth caliph, Mu'awiya, founds the Umayyad caliphate, which will rule the Muslim world from Damascus, Syria, until 750.

680   Husayn, son of Ali (the fourth caliph, assassinated in 661), leads an unsuccessful revolt against Umayyad rule. As a result, his supporters, the Shi'ite Muslims—whose power base is chiefly in Persia—break away from the majority, who are called Sunni Muslims.

711   Moors from North Africa invade Spain, taking over from the Visigoths. Muslims will rule parts of the Iberian Peninsula until 1492.

711   Arabs invade the Sind in western India, establishing a Muslim foothold on the Indian subcontinent.

727   In Greece, the Iconoclasts begin a sixty-year war on icons, or images of saints and other religious figures, which they consider idols. Though the Greek Orthodox Church ultimately rejects iconoclasm, the controversy helps widen a growing division between Eastern and Western Christianity.

732   A force led by Charles Martel repels Moorish invaders at Tours, halting Islam's advance into Western Europe.

The battle firmly establishes the use of armored cavalrymen (in other words, knights) in warfare.

750   A descendant of Muhammad's uncle Abbas begins killing off all the Umayyad leaders and establishes the Abbasid caliphate in Baghdad, Iraq.

751   The Carolingian Age begins when Charles Martel's son Pepin III, with the support of the pope, removes the last Merovingian king from power.

751   Defeated by Arab armies at Talas, China's T'ang dynasty begins to decline. A revolt led by An Lu-shan in 755 adds to its troubles.

756   Pepin defeats the Lombards in Italy and in an act called the Donation of Pepin turns their lands over to the church. This creates the Papal States, which will exist for more than eleven hundred years.

768   Reign of Charlemagne, greatest ruler of Western Europe during the Early Middle Ages, begins.

793   Viking raiders destroy the church at Lindisfarne off the coast of England. Lindisfarne was one of the places where civilized learning had weathered the darkest years of the Middle Ages. Thus begins two centuries of terror as more invaders pour out of Scandinavia and spread throughout Europe.

800   Pope Leo III crowns Charlemagne "Emperor of All the Romans." This marks the beginning of the political alliance later to take shape under Otto the Great as the Holy Roman Empire.

c. 800   The Khmers, or Cambodians, adopt Hinduism under the leadership of their first powerful king, Jayavarman II, founder of the Angkor Empire.

800s   Feudalism takes shape in Western Europe.

820   A group of Vikings settles in northwestern France, where they will become known as Normans.

827   Muslims take Sicily, which they will hold until 1072. Later in the 800s, they very nearly win control of Italy itself.

843   In the Treaty of Verdun, Charlemagne's son Louis the Pious divides the Carolingian Empire among his three

sons. These three parts come to be known as the West Frankish Empire, consisting chiefly of modern France; the "Middle Kingdom," a strip running from what is now the Netherlands all the way down to Italy; and the East Frankish Empire, or modern Germany. The Middle Kingdom soon dissolves into a patchwork of tiny principalities.

862   A group of Vikings called the Varangians invade Eastern Europe, where they come to be known as *Rus,* the first Russians. Under the leadership of Rurik, they establish the city of Novgorod and found a dynasty that will remain in power for more than seven centuries.

907   China's T'ang dynasty comes to an end after almost three centuries of rule, and the empire enters a period of instability known as "Five Dynasties and Ten Kingdoms."

910   Establishment of the Benedictine monastery at Cluny in France signifies a recovery of the church, whose leaders had become increasingly corrupt in the preceding centuries.

911   The last of the Carolingian line in the East Frankish Empire dies. Seven years later, Henry the Fowler of Saxony, father of Otto the Great, takes leadership of the German states.

960   The Oghuz, a group of Turks that includes the Seljuks, convert to Islam.

960   Beginning of the Sung dynasty in China.

962   Having conquered most of Central Europe, Otto the Great is crowned emperor in Rome, reviving Charlemagne's title. From this point on, most German kings are also crowned ruler of the Holy Roman Empire.

987   Russia converts to Greek Orthodox Christianity and gradually begins adopting Byzantine culture after Vladimir the Great marries Anne, sister of Emperor Basil II.

987   The last Carolingian ruler of France dies without an heir, and Hugh Capet takes the throne, establishing a dynasty that will last until 1328.

1000–1300 Era in European history often referred to as the High Middle Ages.

1000s Guilds, which had existed in ancient times but disappeared from Western Europe during the Early Middle Ages, come back into existence.

1001 Vikings led by Leif Eriksson sail westward to North America and during the next two decades will conduct a number of raids on the coast of what is now Canada.

1001 A second Muslim invasion of the Indian subcontinent, this time by Turks, takes place as the Ghaznavids subdue a large region in what is now Afghanistan, Pakistan, and western India.

1025 Basil II dies, having taken the Byzantine Empire to its greatest height since Justinian five centuries earlier; however, it begins a rapid decline soon afterward.

1035 Death of Canute, the last great Viking ruler, who briefly controlled England, Denmark, and Norway.

1054 After centuries of disagreement over numerous issues, the Greek Orthodox Church and the Roman Catholic Church officially separate.

1060 Five years after Turks seize control of Baghdad from the declining Abbasid caliphate, their leader, Toghril Beg, declares himself sultan and thus establishes the Seljuk dynasty.

1066 William the Conqueror leads an invading force that defeats an Anglo-Saxon army at Hastings and wins control of England. The Norman invasion is the most important event of medieval English history, greatly affecting the future of English culture and language.

1071 The Seljuk Turks defeat Byzantine forces at the Battle of Manzikert in Armenia. As a result, the Turks gain a foothold in Asia Minor (today known as Turkey) and the Byzantine Empire begins a long, slow decline.

1071 A Norman warlord named Robert Guiscard drives the last Byzantine forces out of Italy. Byzantium had controlled parts of the peninsula since the time of Justinian.

1072 Robert Guiscard's brother Roger expels the Arabs from Sicily and takes control of the island.

1075–77 Pope Gregory VII and Holy Roman Emperor Henry IV become embroiled in a church-state struggle called the Investiture Controversy, a debate over whether popes or emperors should have the right to appoint local bishops. Deserted by his supporters, Henry stands barefoot in the snow for three days outside the gates of a castle in Canossa, Italy, waiting to beg the pope's forgiveness.

1080 Invaders from Morocco destroy Ghana, the first significant kingdom in sub-Saharan Africa.

1084 Reversing the results of an earlier round in the Investiture Controversy, Henry IV takes Rome and forcibly removes Gregory VII from power. The pope dies soon afterward, broken and humiliated.

1092 Following the death of their sultan Malik Shah, the Seljuk Turks begin to decline.

1094 Norman warrior Bohemond, son of Robert Guiscard, takes control of Rome from Henry IV and hands the city over to Pope Urban II. Fearing the Normans' power and aware that he owes them a great debt, Urban looks for something to divert their attention.

1095 Byzantine Emperor Alexis Comnenus asks Urban II for military assistance against the Turks. Urban preaches a sermon to raise support at the Council of Clermont in France, and in the resulting fervor the First Crusade begins. Among its leaders are Bohemond and his nephew Tancred.

1096–97 A pathetic sideshow called the Peasants' Crusade plays out before the real First Crusade gets underway. The peasants begin by robbing and killing thousands of Jews in Germany; then, led by Peter the Hermit, they march toward the Holy Land, wreaking havoc as they go. In Anatolia a local Turkish sultan leads them into a trap, and most of the peasants are killed.

1097–99 The armies of the official First Crusade conquer Edessa and Antioch, the first of several "crusader states."

1099 The First Crusade ends in victory for the Europeans as they conquer Jerusalem. It is a costly victory, however—one in which thousands of innocent Muslims, as well as many Europeans, have been brutally slaughtered—and it sows resentment between Muslims and Christians that remains strong today.

c. 1100–1300 Many of the aspects of life most commonly associated with the Middle Ages, including heraldry and chivalry, make their appearance in Western Europe during this period. Returning crusaders adapt the defensive architecture they observed in fortresses of the Holy Land, resulting in the familiar design of the medieval castle. This is also the era of romantic and heroic tales such as those of King Arthur.

1100s Beginnings of medieval trading fairs in Champagne and Flanders, a sign of Europe's reawakening.

c. 1100 Inca civilization emerges in South America. Around this time, the Incas establish Cuzco (now in Peru), the oldest continually inhabited city in the New World.

1113 Founding of the first great chivalric order, the Knights Hospitalers.

1119 Founding of the Knights Templars, the second of the three great chivalric orders.

1127 An invasion by the Juchen nomads forces the Chinese to move their capital from Kaifeng southward to Hangchow. This marks the end of the Northern Sung period and the beginning of the Southern Sung.

c. 1140 In Cambodia Khmer emperor Suryavarman II develops the splendid temple complex of Angkor Wat.

1146 After the Muslims' capture of Edessa in 1144, Pope Eugenius III calls on the help of his former teacher, Bernard of Clairvaux, who makes a speech that leads to the launching of the Second Crusade.

1147–49 In the disastrous Second Crusade, armies from Europe are double-crossed by their crusader allies in the Latin Kingdom of Jerusalem. They fail to recapture Edessa and suffer a heavy defeat at Damascus.

c. 1150 Romanesque, the dominant style of architecture in Western Europe since about 1000, gives way to the much more ornate and advanced style of Gothic. Also in this period the art of stained-glass windows reaches its height.

1158 Holy Roman Emperor Frederick I Barbarossa establishes Europe's first university at Bologna, Italy.

1159 Frederick I Barbarossa begins a quarter-century of fruitless, costly wars in which the Ghibellines and Guelphs—factions representing pro-imperial and pro-church forces, respectively—fight for control of northern Italy.

1160 German cities begin banding together to form the Hanseatic League, designed to help them secure greater trade privileges in international markets.

1163 Building begins on the Cathedral of Notre Dame in Paris, perhaps the most well known example of Gothic architecture.

1165 A letter supposedly written by Prester John, a Christian monarch in the East, appears in Europe. Over the centuries that follow, Europeans will search in vain for Prester John, hoping for his aid in their war against Muslim forces. Even as Europe enters the modern era, early proponents of exploration such as Henry the Navigator will remain inspired by the quest for Prester John's kingdom.

1182 France under Philip II Augustus becomes the first European country to expel all its Jews.

1183 Frederick I Barbarossa signs the Peace of Constance with the cities of the Lombard League, thus ending his long war in northern Italy. After this he will concentrate his attention on Germany and institute reforms that make him a hero in his homeland.

1185 For the first time, Japan comes under the rule of a shogun, or military dictator. Shoguns will remain in power for the next four centuries.

1187 Muslim armies under Saladin deal the crusaders a devastating blow at the Battle of Hittin in Palestine.

Shortly afterward, Saladin leads his armies in the re-conquest of Jerusalem.

1189   In response to Saladin's victories, Europeans launch the Third Crusade.

1191   Led by Richard I of England and Philip II of France, crusaders take the city of Acre in Palestine.

1191   Founding of the Teutonic Knights, the last of the great chivalric orders.

1192   Richard I signs a treaty with Saladin, ending the Third Crusade.

1198   Pope Innocent III begins an eighteen-year reign that marks the high point of the church's power. Despite his great influence, however, when he calls for a new crusade to the Holy Land, he gets little response—a sign that the spirit behind the Crusades is dying.

c. 1200 Cambodia's Khmer Empire reaches its height under Jayavarman VII.

1202   Four years after the initial plea from the pope, the Fourth Crusade begins. Instead of going to the Holy Land, however, the crusaders become involved in a power struggle for the Byzantine throne.

1204   Acting on orders from the powerful city-state of Venice, crusaders take Constantinople, forcing the Byzantines to retreat to Trebizond in Turkey. The Fourth Crusade ends with the establishment of the Latin Empire.

1206   Qutb-ud-Din Aybak, the first independent Muslim ruler in India, establishes the Delhi Sultanate.

1206   Genghis Khan unites the Mongols for the first time in their history, and soon afterward leads them to war against the Sung dynasty in China.

1208   Pope Innocent III launches the Albigensian Crusade against the Cathars, a heretical sect in southern France.

1212   The pathetic "Children's Crusade" ends with most of its participants captured and sold into slavery in the Middle East.

1215 In Rome, Pope Innocent III convenes the Fourth Lateran Council. A number of traditions, such as regular confession of sin to a priest, are established at this, one of the most significant ecumenical councils in history.

1215 English noblemen force King John to sign the Magna Carta, which grants much greater power to the nobility. Ultimately the agreement will lead to increased freedom for the people from the power of both king and nobles.

1217–21 In the Fifth Crusade, armies from England, Germany, Hungary, and Austria attempt unsuccessfully to conquer Egypt.

1227 Genghis Khan dies, having conquered much of China and Central Asia, thus laying the foundation for the largest empire in history.

1228–29 The Sixth Crusade, led by Holy Roman Emperor Frederick II, results in a treaty that briefly restores Christian control of Jerusalem—and does so with a minimum of bloodshed.

1229 The brutal Albigensian Crusade ends. Not only are the Cathars destroyed, but so is much of the French nobility, thus greatly strengthening the power of the French king.

1231 Pope Gregory IX establishes the Inquisition, a court through which the church will investigate, try, and punish cases of heresy.

c. 1235 The empire of Mali, the most powerful realm in sub-Saharan Africa at the time, takes shape under the leadership of Sundiata Keita.

1236 Mongol forces enter Russia and within a few years subdue the land, which becomes known as the Empire of the Golden Horde.

1239–40 In the Seventh Crusade, Europeans make another failed attempt to retake the Holy Land.

1241 After six years of campaigns in which they sliced across Russia and Eastern Europe, a Mongol force is poised to take Vienna, Austria, and thus to swarm into Western Europe. But when their leader, Batu Khan, learns that the Great Khan Ogodai is dead, he rushes back to the Mongol capital at Karakorum to participate in choosing a successor.

1243   Back on the warpath, but this time in the Middle East, the Mongols defeat the last remnants of the Seljuk Turks.

1248–54 King Louis IX of France (St. Louis) leads the Eighth Crusade, this time against the Mamluks. The result is the same: yet another defeat for the Europeans.

c. 1250 The Aztecs settle in central Mexico.

1252   In Egypt, a group of former slave soldiers called the Mamluks take power from the Ayyubid dynasty, established many years before by Saladin.

1253   Mongol armies force the Thais from southern China into Southeast Asia, where they are destined to become the dominant power in later centuries.

1258   Hulagu Khan, who controls Mongol forces in southwestern Asia, kills the last Abbasid caliph and declares the region a separate khanate under his leadership as "Il-khan."

1260   The Mamluks become the first force to defeat the Mongols, in a battle at Goliath Spring in Palestine.

1260   Kublai Khan, greatest Mongol leader after his grandfather Genghis Khan, is declared Great Khan, or leader of the Mongols.

1261   Led by Michael VIII Palaeologus, the Byzantines recapture Constantinople from the Latin Empire, and Byzantium enjoys one last gasp of power before it goes into terminal decline.

1270–72 In the Ninth Crusade, last of the numbered crusades, King Louis IX of France again leads the Europeans against the Mamluks, who defeat European forces yet again.

1271   Marco Polo embarks on his celebrated journey to the East, which lasts twenty-four years.

1273 The Hapsburg dynasty—destined to remain a major factor in European politics until 1918—takes control of the Holy Roman Empire.

1273 Italian philosopher and theologian Thomas Aquinas completes the crowning work of his career, the monumental *Summa theologica*. The influential book will help lead to wider acceptance of the idea, introduced earlier by Moses Maimonides, Averroës, and Abelard, that reason and faith are compatible.

1279 Mongol forces under Kublai Khan win final victory over China's Sung dynasty. Thus begins the Yüan dynasty, the first time in Chinese history when the country has been ruled by foreigners.

1281 A Mongol force sent by Kublai Khan on a second attempt to take Japan—a first try, in 1274, also failed—is destroyed by a typhoon. The Japanese call it a "divine wind," or *kamikaze*.

1291 Mamluks conquer the last Christian stronghold at Acre, bringing to an end two centuries of crusades to conquer the Holy Land for Christendom.

1294 At the death of Kublai Khan, the Mongol realm is the largest empire in history, covering most of Asia and a large part of Europe. Actually it is four empires, including the Golden Horde in Russia; the Il-Khanate in the Middle East and Persia; Chagatai in Central Asia; and the Empire of the Great Khan, which includes China, Mongolia, and Korea. Within less than a century, however, this vast empire will have all but disappeared.

1299 Turkish chieftain Osman I refuses to pay tribute to the local Mongol rulers, marking the beginnings of the Ottoman Empire.

1300–1500 Era in European history often referred to as the Late Middle Ages.

1303 After years of conflict with Pope Boniface VIII, France's King Philip the Fair briefly has the pope arrested. This event and its aftermath marks the low point of the papacy during the Middle Ages.

1309 Pope Clement V, an ally of Philip the Fair, moves the papal seat from Rome to Avignon in southern France.

c. 1325 The Aztecs establish their capital at Tenochtitlán, on the site of present-day Mexico City.

1337 England and France begin fighting what will become known as the Hundred Years' War, an on-again, off-again struggle to control parts of France.

1347–51 Europe experiences one of the worst disasters in human history, an epidemic called the Black Death. Sometimes called simply "the Plague," in four years the Black Death kills some thirty-five million people, or approximately one-third of the European population in 1300.

1368 A group of Chinese rebels overthrows the Mongol Yüan dynasty and establishes the Ming dynasty, China's last native-born ruling house.

1378 The Catholic Church becomes embroiled in the Great Schism, which will last until 1417. During this time, there are rival popes in Rome and Avignon; and from 1409 to 1417, there is even a third pope in Pisa, Italy.

1389 Ottoman forces defeat the Serbs in battle at Kosovo Field. As a result, all of Southeastern Europe except for Greece falls under Turkish control.

1392 General Yi Song-ye seizes power in Korea and establishes a dynasty that will remain in control until 1910.

c. 1400 Melaka, or Malaya (modern-day Malaysia), adopts Islam. In later years, it will become a center for Muslim culture in Southeast Asia.

1402 After conquering much of southwestern and central Asia, Tamerlane defeats the Ottoman sultan Bajazed in battle. An unexpected result of their defeat is that the Ottomans, who seemed poised to take over much of Europe, go into a period of decline.

1413 India's Delhi Sultanate comes to an end. As a result, power in the subcontinent is splintered between the Hindu kingdom of Vijayanagar in the south and smaller Muslim states in northern and central India.

1415 English forces under King Henry V score a major victory against the French at Agincourt, one of the most important battles of the Hundred Years' War.

1417 The Council of Constance ends the Great Schism, affirming that Rome is the seat of the church and that Pope Martin V is its sole leader. Unfortunately for the church, the Great Schism has weakened it at the very time that it faces its greatest challenge ever—a gathering movement that will come to be known as the Reformation.

1418 The "school" of navigation founded by Prince Henry the Navigator sponsors the first of many expeditions that, over the next forty-two years, will greatly increase knowledge of the middle Atlantic Ocean and Africa's west coast. These are the earliest European voyages of exploration, of which there will be many in the next two centuries.

1428 In Southeast Asia, Vietnam unites under the leadership of the Le dynasty, which will turn the country into a regional power and control it until 1788.

1429 A tiny French army led by Joan of Arc forces the English to lift their siege on the town of Orléans, a victory that raises French spirits and makes it possible for France's king Charles VII to be crowned later that year. This marks a turning point in the Hundred Years' War.

1430–31 Captured by Burgundian forces, Joan of Arc is handed over to the English, who arrange her trial for witchcraft in a court of French priests. The trial, a mockery of justice, ends with Joan being burned at the stake.

1431 In Southeast Asia, the Thais conquer the Angkor Empire.

1431 The Aztecs become the dominant partner in a triple alliance with two nearby city-states and soon afterward gain control of the Valley of Mexico.

1438 Pachacutec Inca Yupanqui, greatest Inca ruler, takes the throne.

1441   Fourteen black slaves are brought from Africa to Portugal, where they are presented to Prince Henry the Navigator. This is the beginning of the African slave trade, which isn't abolished until more than four centuries later.

1451   The recovery of the Ottoman Empire, which had suffered a half-century of decline, begins under Mehmet the Conqueror.

1453   The Hundred Years' War ends with French victory.

1453   Turks under Mehmet the Conqueror march into Constantinople, bringing about the fall of the Byzantine Empire. Greece will remain part of the Ottoman Empire until 1829.

1455   Having developed a method of movable-type printing, Johannes Gutenberg of Mainz, Germany, prints his first book: a Bible. In the years to come, the invention of the printing press will prove to be one of the most important events in world history. By making possible the widespread distribution of books, it will lead to increased literacy, which in turn creates a more educated, skilled, and wealthy populace. It will also influence the spread of local languages, and thus of national independence movements, and also spurs on the gathering movement for religious reformation.

1455   Just two years after losing the Hundred Years' War to France, England is plunged into the Wars of the Roses, which will last until 1485.

1464   In the last-ever crusade, Pope Pius II attempts to retake Turkish-held Constantinople for Christendom. However, he dies en route to Greece, bringing the crusading movement to an end.

1472   Ivan the Great of Muscovy marries Zoë, niece of the last Byzantine emperor, and adopts the two-headed Byzantine eagle as the symbol of Russia—the "Third Rome" after Rome itself and Byzantium. His grandson, Ivan the Terrible, will in 1547 adopt the title *czar*, Russian for "caesar"—title of Roman and Byzantine emperors for the past fifteen hundred years.

1492 Spain, united by the 1469 marriage of its two most powerful monarchs, Ferdinand II of Aragon and Isabella I of Castile, drives out the last of the Muslims and expels all Jews. A less significant event of 1492, from the Spanish perspective, is the launch of a naval expedition in search of a westward sea route to China. Its leader is an Italian sailor named Christopher Columbus, who has grown up heavily influenced by Marco Polo's account of his travels.

1500 Date commonly cited as the end of Middle Ages, and the beginning of the Renaissance.

1517 Exactly a century after the Council of Constance ended the Great Schism, a German monk named Martin Luther publicly posts ninety-five theses, or statements challenging the established teachings of Catholicism, on the door of a church in Germany. The popes had managed to crush earlier efforts at reform, such as those led by Jan Hus of Bohemia, who was burned at the stake under orders from the Council of Constance. By now, however, the movement called the Reformation is much stronger, and Luther is far from its only leader. Over the next century, numerous new Protestant religious denominations will be established.

1521 Spanish forces led by the conquistador Hernán Cortés destroy the Aztec Empire.

1526 Babur, a descendant of Tamerlane, invades India and establishes what becomes the Mogul Empire.

1533 Francisco Pizarro and the Spanish forces with him arrive in Peru and soon bring about the end of the Inca Empire.

1591 Songhai, the last of the great premodern empires in Africa's Sudan region, falls to invaders from Morocco.

1806 In the process of conquering most of Europe, Napoleon Bonaparte brings the Holy Roman Empire to an end.

1912 More than twenty-one centuries of imperial rule in China end with the overthrow of the government by revolutionary forces, who establish a republic.

1914	On the 525th anniversary of the Serbian loss at Kosovo Field—June 28, 1389—Serbian nationalist Gavrilo Princip fires a shot at Hapsburg heir Franz Ferdinand. This begins World War I.
1918	Among the many outcomes of World War I are the disintegration of several empires with roots in the Middle Ages: the Austro-Hungarian, Ottoman, and Russian empires.
1960s	Nearly a thousand years after Leif Eriksson and other Vikings visited the New World, archaeologists find remains of a Norse settlement in Newfoundland.
1975	The African nations of Mozambique and Angola, former Portuguese possessions, become the last major colonies acquired in the Age of Exploration to gain their independence.
1979	The Shi'ite Muslim movement, which began almost exactly thirteen hundred years before, enters world headlines as Shi'ite fundamentalists seize control of Iran.
1989	As Communism begins to disintegrate, Europe gradually becomes more united than it has been since the Roman Empire began to decline eighteen centuries earlier.
1989	A Serbian commemoration of the 600th anniversary of Kosovo Field on June 28, 1989 marks the beginning of resurgent Serbian nationalism. In the decade that follows, the Balkans will once again be the site of a great religious and ethnic power struggle, with Serbia backed by its Greek Orthodox ally Russia against the Catholic Croatians and Bosnian Muslims.

Words to Know

A

Age of Exploration: The period from about 1450 to about 1750, when European explorers conducted their most significant voyages and travels around the world.

Alchemy: A semi-scientific discipline that holds that through the application of certain chemical processes, ordinary metals can be turned into gold.

Algebra: A type of mathematics used to determine the value of unknown quantities where these can be related to known numbers.

Allegory: A type of narrative, popular throughout the Middle Ages, in which characters represent ideas.

Anarchy: Breakdown of political order.

Ancestor: An earlier person in one's line of parentage, usually more distant in time than a grandparent.

Anti-Semitism: Hatred of, or discrimination against, Jews.

Antipope: A priest proclaimed pope by one group or another, but not officially recognized by the church.

Archaeology: The scientific study of past civilizations.

Archbishop: The leading bishop in an area or nation.

Aristocracy: The richest and most powerful members of society.

Ascetic: A person who renounces all earthly pleasures as part of his or her search for religious understanding.

Assassination: Killing, usually of an important leader, for political reasons.

Astronomy: The scientific study of the stars and other heavenly bodies, and their movement in the sky.

B

Barbarian: A negative term used to describe someone as uncivilized.

Bishop: A figure in the Christian church assigned to oversee priests and believers in a given city or region.

Bureaucracy: A network of officials who run a government.

C

Caliph: A successor to Muhammad as spiritual and political leader of Islam.

Caliphate: The domain ruled by a caliph.

Canonization: Formal declaration of a deceased person as a saint.

Cardinal: An office in the Catholic Church higher than that of bishop or archbishop; the seventy cardinals in the "College of Cardinals" participate in electing the pope.

Cavalry: Soldiers on horseback.

Chivalry: The system of medieval knighthood, particularly its code of honor with regard to women.

Christendom: The Christian world.

Church: The entire Christian church, or more specifically the Roman Catholic Church.

City-state: A city that is also a self-contained political unit, like a country.

Civil service: The administrators and officials who run a government.

Civilization: A group of people possessing most or all of the following: a settled way of life, agriculture, a written language, an organized government, and cities.

Classical: Referring to ancient Greece and Rome.

Clergy: The priesthood.

Clerical: Relating to priests.

Coat of arms: A heraldic emblem representing a family or nation.

Commoner: Someone who is not a member of a royal or noble class.

Communion: The Christian ceremony of commemorating the last supper of Jesus Christ.

Courtly love: An idealized form of romantic love, usually of a knight or poet for a noble lady.

D

Dark Ages: A negative term sometimes used to describe the Early Middle Ages, the period from the fall of Rome to about A.D. 1000 in Western Europe.

Deity: A god.

Dialect: A regional variation on a language.

Diplomacy: The use of skillful negotiations with leaders of other nations to influence events.

Duchy: An area ruled by a duke, the highest rank of European noble below a prince.

Dynasty: A group of people, often but not always a family, who continue to hold a position of power over a period of time.

E

Economy: The whole system of production, distribution, and consumption of goods and services in a country.

Ecumenical: Across all faiths, or across all branches of the Christian Church.

Empire: A large political unit that unites many groups of people, often over a wide territory.

Epic: A long poem that recounts the adventures of a legendary hero.

Ethnic group: People who share a common racial, cultural, national, linguistic, or tribal origin.

Excommunicate: To banish someone from the church.

F

Famine: A food shortage caused by crop failures.

Fasting: Deliberately going without food, often but not always for religious reasons.

Feudalism: A form of political and economic organization in which peasants are subject to a noble who owns most or all of the land that they cultivate.

G

Geometry: A type of mathematics dealing with various shapes, their properties, and their measurements.

Guild: An association to promote, and set standards for, a particular profession or business.

H

Hajj: A pilgrimage to Mecca, which is expected of all Muslims who can afford to make it.

Heraldry: The practice of creating and studying coats of arms and other insignia.

Heresy: A belief that goes against established church teachings.

Holy Land: Palestine.

Horde: A division within the Mongol army; the term "hordes" was often used to describe the Mongol armies.

I

Icon: In the Christian church, an image of a saint.

Idol: A statue of a god that the god's followers worship.

Illumination: Decoration of a manuscript with elaborate designs.

Indo-European languages: The languages of Europe, India, Iran, and surrounding areas, which share common roots.

Indulgence: The granting of forgiveness of sins in exchange for an act of service for, or payment to, the church.

Infantry: Foot soldiers.

Infidel: An unbeliever.

Intellectual: A person whose profession or lifestyle centers around study and ideas.

Interest: In economics, a fee charged by a lender against a borrower—usually a percentage of the amount borrowed.

Investiture: The power of a feudal lord to grant lands or offices.

Islam: A religious faith that teaches submission to the one god Allah and his word as given through his prophet Muhammad in the Koran.

J

Jihad: Islamic "holy war" to defend or extend the faith.

K

Khan: A Central Asian chieftain.

Koran: The holy book of Islam.

L

Legal code: A system of laws.

Lingua franca: A common language.

M

Martyr: Someone who willingly dies for his or her faith.

Mass: A Catholic church service.

Medieval: Of or relating to the Middle Ages.

Middle Ages: Roughly the period from A.D. 500 to 1500.

Middle class: A group whose income falls between that of the rich and the poor, or the rich and the working class; usually considered the backbone of a growing economy.

Millennium: A period of a thousand years.

Missionary: Someone who travels to other lands with the aim of converting others to his or her religion.

Monastery: A place in which monks live.

Monasticism: The tradition and practices of monks.

Monk: A man who leaves the outside world to take religious vows and live in a monastery, practicing a lifestyle of denying earthly pleasures.

Monotheism: Worship of one god.

Mosque: A Muslim temple.

Movable-type printing: An advanced printing process using pre-cast pieces of metal type.

Muezzin: A crier who calls worshipers to prayer five times a day in the Muslim world.

Mysticism: The belief that one can attain direct knowledge of God or ultimate reality through some form of meditation or special insight.

N

Nationalism: A sense of loyalty and devotion to one's nation.

Nation-state: A geographical area composed largely of a single nationality, in which a single national government clearly holds power.

New World: The Americas, or the Western Hemisphere.

Noble: A ruler within a kingdom who has an inherited title and lands, but who is less powerful than the king or queen; collectively, nobles are known as the "nobility."

Nomadic: Wandering.

Novel: An extended, usually book-length, work of fiction.

Nun: The female equivalent of a monk, who lives in a nunnery, convent, or abbey.

O

Order: An organized religious community within the Catholic Church.

Ordination: Formal appointment as a priest or minister.

P

Pagan: Worshiping many gods.

Papacy: The office of the pope.

Papal: Referring to the pope.

Patriarch: A bishop in the Eastern Orthodox Church.

Patron: A supporter, particularly of arts, education, or sciences. The term is often used to refer to a ruler or wealthy person who provides economic as well as personal support.

Peasant: A farmer who works a small plot of land.

Penance: An act ordered by the church to obtain forgiveness for sin.

Persecutions: In early church history, Roman punishment of Christians for their faith.

Philosophy: An area of study concerned with subjects including values, meaning, and the nature of reality.

Pilgrimage: A journey to a site of religious significance.

Plague: A disease that spreads quickly to a large population.

Polytheism: Worship of many gods.

Pope: The bishop of Rome, and therefore the head of the Catholic Church.

Principality: An area ruled by a prince, the highest-ranking form of noble below a king.

Prophet: Someone who receives communications directly from God and passes these on to others.

Prose: Written narrative, as opposed to poetry.

Purgatory: A place of punishment after death where, according to Roman Catholic beliefs, a person who has not been damned may work out his or her salvation and earn his or her way to heaven.

R

Rabbi: A Jewish teacher or religious leader.

Racism: The belief that race is the primary factor determining peoples' abilities and that one race is superior to another.

Reason: The use of the mind to figure things out; usually contrasted with emotion, intuition, or faith.

Reformation: A religious movement in the 1500s that ultimately led to the rejection of Roman Catholicism by various groups who adopted Protestant interpretations of Christianity.

Regent: Someone who governs a country when the monarch is too young, too old, or too sick to lead.

Relic: An object associated with the saints of the New Testament, or the martyrs of the early church.

Renaissance: A period of renewed interest in learning and the arts that began in Europe during the 1300s and continued to the 1600s.

Representational art: Artwork intended to show a specific subject, whether a human figure, landscape, still life, or a variation on these.

Ritual: A type of religious ceremony that is governed by very specific rules.

Rome: A term sometimes used to refer to the papacy.

S

Sack: To destroy, usually a city.

Saracen: A negative term used in medieval Europe to describe Muslims.

Scientific method: A means of drawing accurate conclusions by collecting information, studying data, and forming theories or hypotheses.

Scriptures: Holy texts.

Sect: A small group within a larger religion.

Secular: Of the world; typically used in contrast to "spiritual."

Semitic: A term describing a number of linguistic and cultural groups in the Middle East, including the modern-day Arabs and Israelis.

Serf: A peasant subject to a feudal system and possessing no land.

Siege: A sustained military attack against a city.

Simony: The practice of buying and selling church offices.

Sultan: A type of king in the Muslim world.

Sultanate: An area ruled by a Sultan.

Synagogue: A Jewish temple.

T

Technology: The application of knowledge to make the performance of physical and mental tasks easier.

Terrorism: Frightening (and usually harming) a group of people in order to achieve a specific political goal.

Theologian: Someone who analyzes religious faith.

Theology: The study of religious faith.

Trial by ordeal: A system of justice in which the accused (and sometimes the accuser as well) has to undergo various physical hardships in order to prove innocence.

Tribal: Describes a society, sometimes nomadic, in which members are organized by families and clans, not by region, and in which leadership comes from warrior-chieftains.

Tribute: Forced payments to a conqueror.

Trigonometry: The mathematical study of triangles, angles, arcs, and their properties and applications.

Trinity: The three persons of God according to Christianity—Father, Son, and Holy Spirit.

U

Usury: Loaning money for a high rate of interest; during the Middle Ages, however, it meant simply loaning money for interest.

V

Vassal: A noble or king who is subject to a more powerful noble or king.

Vatican: The seat of the pope's power in Rome.

W

West: Generally, Western Europe and North America, or the countries influenced both by ancient Greece and ancient Rome.

Working class: A group between the middle class and the poor who typically earn a living with their hands.

Research and Activity Ideas

The following list of research and activity ideas is intended to offer suggestions for complementing social studies and history curricula, to trigger additional ideas for enhancing learning, and to suggest cross-disciplinary projects for library and classroom use.

- Obtain a list of movies about the medieval period. Sources include the *Medieval Sourcebook* Web site, "Medieval History at the Movies" (http://www.fordham.edu/ halsall/medfilms.html) or *Videohound's Golden Movie Retriever,* published by Visible Ink Press, 2001. Watch several movies about the era and discuss them. How accurately do they portray events in the Middle Ages?

- One of the signs of Europe's recovery during the 1100s was the emergence of international fairs at Champagne and in Flanders. Hold a class "fair," with each student assigned to bring in an item for "sale." What do students learn about one another by doing business together?

- Divide into two groups, representing the people of Europe and those of the Middle East. The Europeans are preparing to go on a crusade to seize the Holy Land from the Muslims to place it under Christian control. Debate this issue, considering it from as many viewpoints as possible. Is a crusade justified according to the Christian religion? What is the justification for Muslim control of the Holy Land? How could a crusade be avoided?

- Obtain a world map, and use colored pins to indicate the different locations mentioned in this book, including such routes as those of the crusaders, Marco Polo, or invaders of Europe from Central Asia. Discuss the natural features that may have helped Europe become dominant in the period after 1500, as well as the natural barriers that prevented some civilizations from interacting with those of Europe and the Middle East.

- Pretend that you are living in the Middle Ages and describe a typical day. Keep in mind that you would possess virtually none of the modern conveniences that make life easy. There would be no electricity, hardly any commercially manufactured products, and no transportation other than by animal or foot. Few people would be able to read and write, and modern standards of hygiene—for instance, bathing every day—would not be observed. The last two facts were most true for Western Europeans rather than for Byzantines, Arabs, or Chinese. How would people of those cultures look upon an unwashed, illiterate Western European? How would a medieval person seem to someone now and vice versa?

- Most of the famous women from premodern times were queens, and in fact very few women ever had an opportunity to achieve fame of any kind. Discuss the reasons why this was the case, particularly in light of the conditions involved in having children and of taking care of a household. Keep in mind there was very little medical help for problems in pregnancy—nor were there anesthetics to ease the pain of childbirth. There were no disposable diapers, no pediatricians, no baby formula or prepared foods for infants. On top of all these challenges, a woman had to cook and clean without the benefit of modern conveniences. Consider the ways things have changed, not only from the standpoint of technology, but also with regard to attitudes about women's and men's roles.

- The list of Arab or Muslim scientists and mathematicians from the Middle Ages is a long one. Starting with this book, compile a list of such figures and arrange for each member of the class to prepare a brief report on that person's achievements. If possible, include visual aids or models as well. Then, after the presentations, discuss the relative level of technological advancement in Western Europe during the Middle Ages and the Arabs' view of Europeans. Also, consider the relative levels of technological advancement in Europe and the Middle East today. Why and how did things change? Sources for information about Muslim scientists include the U•X•L books *Science and Technology Breakthroughs: From the Wheel to the World Wide Web* and *Math and Mathematicians: The History of Math Discoveries around the World,* as well as these Web sites:

  - "Index of Biographies" (Mathematicians). [Online] Available http://www-groups.dcs.st-andrews.ac.uk/%7Ehistory/BiogIndex.html (last accessed August 9, 2000).

  - *Medieval Technology Pages.* [Online] Available http://scholar.chem.nyu.edu/technology.html (last accessed August 9, 2000).

  - *Muslim Scientists and Islamic Civilization.* [Online] Available http://users.erols.com/zenithco/index.html (last accessed August 9, 2000).

- Hold a "Medieval Biography" day, on which each member of the class takes on the role of an important person from medieval history. Perhaps using the biography and sidebar subjects from *Middle Ages: Biographies,* which offers names from a range of world cultures, start with a drawing in which each person is assigned a "character." Then, in addition to creating a costume appropriate to that person (makeshift armor, for instance, or royal robes), each student should research the person's biography and be prepared to discuss his or her life and significance.

- Go through recent newspapers or newsmagazines and cut out or copy stories relating to issues that concerned people in the Middle Ages as much as they do people today. Such issues would include the conflict of church and state, as well as freedom *for* and freedom *from* religious beliefs; the relationship between science and religious faith; the differences between Christianity, Islam, and Judaism; and the clash between societies that have achieved radically different levels of technological advancement.

- Most books and courses of study relating to the Middle Ages place a greater emphasis on Europe than on the cultures of the Middle East, Asia, Africa, and the Americas. Why do you think that is so? Does it seem strange, given the fact that Western Europe at the beginning of the Middle Ages was far less advanced than many other regions at the same time? Do you think it is right or wrong to place such an emphasis on Europe? How would you feel about that question if you had been raised in a society that had hardly been influenced by Europe? Take a position, pro or con, and explain your reasoning in a short paper or debate it as a class. (As you discuss this, keep in mind that almost all societies throughout history have believed that they were the "best.")

- During the Middle Ages superstition often took the place of science, and when people could not explain the causes behind something they often made up superstitious explanations that seem silly to people today. Research the history of a superstition—for instance, fear of the number 13. With superstitions that relate to science in some way, compare the superstition with the actual facts about a subject: for instance, in the Middle Ages people believed in spontaneous generation, but now people know that when food is left out to spoil vermin are drawn to it, rather than the food actually turning into the vermin. Choose some sort of everyday phenomenon, such as wind blowing trees or the operation of a car, and make up a fanciful, superstitious explanation for it of the type a medieval person might have believed. Then compare this superstition with the actual facts regarding the subject—in this case, how the wind blows trees, or how cars operate.

- Medieval history is filled with "what ifs" and things that almost happened. Consider how Europe—and thus America and the world—might have been changed, for instance, if the Muslims had succeeded in taking Constantinople in 718, or had defeated the Franks at Tours in 732; or if the Mongols had kept moving westward into Vienna in 1241; or if Tamerlane had not temporarily halted the Turks' conquest of the Balkans in 1402. Conversely, discuss ways that various events or phenomena could have been avoided. Examples include the fall of the Western Roman Empire; the destruction of the gold-rich kingdoms of West Africa; the European conquest of the Aztecs and Incas; or the failure of the Arabs or Chinese to maintain their technological advantages over Europeans.

The Middle Ages

The Middle Ages, or medieval (med-EE-vul) period, lasted roughly from A.D. 500 to 1500. It was an era of great changes in civilization, a transition between ancient times and the modern world. With the rise of the Roman Catholic Church and other institutions, Western Europe during this period grew apart from Eastern Europe, which centered around Greece and its Orthodox Church. The Middle East at the same time experienced the explosion of the Muslim, or Islamic, faith, and the region became home to a series of Arab and Turkish empires. Farther east, and in Africa and the Americas, other great empires—among them those of the Chinese, the Mongols, and the Incas—rose and fell.

Most historians link the beginning of the Middle Ages with the fall of the Roman Empire, the long decline of which can be traced to the A.D. 200s. By the 300s, Rome had adopted many practices that would come to characterize medieval life. Whereas ancient Romans had worshiped the old pagan gods such as Jupiter, now the official religion of Rome was Christianity—though a form of Christianity heavily mixed with pagan practices. And whereas the ancient

Words to Know: The Middle Ages

Age of Exploration: The period from about 1450 to about 1750, when European explorers conducted their most significant voyages and travels around the world.

Ancestor: An earlier person in one's line of parentage, usually more distant in time than a grandparent.

Barbarian: A negative term used to describe someone as uncivilized.

Chivalry: The system of medieval knighthood, particularly its code of honor with regard to women.

Church: The entire Christian church, or more specifically the Roman Catholic Church.

Civilization: A group of people possessing most or all of the following: a settled way of life, agriculture, a written language, an organized government, and cities.

Dark Ages: A negative term sometimes used to describe the Early Middle Ages, the period from the fall of Rome to about A.D. 1000 in Western Europe.

Economy: The whole system of production, distribution, and consumption of goods and services in a country.

Empire: A large political unit that unites many groups of people, often over a wide territory.

Feudalism: A form of political and economic organization in which peasants are subject to a noble, who owns most or all of the land that they cultivate.

Leprosy: A disease involving the gradual wasting of muscles, deformity, and paralysis; relatively common until modern times.

Medieval: Of or relating to the Middle Ages.

Middle Ages: Roughly the period from A.D. 500 to 1500.

Millennium: A period of a thousand years.

Pagan: Worshiping many gods.

Papacy: The office of the pope.

Peasant: A farmer who works a small plot of land.

Reformation: A religious movement in the 1500s that ultimately led to the rejection of Roman Catholicism by various groups in Europe.

Renaissance: A period of renewed interest in learning and the arts that began in Europe during the 1300s and continued to the 1600s.

Technology: The application of knowledge to make the performance of physical and mental tasks easier.

West: Generally, Western Europe and North America, or the countries influenced both by ancient Greece and ancient Rome.

The remains of the Roman Forum. Completed in A.D. **118, the Forum was built several hundred years before the fall of the Western Roman Empire.** *Reproduced by permission of Popperfoto/ Archive Photos.*

Roman economy had been based on slavery, Rome in the 300s already had the beginnings of a new system called feudalism (FYOO-dul-izm).

The Western Roman Empire fell in 476, but the Eastern Roman Empire continued as the Byzantine (BIZ-un-teen) Empire throughout the Middle Ages. By the time the Byzantine Empire fell in 1453, the medieval period was coming to an end as Europe began experiencing a full-scale transformation in the arts, science, politics, and even religion. The awakening in the arts and science was called the Re-

naissance (REN-uh-sahnts), or "rebirth"; similarly, the Reformation (ref-ur-MAY-shun) heralded the re-formation of religion and even politics. The Renaissance and Reformation had their beginnings in the 1300s, and gathered steam after 1450 with the invention of the printing press, which made it possible to spread ideas much more quickly. Around the same time, the Age of Exploration began with the first European voyages around the coast of Africa. These events collectively brought about the end of the Middle Ages, and the beginning of the modern world.

Many people think of the Middle Ages in terms of romance and chivalry: kings, castles, and knights battling over the hand of a fair maiden. *Reproduced by permission of the Corbis Corporation.*

Understanding medieval times

People in the Middle Ages did not think of their time as "a middle period" between ancient and modern times; that idea only arose during the Renaissance. As Europe reawakened in the 1500s, it was hard not to view the Middle Ages as a time of ignorance and confusion, an interruption in the progress of humankind. This was particularly true of the millennium's first half, from about 500 to about 1000.

People began to refer scornfully to medieval times as "the Dark Ages," and for many centuries thereafter, this remained the accepted view.

In the twentieth century there was a backlash against this interpretation, and indeed it became almost "politically incorrect" to refer to the medieval period as the Dark Ages. Yet the Dark Ages viewpoint is not necessarily inaccurate. There can be no question that, in terms of political organization and technology, Western Europe took many steps backward during the centuries leading up to and following the fall of Rome.

The Dark Ages interpretation, however, fails to take into account the many great achievements made by Western Europeans during the Middle Ages—from the beauty of manuscript illumination and Gothic architecture to the literary classics of Augustine and Dante. On the political and social level, the Middle Ages laid the groundwork for modern times, bringing into being the first nation-states such as France and England, and establishing the conditions for explosive economic growth in future centuries. The medieval period was far from a dead spot between ancient and modern times.

The Middle Ages around the world

The idea of the Middle Ages in general, and of the Dark Ages in particular, is specifically European in origin— or rather, Western European. In contrast to Western Europe, Eastern Europe

Knights, Castles, and Bad Teeth

The view of the medieval period as the "Dark Ages" is a stereotype, or oversimplified image; so, too, is the other extreme, which one might describe as the "knights in shining armor" viewpoint. This is the idea created by fairy tales and sustained by movies, an impression of the Middle Ages as a time of beauty, romance, and mystery. This view centers around images of chivalry—for instance, the knight rescuing the fair maiden from a dragon or an enemy, and carrying her on his horse to a castle gleaming in the distance.

In fact, if a modern person actually got a chance to meet a real medieval knight and his fair maiden, they would probably be more than a little disappointed—maybe even revolted. Whereas people in ancient Greece and Rome had been reasonably clean according to modern standards, by the time of the Middle Ages most of Western Europe had come to believe that baths were only good as a cure for sickness. If one were not sick, then there was no need for a bath. Therefore the knight and his maiden would be fairly smelly; furthermore, no one

had any concept of brushing their teeth, let alone the idea of preventing tooth decay. Teeth simply fell out, and therefore the smile of the fair maiden would indeed be a sight to behold.

At some point, either the knight or his maiden were likely to come into contact with a terrible illness for which there was no cure. Certainly if one got sick, it was a bad idea to visit a so-called "doctor." Doctors in medieval Europe were actually just moonlighting barbers, and they proposed all sorts of hideous "cures" such as bleeding the patient to release impurities from the body. Not surprisingly, life expectancy during much of the Early Middle Ages was only about twenty-five or thirty years. Not only were lives short; *people* were short. Due to a number of factors, most notably poor diet and medical care, the average-sized man was between five and five-and-a-half feet tall, as opposed to six feet tall today. There were also far more people with physical problems of one kind or another: hunchbacks, persons with the dreaded disease leprosy, and others.

experienced no dark age, and indeed became home to a splendid reminder of ancient Greek and Roman glory in the form of the Byzantine Empire.

Nor did the Arabs of the Middle East view the period as a "dark age": beginning in the 600s, Arabia ex-

perienced a cultural flowering on a scale seldom equaled in human history. While the ancestors of the English and French were still mostly illiterate peasants living in drafty huts, the Arabs enjoyed a degree of civilization that easily put them on a level with ancient Rome. It is not surprising that when they first encountered Western Europeans during the Crusades beginning in 1095, the Arabs viewed them as ignorant, foul-smelling brutes. Even in modern times, Arab historians do not typically view the millennium that began in A.D. 500 as a "middle age," especially since the Muslim world does not use the same calendar as Europe: instead of dating their years from the birth of Jesus Christ, Muslims begin with the prophet Muhammad's escape from the city of Mecca in A.D. 622.

Much farther east, the Chinese not only had their own calendar, but their own long and distinguished history—a history that had nothing to do with Europe. In fact, prior to about A.D. 100, the Chinese did not know that Greece or Rome existed, nor did they much care when they did learn of the fact. In their view, China was the center of the world, and all other peoples were barbarians to varying degrees. Just how barbarian the Chinese thought others were, of course, had a great deal to do with how much or how little their culture was influenced by that of China.

Moving farther east—so far east, in fact, that it is considered west—one finds the Mayan civilization in what is now Mexico and Guatemala. The Maya had never heard of Western Europe, Arabia, *or* China, placing them even farther from the Western European world of knights and castles. Nonetheless, the peoples of America, as well as Africa and other regions covered in this series, had their own unique experience of the period that in the West is known as the Middle Ages.

The Fall of the Roman Empire

2

The fall of the Roman Empire is usually considered the starting point for the Middle Ages. In ancient times, Rome—a term that stood not only for the city of Rome, but for the entire world dominated by the Romans—was one of the world's great civilizations. The city itself was founded, according to tradition, in 753 B.C., and over the years that followed, it gradually began to dominate other cities in Italy. In 507 B.C. the Roman Republic, comprising Rome itself and surrounding areas, was established. In 390 B.C. a nomadic group from the north called the Gauls, or Celts, invaded Rome, and this led the Romans to begin building up their military. The next five centuries saw near-constant warfare, during which Rome expanded its territory to include much of Europe, the Middle East, and North Africa. There was also nearly constant warfare among the Roman leaders themselves in the century leading up to 31 B.C., when the Roman Empire was established. During the next two centuries, the Roman world enjoyed a period of prosperity and contentment known as the *Pax Romana,* or "Roman peace."

Words to Know: The Fall of the Roman Empire

Assassination: Killing, usually of an important leader, for political reasons.

Bishop: A figure in the Christian Church assigned to oversee priests and believers in a given city or region.

Cavalry: Soldiers on horseback.

Convert: A new believer in a religion.

Ecumenical: Across all faiths, or across all branches of the Christian Church.

Heresy: A belief that goes against established church teachings.

Infantry: Foot soldiers.

Legion: A unit in the Roman military, consisting of between 3,000 and 6,000 soldiers; used collectively to refer to the entire Roman army.

Martyr: Someone who willingly dies for his or her faith.

Nomadic: Wandering.

Persecutions: In church history, Roman punishment of Christians for their faith.

Pope: The bishop of Rome, and therefore the head of the Catholic Church.

Sack: To destroy, usually a city.

Theologian: Someone who analyzes religious faith.

Tribal: Describes a society, sometimes nomadic, in which members are organized by families and clans, not by region, and in which leadership comes from warrior-chieftains.

The decline of the Roman Empire (A.D. 180–c. 350)

From A.D. 96 to 180, a series of able emperors ruled Rome, but the quality of emperors in the next half-century would be uneven, and several were assassinated. Over the coming years, that method of replacing Roman emperors would become common. Between 235 and 285, Rome had twenty emperors, many of them promoted to their positions by the army. Few died a natural death.

During the third century, an increasing tax burden, a slave-based economy, and other deep-seated economic problems created an ever-widening gap between rich and poor, until there was no one in between. The few Romans who were fabulously wealthy gave themselves up to lives of pleasure, while the many living in poverty faced a future of unrelieved misery. Neither group was having children, the rich because they could not be bothered, the poor because they could not afford them. Both groups practiced widespread abortion and infanticide, or the murder of children. Soon the Roman population began to decrease, and

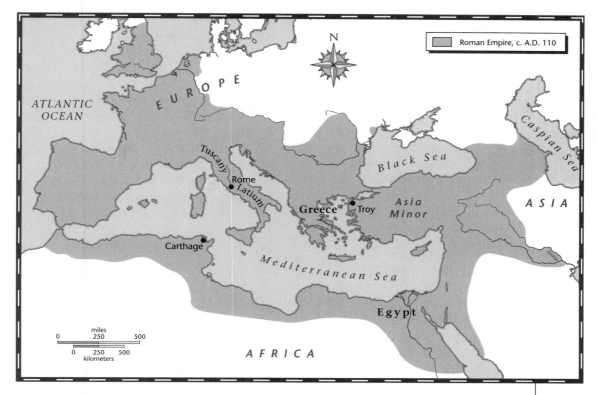

A map of the Roman Empire at its height, c. A.D. 110. *Illustration by XNR Productions. Reproduced by permission of the Gale Group.*

the Italian countryside was filled with empty houses.

The empire stopped growing along with the population. For centuries, Rome had survived on constant warfare, which brought in slaves and captured treasures. No one thought about expanding the economy by learning better ways to cultivate crops or by creating more goods to sell; therefore once there were no more nations to attack, there would be no more wealth. Up to the A.D. 100s, the system of growth by conquest had worked fair-

ly well; then Rome came to the limits of its power.

All around it, the empire faced natural or manmade boundaries: deserts in North Africa and the Middle East, the military force of the Persians and others on its southeastern borders, the Atlantic Ocean to the west, and the North Sea to the northwest. Worst of all, along its northern and northeastern frontiers, formed by the Rhine (RYN) and Danube (DAN-yoob) Rivers respectively, were dozens and dozens of tribal "barbarians." The mission of Rome's armies turned from conquest to mere survival, as they tried to hold on to lands they had won centuries before. But Romans themselves had lost their will to fight; therefore as time went on, the ranks of their legions were increasingly filled with foreigners—primarily barbarians.

Barbarians and Christians

The barbarians would later bring down the empire, but the decline of Roman society itself made possible the barbarian takeover. The Romans had grown weak, but the tribes around their borders were strong; and whereas the Romans were cowardly, the barbarians were brave. In many ways, the barbarians—who, despite their brutality, were often honest and noble in their behavior—most resembled the ancient Romans who had built the great society that was now crumbling.

Only one group within Rome could match the barbarians' vigor and energy: a small group of religious believers called Christians, so named because they followed the teachings of Jesus Christ. The Christian religion had originated in the Middle East during the first century A.D. and spread to Rome through the efforts of numerous apostles, or teachers, including Paul, Peter, and others. Most likely Peter and Paul died in Rome during the reign of Emperor Nero (ruled A.D. 54–68), who conducted the first wave of persecutions against Christians.

Over the next two-and-a-half centuries, Rome treated its Christian minority mercilessly: for instance, Christians were fed to lions while cheering spectators watched. One reason for this treatment was Christians' rejection of Roman ways, in particular the pagan religion. Whereas the Romans worshiped many gods, represented with statues everywhere, the Christians had just one god, and it was against their religion to worship statues. The gods of Rome were such a part of life that to reject them was to reject Rome itself: therefore Christians were scorned as "atheists" and dangerous anti-Roman activists.

The Christians meanwhile had their own type of government, with leaders called bishops presiding over each major city. According to tradition, in his last days the apostle Peter became the bishop of Rome, and because Rome was the center of the world at the time, Peter's office came to have a great significance. Therefore the bishop of Rome took on a special title: father, or *papa*—that is, pope. During the Middle Ages, hundreds of men would hold the title of pope, or leader of the Roman Catholic Church, and the papacy (office of the pope) would come to hold great power.

The early popes, however, were far from powerful; and whereas many popes in the Middle Ages did things that Jesus Christ would have condemned—for instance, living on wealth that they had taken from the poor—the early popes typically led lives of poverty. As for the Christians as a whole, it seems that persecution made them more sincere in charity and love, concepts taught by Christ, and indeed it would be hard to find a class

This painting, *The Apparition of the Cross to Constantine,* by Giulio Romano, depicts the event that persuaded Constantine to convert to Christianity. *Reproduced by permission of the Corbis Corporation.*

of people more heroic than the early Christian martyrs (MAR-turz) who sacrificed their lives for their faith.

The age of Constantine

Rome may have lost its will to rule the world, but it did not die easily. From the late 200s to the early 300s, the empire recovered under the leadership of Diocletian (die-oh-KLEE-shun; ruled A.D. 284–305) and later Constantine. Diocletian was the last emperor to persecute Christians. Constantine later claimed that before going into battle at the Milvian Bridge along the River Tiber (TY-bur) on Oc-

tober 28, A.D. 312, he saw a cross in the sky superimposed over Greek words meaning "In this sign [you shall] conquer." He won the battle and accepted Christianity.

Constantine's version of the Christian faith, however, was mixed with a heavy dose of the old-time Roman religion, and as emperor he remained high priest of the pagan gods. Nonetheless, under his rule, Christianity became not only legal, but socially acceptable. At the same time church leaders, seeing the advantages of working with the Roman system rather than against it, eased restrictions against Christians taking part in public life.

Meanwhile more and more people converted to the new religion, and this rising popularity—combined with imperial support and the church's new openness to participation in political affairs—soon gave Christians considerable power. Many church leaders used their influence to foster the principles of brotherhood and tolerance taught by Jesus, but many others seemed eager to turn the tables on the pagans who had mistreated them for so long. Indeed, in many cases, the formerly persecuted Christians themselves became persecutors. One of their most notable victims was Hypatia (hy-PAY-shuh; A.D. 370–415), the only known female philosopher of ancient times, who in 415 was brutally attacked and killed by a group of "Christians" opposed to her pagan teachings.

Constantine made a number of valuable contributions to early Christianity, particularly by linking the power of the church with the power of the state—in this case, the Roman government. He also called an extremely important conference of Christian bishops, who met in the city of Nicaea (nie-SEE-uh) in Asia Minor in 325 to discuss a problem that threatened to destroy Christian unity at the very moment of triumph.

A Greek named Arius (AR-ee-uhs; c. A.D. 250–337) had been preaching that God was separate from all of his creation—and that Christ was one of those creations; this idea came to be called Arianism. Mainstream Chris-

tians, by contrast, believed that God the Father and God the Son (Jesus) were one and the same being. Arianism had by then gained a number of converts, particularly in Greece and Egypt. In response, the 220 bishops at the Council of Nicaea declared Arianism a heresy (HAIR-uh-see)—a belief that went against the Christian faith. The bishops also adopted the Nicene (ny-SEEN) Creed, a form of which is still recited in churches today: "We believe in one God, the Father Almighty, maker of all things visible or invisible; and in one Lord Jesus Christ, the Son of God, begotten ... not made...."

Nicaea was the first ecumenical (ek-yoo-MIN-i-kul) council, a meeting of all believers at which church leaders established the official Christian position on a variety of issues. In the view of Constantine and later church leaders, in order for Christianity to survive and grow, there could be no diversity of opinion. Gradually the church began to call itself "catholic," which means universal. Indeed, for many centuries the church would maintain a semblance of unity, though in fact there were many varieties of Christianity.

Constantine in his later years placed his stamp all over Christianity and the medieval world. Adapting a type of Roman building called the basilica (buh-SIL-i-kuh), he made its open floor plan a model for church design that is still used today. He also established the city of Constantinople (kahn-stan-ti-NOH-pul), which became the capital of the Eastern Roman Empire. Realizing that the empire had become too big to control from one city, in 330 he established a second capital at a Greek city formerly called Byzantium (bi-ZAN-tee-um). Thus he restored the empire for a time, but he could not arrest its steady decline. By the mid-300s, the threat to Rome's borders had become too severe to ignore.

The fall of Rome (c. 350–476)

The ultimate source of Rome's downfall lay many centuries and many thousands of miles away. When the Chinese began building their Great Wall in 221 B.C. to keep out barbarian invaders, they displaced a number of nomadic peoples who had long threatened them from the north. Among these were the Hsiung-Nu (shung-NOO), a group of extremely able horsemen and warriors. The Hsiung-Nu began moving westward, leaving a trail of death and destruction as they went. The first Europeans unfortunate enough to cross their paths in the A.D. 300s gave them a new name: Huns. For more than a century, the very word "Hun" was a synonym for terror.

Meanwhile, a number of other tribal groups emerged in Europe. There were the Gauls, or Celts (KELTZ), who lived in what is now France and the British Isles. Farther east and north were other groups, so many that the Romans had long before given up trying to distinguish between them. They all seemed to have blond hair and blue eyes; therefore the Romans called them by a word that, in the Latin language, meant "related": *Germanus*.

 Roman Numerals

The Romans had their own number system, quite unlike the Arabic numerals (1, 2, 3, etc.) used throughout the world today. The symbols included:

I = 1
V = 5
X = 10
L = 50
C = 100
D = 500
M = 1,000

All other numbers were created by combinations of these seven numbers; for example, the numbers from 1 to 10 are: I, II, III, IV, V, VI, VII, VIII, IX, X. From 11 to 20, the pattern repeated, but with an X at the front, standing for 10: XI, XII, XIII, XIV, XV, XVI, XVII, XVIII, XIX, XX.

A German group known as the Goths began moving southeastward in the A.D. 200s, and as they did, they split into two groups. The eastern Goths or Ostrogoths settled in what is now Ukraine, and the western Goths or Visigoths put down roots in northeastern Greece and modern-day Romania. No one knew it then, but these two tribes would become key players in the chain of events that brought about the fall of Rome.

Though the Romans called them barbarians and thought of them as uncivilized, in fact the Goths had a

The Great Wall of China, which the Chinese began building in 221 B.C., was built to repel barbarian invaders. *Reproduced by permission of AP/Wide World Photos.*

great respect for Roman civilization. They seemed to understand that the Roman Empire was on the decline, and they hoped to preserve what was best about Rome. Thus it was a particular tragedy when, in 372, the Huns crossed the Volga River and attacked the Ostrogoths. They then moved westward and dealt the Visigoths a harsh blow as well.

The Visigoths begged the Roman emperor Valens (VAY-luhnz; ruled 364–378) for permission to cross the Danube into the empire. Up to that point, Rome had seldom willingly allowed barbarian tribes inside its borders; but Valens agreed to let them in if they would surrender their weapons and give up their children as hostages. The Romans took advantage of the Visigoths' desperation to charge them outrageous prices for food—a loaf of bread, for instance, went for ten pounds of silver—and sold most of the Visigoths' children into slavery.

Because the Visigoths were relatively peaceful and civilized—though that would change in time—the Romans' treatment of them was particularly cruel. This says a great deal about the moral character of the Romans; so too does the fact that the Visigoths were able to bribe Roman officials into letting them keep their weapons. In the end, the Visigoths revolted, and began overrunning the region, burning and looting as they went.

In 378, Valens lost his life in a battle with the Visigoths, a battle that according to one historian was the worst Roman defeat in nearly six hundred years. The victory of the Gothic cavalry also marked the beginning of medieval military tactics: whereas foot soldiers (or infantry) had dominated for more than a millennium, horsemen would now control the battlefield.

The Visigoths sack Rome

It was the beginning of the end for Rome. Theodosius (ruled 379–395) was the last emperor to rule a united realm; thereafter the Eastern Roman Empire would chart a separate course. Among Theodosius's generals was a

Augustine and the *City of God*

One of the greatest minds of the Middle Ages, and indeed in Western history, was the theologian and church leader Augustine (aw-GUS-tin; 354–430). Raised in North Africa, he experimented with loose lifestyles and the Manichaean faith, an obscure Persian religion that viewed all existence as a battle between good and evil, before embracing Christianity in 386. Later he became bishop at the Mediterranean port city of Hippo, now part of northeastern Algeria. Augustine wrote a number of important books, including the *Confessions* and *De civitate Dei,* or the *City of God.* The former, the world's first autobiography, was a deeply personal work, whereas the latter discussed the whole history of the world.

Augustine wrote the *City of God* after the Visigoths sacked Rome in 410. This event was far more devastating than the actual end of the Western Roman Empire sixty-six years later, and wise men throughout the Roman world looked for reasons why it had happened. They did not try to provide a military or political explanation, as modern analysts would; in a fashion more typical of premodern people, they saw the event purely in religious terms. The gods of Rome, many claimed, were angry at the Romans for turning away from them in favor of Christianity.

Not so, claimed Augustine in the *City of God;* in fact, quite the opposite was

Augustine. *Reproduced by permission of the Corbis Corporation.*

true. The Visigoths were a punishment from the Christian God for the Romans' continued sinfulness. He then went on to outline a number of ideas that would become essential to medieval European thought. The world was divided into two groups, he wrote: the city or society of people who were loyal to God on the one hand, and those loyal to earthly existence—which was the same thing as loyalty to Satan—on the other. The City of God, as he called the first group, was destined to triumph over the City of Man. This idea provided a basis for later claims by the popes that the church, as the City of God, should dominate the state, or the City of Man.

Attila, leader of the Huns, spread fear throughout Western Europe, though Pope Leo I was able to convince him not to attack Rome. *Reproduced by permission of the Corbis Corporation.*

brilliant Visigoth king named Alaric (AL-uh-rik; c. 370–410). After Theodosius died, Alaric turned against Rome.

To protect themselves against invasion, the Romans had moved their capital from Rome itself to Ravenna, a city in northeastern Italy surrounded by marshes. Yet Rome still remained the center of the Western world, and one of its greatest defenders was a "barbarian" named Stilicho (STIL-i-koh; c. 365–408). Stilicho's people were the Vandals, a Germanic

tribe that, following their defeat by the Visigoths in Constantine's time, had requested and received permission to settle within the empire. Stilicho himself had proven such an able commander and administrator that he essentially ruled the Western Roman Empire, and he was able to repel an earlier attack by Alaric. However, a rival managed to convince the reigning emperor that Stilicho was a traitor, and he was executed in 408—two years before Alaric's troops returned.

The Romans tried to bribe Alaric, who had surrounded the city and cut off all food supplies. For a time, Alaric considered it, but in the end he invaded the city. For three days in August 410, Rome experienced a terror it had not known since the Gauls' invasion exactly eight hundred years before. The Visigoths and their army, which included Huns and runaway Roman slaves, looted, burned, and killed, virtually destroying the city.

Later a rumor would spread that the Visigoths had destroyed Rome because they were pagans and resented Rome's acceptance of Christianity. This rumor helped bring about one of the most important books of the Middle Ages (see box, "Augustine and the *City of God*"), but it was not true: the Visigoths were Christians, though they subscribed to the Arian heresy. They even spared the Church of St. Peter, center of the pope's authority.

Huns and Vandals

Certain barbarian leaders, despite their reputations for cruelty and ruthlessness, had an odd respect for religion—including the religions of other peoples. Certainly that was true of the Huns, particularly their leader, Attila (c. 400–453). For a few years in the mid-400s, Attila held Western Europe in terror, and when he invaded Gaul in 448, it looked as though he were poised to deal the Roman Empire a fatal blow.

A combined force of Romans and barbarians actually scored a military victory over Attila—Rome's last—in 451, but in the following year he appeared with his troops right outside Rome itself. However, he allowed Pope Leo I, or Leo the Great (ruled 440–461), to talk him out of attacking. This incident was an example of how much political authority the church could wield, establishing an important pattern for later popes. Attila withdrew and died a year later, and after that the Huns faded into the larger European population. Only the name of the country where they briefly settled in the early 400s, Hungary, serves as a reminder that they existed.

In the time between Alaric and Attila, Western Europe had been ravaged by a new threat, the formerly peaceable Vandals. Impressed by Alaric's victories, the Vandals and other tribes plundered and pillaged their way through Gaul and into Spain. By 429, they had crossed the Mediterranean Sea and landed in North Africa, which had been under Roman control for centuries. Led by Gaiseric (GY-zu-rik; ruled 428–477), they quickly subdued the fertile coast, where most of Rome's food was

Gaiseric, leader of the Vandals, led a devastating attack on Rome in 455, contributing greatly to the fall of the Roman Empire. *Reproduced by permission of Archive Photos, Inc.*

grown. For a time, the Romans were able to bribe Gaiseric, but in 455 his forces sailed across the Mediterranean for Rome itself. This time Pope Leo could not convince the invaders to turn away: they devastated Rome, and ever since, the term "vandal" has been used to describe a destructive person.

The final hours

The Western Roman Empire was in its final hours, and after the

Vandals, it was just a matter of time before it caved in completely. Rome itself, once home to some 1.5 million people, had shrunk to one-fifth that size, and it would be more than a thousand years before another Western European city grew larger than ancient Rome. A parade of leaders, each more forgettable than the one before, gained control of the empire's remains; then in 475 a general named Orestes (ohr-ES-teez) placed his son on the throne with the imposing title of Romulus Augustulus.

Around the same time, a new wave of German invaders swarmed over the Italian Peninsula. When Orestes refused to give them one-third of Italy, they replaced his son with their own elected leader, Odoacer (oh-doh-AY-sur; c. 433–493). Thus the Western Roman Empire came to an end on August 23, 476. At the time, however, few perceived the event as particularly significant.

Odoacer sent a message to Zeno (ruled 474–491), ruler of the Eastern Roman Empire—thenceforth the Byzantine Empire—promising that Zeno would have the title of ruler over the West as well if he would allow Odoacer to govern in his place. Zeno had no reason to refuse, and no power in Italy to back him up, so he accepted. To many it seemed as though the empire had been reunited, not destroyed; but in fact Odoacer ruled Italy as a kingdom entirely separate from the Byzantine Empire.

For More Information

Books

Bardi, Piero. *The Atlas of the Classical World: Ancient Greece and Ancient Rome.* Illustrations by Matteo Chesi, et al. New York: Peter Bedrick Books, 1997, pp. 34–59.

Burrell, Roy. *Oxford First Ancient History.* New York: Oxford University Press, 1991, pp. 206–315.

Caselli, Giovanni. *The Roman Empire and the Dark Ages.* New York: P. Bedrick Press, 1985.

Dijkstra, Henk, editor. *History of the Ancient and Medieval World,* Volume 8: *Christianity and Islam.* New York: Marshall Cavendish, 1996, pp. 1015–32.

Martell, Hazel Mary. *The Kingfisher Book of the Ancient World.* New York: Kingfisher, 1995, pp. 76–87.

Severy, Merle, editor. *The Age of Chivalry.* Washington, D.C.: National Geographic Society, 1969, pp. 13–42.

Web Sites

"EAWC: Ancient Rome." *Exploring Ancient World Cultures.* [Online] Available http://eawc.evansville.edu/ropage.htm (last accessed July 28, 2000).

Imperium Romanorum. [Online] Available http://wwwtc.nhmccd.cc.tx.us/people/crf01/rome/ (last accessed July 28, 2000).

Roman Emperors: De Imperatoribus Romanis: An Online Encyclopedia of Roman Emperors. [Online] Available http://www.salve.edu/~romanemp/startup.htm (last accessed July 28, 2000).

Roman Sites—Gateway to 1,849 Websites on Ancient Rome. [Online] Available http://www.ukans.edu/history/index/europe/ancient_rome/E/Roman/RomanSites*/home.html (last accessed July 28, 2000).

Rome Resources. [Online] Available http://www.dalton.org/groups/rome/ (last accessed July 28, 2000).

The Merovingian Age

3

Western Europe includes what is now Germany and Italy, the countries between them such as Switzerland and Austria, and lands to the west, including France, Britain, and Spain. At the beginning of medieval times, however, few of these nations existed; only during the course of the Early Middle Ages (c. 500–c. 1000) would they emerge from the ruins of the Western Roman Empire. The first half of the Early Middle Ages began with great unrest, as barbarian tribes swept over the region. Only the Catholic Church served to provide the area with a unifying culture. The church would in turn lend its support to one of those tribes, whose royal dynasty would give a name to an entire era: the Merovingian Age (481–751).

Dividing up Western Europe (400s–500s)

Europe in the late 400s and early 500s was a confusing mass of tribes, mostly Germanic (i.e., from a group of related tribes in northern Europe) and mostly moving westward and southward. More than a few of these peoples gave their names to regions and entire nations, names that would long outlast

Words to Know: The Merovingian Age

Abstract art: Painting or other artwork that shows forms or designs, but does not represent objects as they really appear.

Aristocracy: The richest and most powerful members of society.

Ascetic: A person who renounces all earthly pleasures as part of his or her search for religious understanding.

Canonization: Formal declaration of a deceased person as a saint.

Cloister: A monastery, or sometimes the inner part of a monastery.

Convent: A dwelling in which nuns live.

Dialect: A regional variation on a language.

Divine: Godlike.

Dynasty: A group of people, often but not always a family, who continue to hold a position of power over a period of time.

Excommunicate: To banish someone from the church.

Illumination: Decoration of a manuscript with elaborate designs.

Manorialism: An early form of feudalism that lasted from the late Roman Empire into the Merovingian age.

Monastery: A place in which monks live.

Monasticism: The tradition and practices of monks.

Monk: A man who leaves the outside world to take religious vows and live in a monastery, practicing a lifestyle of denying earthly pleasures.

Nomadic: Wandering.

Nun: The female equivalent of a monk, who lives in a nunnery, convent, or abbey.

Order: An organized religious community within the Catholic Church.

Papal: Referring to the pope.

Purgatory: A place of punishment after death where, according to Roman Catholic beliefs, a person who has not been damned may work out their salvation and earn their way to heaven.

Relic: An object associated with the saints of the New Testament, or the martyrs of the early church.

Representational art: Artwork intended to show a specific subject as it really appears, whether a human figure, landscape, still life, or a variation on these.

Rome: A term sometimes used to refer to the papacy.

Serf: A peasant subject to a feudal system and possessing no land.

Trial by ordeal: A system of justice in which the accused (and sometimes the accuser as well) has to undergo various physical hardships in order to prove innocence.

Tribal: Describes a society, sometimes nomadic, in which members are organized by families and clans, not by region, and in which leadership comes from warrior-chieftains.

Villa: A type of country estate in Roman times; more generally, any kind of large, wealthy estate.

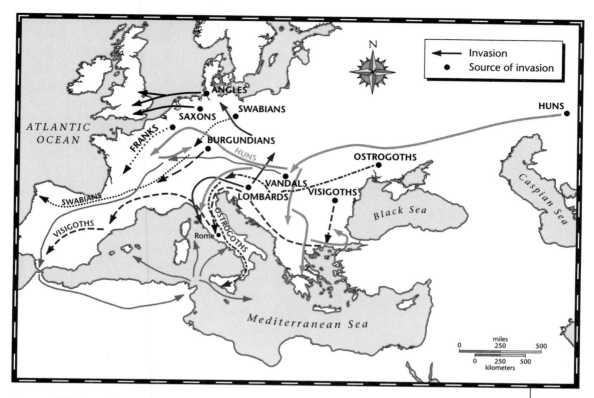

A map of Western Europe, c. A.D. 500, showing the movements of the various tribes across the continent. *Illustration by XNR Productions. Reproduced by permission of the Gale Group.*

the tribes themselves. Though the Western Roman Empire was finished, out of its collapse would come many beginnings.

Such was the case, for instance, with the Burgundians, for whom a region—later to emerge as an important French kingdom—was named. They came in the 400s, only to be subdued by the powerful Franks, another Germanic tribe, in 534. And there were the Lombards, who in the 500s stormed out of Eastern Europe and into the part of Italy that came to be known as Lombardy. They, too, succumbed to the Franks in

774. As for the Franks, they settled in Gaul—which, because of them, would thenceforth be known as France.

The Franks in time dropped their Germanic language and adopted Latin, which would emerge as a local dialect and then as a full-fledged language, French. Before the Franks and before the Romans, however, Gaul had been controlled by the Celts, a group whose language had little relation to either Latin or German. Celts had spread from the European continent to the isle of Britain, where they came to be known as Britons; and beyond

Hadrian's Wall, built between A.D. 122 and 128, stretches across some seventy-three miles of Scotland. *Reproduced by permission of the Corbis Corporation.*

tended some seventy-three miles across what is now Scotland and was designed to keep out a native Scottish people called the Picts. The Picts overran it several times, however, and threatened to do so again after the Romans permanently withdrew their legions in 410 to protect Rome itself from the Visigoths—another failed project.

By then the Britons had become Romanized and had accepted the Christian religion. They saw themselves as the last line of defense between civilization and barbarism. To assist their defense against the Picts, one of the Britons' leaders asked the help of three Germanic tribes—the Angles, the Saxons, and the Jutes—living in what is now northern Germany and Denmark. But once they arrived, the Germans realized how defenseless the natives were, so they simply took over the island.

Today the greater part of Britain is named England after the Angles, and the term "Anglo-Saxon" is used to describe persons of English descent. The German invaders' language, which completely replaced the Britons' Celtic tongue, ultimately became English, or rather Old English. An English-speaker today would have trouble recognizing Old English, yet modern English maintains many words from the distant past—usually short, highly direct terms such as "hit" or "gold."

Britain to Ireland, where the Celtic language of Gaelic is still spoken today.

Britain becomes England

When Rome added Britain to its empire in the first century A.D., Roman power had seemed limitless. Yet it was in Britain that the emperor Hadrian (ruled 117–138) had given physical form to the idea that Rome's power did indeed have limits: Hadrian's Wall. Built between 122 and 128 and possibly inspired by travelers' tales of the Great Wall of China, the wall ex-

Barbarian kingdoms of Western Europe

To varying degrees, the Germans of Western Europe were true barbarians. In place of Rome's highly sophisticated system of justice, they practiced trial by ordeal (see box, "Trial by Ordeal"). They had turned from their own brand of paganism to Christianity; but they possessed little concept of Christian mercy or kindness.

More advanced were the Visigoths in Spain, who chased out the Vandals in the mid-400s and established a kingdom that would rule until the arrival of the Moors in 711. The Visigoths adopted Latin and, like the Franks, developed their own dialect. This became the foundation for one of the most widely spoken languages today: Spanish.

Meanwhile in Italy, the Ostrogoths under Theodoric (c. 454–526) invaded, killed Odoacer, and briefly established the most advanced of the early barbarian kingdoms. Raised with a profound respect for Roman civilization, Theodoric tried to preserve what was best about Rome. To do this, he kept his own people separate from the Romans, and put Romans in charge of Italy's civil administration while his own forces oversaw the military. Not long after Theodoric's death, however, Byzantine armies would eliminate the Ostrogoth kingdom.

The Byzantines, as it turned out, were unable to hold on to Italy, which succumbed to the Lombards a few years later. Italy would never again be the center of power in Europe that it had once been; that center had shifted northward, to what is now France and Germany. There the Franks

Trial by Ordeal

The system of law practiced by the Germanic tribes of Europe in the 400s and 500s often demanded trial by ordeal. This meant that in order to prove his innocence, the accused had to walk over hot coals, stand with his arms outstretched for long hours, or endure some other form of torture. If the person was innocent, the logic went, he would be able to withstand these pains.

Sometimes the reasoning was even more twisted—and deadly. In some scenarios, the accused would be bound hand and foot and thrown into a river. A priest prayed that the water would reject the evildoer, meaning that if a person drowned, he was innocent. Those who survived, on the other hand, were guilty—and therefore were executed. Another form of ordeal was trial by combat. Accused and accuser underwent hand-to-hand combat, and whoever survived was judged the innocent party. The only advantage to this system was that it probably kept down the number of false or petty accusations.

would establish the first significant Western European kingdom of the Middle Ages, the Merovingian (mair-oh-VIN-jee-un) dynasty.

The church

The north was on the rise, but Italy still had a few things going for

St. George, patron saint of England, is usually depicted as he is here: on horseback, slaying a dragon. *Reproduced by permission of the Corbis Corporation.*

it—in fact, two big things. There was the legacy of the Roman Empire on the one hand, and on the other hand the spiritual empire of Christianity, led by the pope. Thanks to Constantine, the church had become tied to the Western Roman Empire, and with the fall of the latter, popes had increasingly taken on the Roman emperors' role as leaders of Western Europe. Popes drew their power in part from the influence of Christianity, but to a perhaps greater extent from the thousand-year influence of Rome. No doubt the apostles

Peter and Paul would have been shocked to see this alignment between the church they had helped establish and the empire that had killed them; but much had changed in the five centuries since their time.

The Bible's New Testament had referred to all Christians as "saints," but by the A.D. 100s, believers in Rome and elsewhere had come to recognize certain figures as special. These people were canonized, or formally declared as saints, and thenceforth referred to as such—for example, "St. Peter." By the year 1000, there were more than 25,000 saints.

The saints would eventually come to be worshiped in their own right, complete with pictures and statues representing them, a practice that recalled Roman paganism. Just as there had been a god assigned to nearly every town and every profession—for instance, Vulcan was the god of blacksmiths—now there was a patron saint for each. Later, as nations emerged during the High Middle Ages, each would have its own patron saint; for instance, St. George was England's patron saint.

The identity of Jesus Christ

Belief in saints as intercessors, or go-betweens for God and people, arose in part because of church teachings that encouraged believers to think of God as so holy and so pure that no sinner could dare approach him directly in prayer. The Old Testament had taught the same thing; but according to the New Testament,

Jesus, as God's son, was humankind's intercessor. The early Church, however, placed heavy emphasis on the fact that Jesus *was* God, and therefore downplayed the intercessor role.

This emphasis arose in response to heresies such as Arianism (the belief that Jesus Christ was not God) and Nestorianism. A Persian priest named Nestorius (died 451), who became bishop at Constantinople, had declared that Jesus had two separate identities, one human and one divine. The Council of Ephesus (EF-uh-sus) in 431 declared Nestorianism a heresy, but the belief found many adherents in the East—most notably the Far East, where it established a firmer foothold than any other branch of Christianity.

In 451, the Council of Chalcedon (KAL-suh-dahn) declared that Jesus had two natures, both human and divine, in one. This became the accepted position of western Christianity; but the Monophysites (muh-NAH-fu-zytz) in the Middle East, reacting to Nestorianism, began preaching that Christ was *only* divine and not human at all. This led the pope to excommunicate, or banish from the church, most believers in that region. Whole branches of Christianity, most notably the Armenian and Coptic (Egyptian) churches, split with Rome for good.

Jesus had become so removed from humanity that now Christians needed an intercessor to go *to him*, and the Council of Ephesus named one: Mary, mother of Jesus. In declaring Mary "Mother of God," the Council set her up as a potential figure of worship, allowing her to be linked with pagan mother goddesses such as the Greeks' Artemis or the Romans' Diana. The worship of Mary, still practiced in some parts of the world today, gained force during the High Middle Ages. It should be said, however, that for the most part the church did not officially encourage Mary-worship: as with the saints, it was a practice that arose from the people, and the church merely sought to make a place for it.

Monasticism

The 500s saw the appearance of two key figures in church history. The first was Benedict (c. 480–547), who established the tradition of monasticism (moh-NAS-ti-sizm), or the life of monks, men who leave the outside world to live in a monastery or cloister. There had been monks before Benedict, and indeed the idea of the ascetic (uh-SET-ik)—someone who gives up comfort to pursue spiritual wisdom—is an old one. Before Benedict, however, monks and ascetics were inclined to be undisciplined, practicing what amounted to self-torture. Benedict called for an end to such excesses.

In 529, Benedict and his followers demolished a pagan temple to build Monte Cassino, a high mountain retreat where they established the Benedictine (ben-uh-DIK-teen) Order. Not only were they the first true order of monks, and one that exists today, the Benedictines were the first to require that their members swear vows. Thus a man wanting to become a monk would live in the monastery,

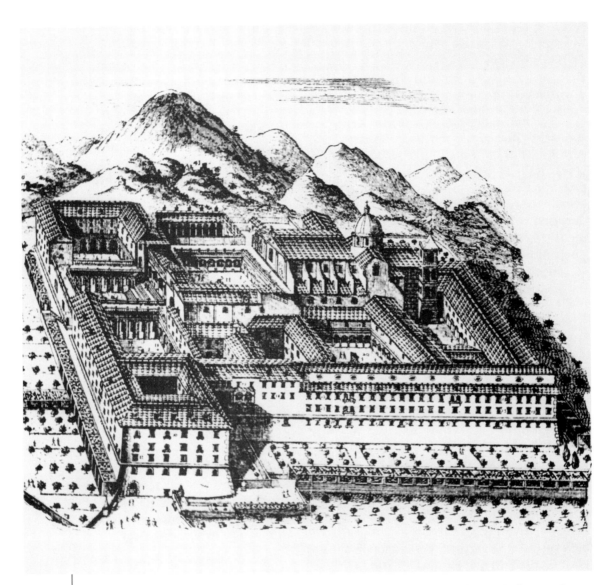

Monte Cassino was built by Benedict and his followers in 529. The Benedictine Order was the first true order of monks, and it still exists today. *Reproduced by permission of the Corbis Corporation.*

enduring all kinds of hardships; then if he chose to go on, after a time he would take the vows. Among the things monks vowed to give up were sex, laughter, and possessions. They agreed to eat only one meal a day in winter and two in summer when days were longer; to speak only when necessary; to walk with their eyes turned to the ground; not to joke or laugh; and to let their sleep be interrupted for prayer.

Benedictine monasteries spread throughout Europe; meanwhile, the tradition of nuns and convents developed for women who chose to take vows of poverty and chastity. According to legend, the first convent was founded by Benedict's twin sister, Scholastica, near Monte Cassino in 530. Whatever the case, the first order of nuns was the Benedictine, and soon there were as many nuns as there were monks. Over the centuries that followed, these men and women would serve as a symbol of Christian meekness and kindness, often providing shelter and care for the poor. And at about the same time Benedict founded his order, another group of monks did nothing less than preserve Western civilization (see box, "How the Monks Saved Civilization").

Gregory the Great

Another key figure in early medieval Christianity was Pope Gregory I (the Great; ruled 590–604). Gregory's name is today associated with Gregorian chants, a type of prayerful singing in Latin with minor variations in tone, performed by Benedictine monks throughout the Middle Ages. Though he did not invent the chants, Gregory ordered that they be written down for future use.

In his writings, Gregory approved of the veneration, or admiration, of relics. Like belief in the saints, the idea that an object could be sacred because of its association with Jesus or the saints had little to do with the Bible, and everything to do with pop-

This image depicts the Holy Grail, the cup Jesus drank from the night before he was crucified. This religious relic has never been found. *Reproduced by permission of the Corbis Corporation.*

ular beliefs. But that did not stop Gregory from asserting, for instance, that eyesight could be restored by contact with a set of chains supposedly used to imprison Peter and Paul. As the Middle Ages went on, relics abounded, none more venerated than the Holy Grail and the "True Cross." The former was the cup from which Jesus drank on the night before his crucifixion, the latter the cross on which he was killed. Despite many claims to the contrary, neither was ever found.

How the Monks Saved Civilization

One popular misconception concerning the Middle Ages is the idea that the church squelched learning, which it associated with the pagan societies of Greece and Rome. Quite the opposite is true. With the Roman Empire gone and the barbarian tribes threatening to extinguish the candle of civilization, only the church kept it lit.

Much of that light came from Rome, of course, but Rome itself was threatened when the Lombards invaded Italy in 568. Around the same time, a group of monks traveled to the farthest reaches of the Western world—the British Isles. There, in dank, cold monasteries on the harsh coasts of the North Sea and the Atlantic, they copied down the Bible and early church writings. But they did not simply copy; the books they produced were works of art in themselves, with lavishly illuminated lettering that served to illustrate the fact that to these scholars, words were sacred.

Ireland was converted to Christianity by St. Patrick in the 400s, and in the following century, monks began arriving on the British Isles from continental Europe. The first major monastic settlement in the area was founded by the Irish missionary St. Columba (c. 521–597) at Iona, off the coast of Scotland, in 563. Monks from the Iona community in turn founded Lindisfarne off the coast of England in 634. The latter community would become famous for the Lindisfarne Gospels, and Iona became famous for the Book of Kells. Both were gorgeously illuminated manuscripts.

The communities of Iona and Lindisfarne were destroyed by the last great wave of Germanic barbarians in the Middle Ages, the Vikings, in the 790s. Many of the monks left before the Vikings arrived; in any case, they and their brethren had managed to keep learning alive during the darkest years of the Middle Ages.

Eventually the stature of the popes would become such that they created relics of their own, making water or oil "holy" simply by praying over them. By that time, the pope was the most powerful man in Christendom (KRIS-in-dum), or the Christian world, and for that, too, later popes had Gregory to thank. Under his shrewd leadership, the papacy became firmly established as something much more than the office of Rome's bishop; gradually the pope became not just the spiritual, but the political leader of Western Europe.

Gregory reinforced the church's power by teaching that the Bible was a difficult book that required interpretation by those trained to do so: priests and other leaders of the church. A version of the Bible had been translated by St. Jerome (c. 347–c. 419), and its name, the Vulgate, a term referring to the language spoken by common people, implied that it was meant to be understood by the masses. The Vulgate, however, was in Latin, a language that had long since been replaced by local dialects for everyday use. Yet it remained strong as a written language, and virtually every educated person in early medieval Europe understood Latin. The problem was that hardly anyone, outside of a tiny minority within the church, was educated: for many centuries, even most kings were illiterate. Eventually people had no idea of what the Bible said, and the church actively discouraged believers from attempting to read the Scriptures.

Finally, from Augustine's writings Gregory adopted the idea of Purgatory, a place for people who were too good to go to Hell, but had not quite made it to Heaven. He took this concept and added to it, suggesting that the loved ones of a deceased person pray for his or her soul. By the 1000s, the concept of Purgatory had become firmly established.

The Merovingians (481–751)

An earlier Frankish king gave his name to a dynasty that emerged among the Franks in the 400s, the Merovingians, but Clovis (ruled 481–511) was its first important king. By accepting mainstream Christianity in 496, he gained the support both of Rome (that is, the pope and the Church) and of powerful local priests.

Clovis, a Frankish king who ruled from 481 to 511, was the greatest ruler of the Merovingian dynasty. *Reproduced by permission of the Corbis Corporation.*

He was also the only notable Merovingian ruler. This was because Clovis, like many German chieftains, believed that a king should divide his

Merovingian Art

Ancient Greek and Roman artists had tried to depict human beings and other subjects as accurately as possible, and representational art became amazingly precise. Then as Rome began to decline in the A.D. 200s, so did Roman portrayals of the human figure. Faces and bodies began to look all the same, and artists' depictions of people looked more and more primitive.

With the rise of the Merovingians after Rome's fall, art took a sharp turn away from representation and toward abstract images. It was as though Merovingian artists realized that they had lost the ability to accurately represent subjects, so they moved in the opposite direction, producing gorgeous designs with only limited representative quality.

The artwork itself may have been abstract, but the objects produced by the Merovingians—belt buckles, decorative pins for fastening clothing—were decidedly practical. Much Merovingian art was intended to be portable, reflecting their still somewhat unsettled lifestyle, but the Merovingians also made a significant contribution to architecture by introducing the idea of a church bell tower. Monks in Merovingian France illuminated manuscripts and developed an elegant type of lettering called majuscule (MAJ-uh-skyool).

realm equally between all his sons instead of passing it on to the firstborn. While this was a generous idea, in practice it meant that a kingdom's power would be diluted quickly.

Nonetheless, the Merovingians were important in a number of regards. Under Clovis, they conquered much of what is now France—formerly home to the Burgundians and Visigoths, as well as other Frankish tribes—and western Germany. With the support of Rome, they were able to establish themselves as a stronghold of Christianity, a fact that became more important with the rise of Islam in the 600s. This papal-royal alliance set the tone for the Middle Ages. In the realm of the arts, the Merovingians were also trailblazers (see box, "Merovingian Art").

Manorialism

The Franks adopted few aspects of Roman law and administrative rule, but they did maintain one significant link with a late Roman practice. When Roman power was fading and the people could no longer look to the legions, or army, for protection, they had turned to the owners of large villas, or country estates, who controlled private armies. The serfs gathered their dwellings around the villa in what came to be called villages.

Villas were also known as manors (source of the word "mansion"), and the Frankish version of the late Roman system came to be known as manorialism (muh-NOHR-ee-ul-izm). Under manorialism, large numbers of serfs became dependent on a large landowner for protection. A serf was like a peasant, a farmer with a small plot of land; but serfs, whose name comes from the same root as "serve," were more like slaves.

The manorial system provided the framework for feudalism. This system helped bring an end to the Merovingians as power shifted from Merovingian kings to the Frankish aristocracy, who exerted influence through the office of majordomo.

The house of Charles Martel

Today the term majordomo, meaning "mayor of the palace," refers to someone who takes charge in place of another, which is essentially what the majordomos did. The later Merovingian kings lived lives of pleasure, and could hardly be bothered to run their kingdoms, but the majordomos were more than happy to assume that job—and the authority that went with it.

This was particularly true of the greatest majordomo, Charles Martel (c. 688–741). Martel, which meant "hammer"—thus suggesting Charles's power—was not a family name, or surname; the custom of surnames would not arise until centuries later. Under his leadership, beginning in 714, the kingdom withstood invasions by the Saxons and Frisians (FREE-zhunz), a Germanic people from what is now Holland.

Even more significant was his defense against invaders from the

Charles Martel was a great leader of the Frankish kingdom during the Merovingian Age, and it was his grandson, Charlemagne, who gave his name to the next great dynasty: the Carolingians. *Reproduced by permission of Archive Photos, Inc.*

south: the Moors, Muslims who had conquered Spain and were ready to take over France. Had the Moors succeeded in their invasion of France, which they began in 719, Europe might be quite different today; as it was, a force led by Charles drove back the Muslims at Tours (TOOR) in 732. Given his vital role in the Frankish leadership, it is not surprising that Charles judged it was time for his family to take full control.

For More Information

Books

Clark, Kenneth. *Civilisation: A Personal View.* New York: Harper, 1969, pp. 1–32.

Dijkstra, Henk, editor. *History of the Ancient and Medieval World,* Volume 8: *Christianity and Islam.* New York: Marshall Cavendish, 1996, pp. 1032–44.

Dijkstra, Henk, editor. *History of the Ancient and Medieval World,* Volume 9: *The Middle Ages.* New York: Marshall Cavendish, 1996, pp. 1159–64.

Hanawalt, Barbara A. *The Middle Ages: An Illustrated History.* New York: Oxford University Press, 1998.

Langley, Andrew. *Medieval Life.* New York: Knopf, 1996.

Severy, Merle, editor. *The Age of Chivalry.* Washington, D.C.: National Geographic Society, 1969, pp. 13–42.

Web Sites

Book, Manuscript, and Printing History. [Online] Available http://historymedren.about.com/education/history/historymedren/msubprint.htm (last accessed July 28, 2000).

The Catholic Encyclopedia. [Online] Available http://www.newadvent.org/cathen/ (last accessed July 28, 2000).

"The Franks." [Online] Available http://www.btinternet.com/~mark.furnival/franks.htm (last accessed July 28, 2000).

The Carolingian Age | 4

Whereas the Merovingian Age had begun in turmoil, but had led to the establishment of Europe's first stable dynasty in centuries, the period from 750 to 1000 started with the establishment of a new dynasty and ended in turmoil. The Carolingians' magnificent empire seemed to recall that of Rome, but their power largely centered around one man: Charlemagne. Once he was gone, the empire began disintegrating. Europe faced new terrors as well, not least of which was the last wave of Germanic barbarians: the Vikings. Other invaders came as well, and it seemed that Europe was on the verge of another dark age.

The Carolingian Age (751–987)

A turning point in the history both of Western Europe and of church-state relations occurred in 751, when Charles Martel's son Pepin III (c. 714–768) sent a message to the pope asking if it would be a sin to remove the Merovingian king from power. The pope, who needed Frankish help to defend against the Lombards, sent word that it would not, where-

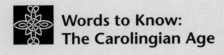

Words to Know:
The Carolingian Age

Astronomy: The scientific study of the stars and other heavenly bodies, and their movement in the sky.

Chain mail: A lightweight, flexible armor made of interlocking metal rings.

Christendom: The Christian world.

Communion: The Christian ceremony of commemorating the last supper of Jesus Christ.

Epic: A long poem that recounts the adventures of a legendary hero.

Geometry: A type of mathematics dealing with various shapes, their properties, and their measurements.

Mace: A club with spikes on the end, typically used for breaking armor.

Mead: An intoxicating drink of fermented honey, popular among Vikings and other Germanic peoples of Northern Europe.

Noble: A ruler within a kingdom who has an inherited title and lands, but who is less powerful than the king or queen; collectively, nobles are known as the *nobility.*

Nomadic: Wandering.

Vatican: The seat of the pope's power in Rome.

upon Pepin ordered that the last of the Merovingians be thrown into a monastery. Thus once again a pope blessed the establishment of a new dy-

nasty, the Carolingians (kayr-uh-LINJ-ee-unz).

The name came from that of Pepin's son Charles, sometimes known as Carolus Magnus, meaning "Charles the Great." He is better known as Charlemagne (SHAR-luh-main; 742–814; ruled 768–814), and he was the single most important Western European leader of the Early Middle Ages. Under Charlemagne, Western Europe had something it had not seen for centuries: a vibrant, growing empire. Already the Frankish territories comprised most of what is now France and western Germany, but Charlemagne started expanding the boundaries, first by defeating the Saxons to the north in 777. He saw himself as more than a conqueror, however, and with the conquest came the forced conversion of the Saxons to Christianity.

His father Pepin had already dealt the Lombards a harsh blow in 756, after which he turned their territories in eastern Italy over to the church in an act known as the Donation of Pepin. Thenceforth these were called the Papal States, and would exist as such until the 1800s. Charlemagne completed the conquest of the Lombards, receiving their crown as his own in 774. He then turned his attention to Spain, where in 778 he tried unsuccessfully to win back Muslim-held territories for Christendom. Further campaigns resulted in Charlemagne unifying virtually all German territories, including the kingdom of Bavaria in southern Germany.

In 794, Charlemagne established his capital at Aachen (AH-ken;

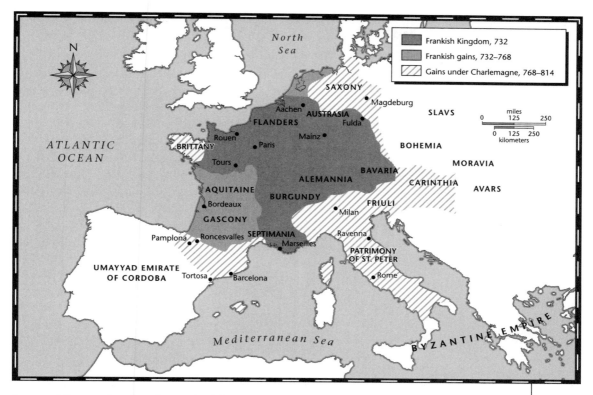

A map of Europe showing the territorial gains made under Charlemagne's rule. *Illustration by XNR Productions. Reproduced by permission of the Gale Group.*

in modern-day Germany), a city famous for its mineral baths. The year 800 marked the high point of his career, when he became the first European emperor to visit Rome in three centuries. The Byzantine rulers had cut themselves off from Rome; therefore Pope Leo III crowned Charlemagne Carolus Augustulus, Emperor of the Romans, on Christmas Day. This was in effect the beginning of the Holy Roman Empire, which, though it never lived up to its magnificent name, was destined to become a significant part of the Middle Ages.

The Carolingian Renaissance

While in Italy, Charlemagne visited the former imperial capital of Ravenna, including the Church of San Vitale. Built by the Byzantine invaders, the church must have inspired him, because upon his return to Aachen, he ordered his architect, Odo of Metz, to design a replica. The chapel at Aachen, as it turned out, was not an exact reproduction: it was a much firmer, less delicate building than the original—and thus it helped establish the essentials of Carolingian architecture.

Charlemagne, who ruled from 768 to 814, was the most significant Western European ruler of the Early Middle Ages. *Reproduced by permission of the Corbis Corporation.*

and laid the groundwork for both Romanesque and Gothic architecture.

The period of Charlemagne's rule saw a rebirth in the arts and learning; hence it is sometimes called the "Carolingian Renaissance." Much of the credit goes to Alcuin (AL-kwin; c. 732–804), an Anglo-Saxon scholar who at Charlemagne's request became head of the school at Aachen. Surveying the deplorable state of education among the future Carolingian leaders, Alcuin called for a return to the study of Latin and of what the Romans had called the seven liberal arts: grammar, rhetoric (the art of writing and speaking), logic, arithmetic, geometry, music, and astronomy.

Charlemagne himself could barely read and write, yet literacy thrived among the upper classes during his reign. By then parchment, a durable type of paper made from sheepskin, had come into use. Many of the Greek and Roman classics had been saved earlier by monks in the British Isles, but Carolingian monks copied so many manuscripts themselves that many took their versions for the originals. The monks had developed the Merovingian majuscule into a highly readable script called minuscule. Later, they created a more square version of this script that, because people mistook their manuscripts for Roman originals, came to be called "Roman." A slanted version of "Roman" lettering, used at the Vatican, became the basis for italic—that is, Italian—script.

A number of qualities distinguished the architecture of Carolingian times from that of the Merovingian era, when civilization was still hanging by a thread. Merovingian buildings were small and boxlike— like a hut, only bigger and more permanent. Carolingian design, by contrast, incorporated the graceful, open basilica floorplan used by Constantine (emperor of the Roman Empire; ruled 310–37). Thus the Carolingians borrowed Italian concepts for a rougher, hardier northern kingdom,

The divided kingdom

Charlemagne's empire did not long outlast him. His son Louis the

Pious succeeded him in 814, but Louis was no Charlemagne, and his rule was marked by quarrels. The Treaty of Verdun in 843 arranged for the division of the empire into three parts, one for each of Louis's sons.

One son received an area that came to be known as the West Frankish Empire, later to become the nation of France. A second son received what was dubbed the East Frankish Empire, which would unify under the name Germany more than a thousand years later. In between was the "Middle Kingdom," the inheritance of the other son. This comprised a strip running from what is now Holland all the way down to Italy.

Through inheritance, the "Middle Kingdom" would soon be dissolved into a patchwork of tiny principalities. The western and eastern empires, by contrast, lasted a bit longer. Descendants of Charlemagne ruled France until 887, and off and on for exactly 100 more years; however, the real power rested in the hands of various feudal lords. Much the same happened in the East Frankish Empire, where in 911 the nobility chose their own king from outside the Carolingian line of succession.

Feudalism

One of the most important legacies of the Carolingian dynasty was feudalism, an economic and political system based on land and loyalty that evolved into a fully defined way of life in the 800s. Central to this evo-

 Abu al-Abbas

During Charlemagne's time, fame of the great Frankish emperor spread to Arabia, from whence the powerful caliph Harun al-Rashid sent him an unusual gift in 802: an elephant called Abu al-Abbas. The king and the beast soon became inseparable, and wherever Charlemagne went on his conquests, Abu went as well. Abu died in 810, while his master was on a campaign against the Danes in northern Europe. Abu's ivory tusks were made into chess pieces.

lution were knights, heavily armed cavalry soldiers who could fight either in massed formations or one on one. As such, they represented centuries of change and development in society as a whole.

In early Merovingian times, all soldiers were more or less the same. Many were farmers who had simply left their fields to fight, and most were infantrymen, or foot soldiers. This was a pattern that went back to the ancient Greeks. Then in the late 500s, one of the most important inventions in human history made its appearance: the stirrup.

Actually, a form of stirrup had been used in India since before the time of Jesus Christ, and perhaps the Huns picked up the idea as they moved across Asia toward Rome. Whatever the case, the power of Attila's armies can be attributed in part to the fact that riders were equipped with hanging rings to hold their feet. This may not sound terribly important, but it made all the difference in battle. A rider without stirrups could use only the strength of his arm to deliver a blow with a sword or lance; if he struck with his full weight, he would be thrown from his horse. A soldier firmly anchored in stirrups, by contrast, could strike with his whole weight and that of his horse as well.

More than a century after Attila, stirrups—and the types of tactics they permitted—took hold among the Merovingians. Soldiers began protecting themselves with armor, typically chain mail, a lightweight, flexible covering made of interlocking metal rings. The first battle using armored cavalrymen was probably a fight between the Franks and Saxons in 626; but it was Charles Martel's victory at Tours in 732 over the Muslims (who had no stirrups) that firmly established the new technology.

How the feudal system worked

To equip a knight was costly: not only did he have his armor and his weapons (sword, lance, mace, and sometimes crossbow), but he needed more than one horse in case the first one was hurt in battle. He also needed a group of servants to assist him, along with food for his horses, his servants, and himself—not to mention years of freedom from other responsibilities in order to train for warfare. Not even a king could afford to support more than a few knights; for this,

he had to depend on the nobles within his kingdom.

In early medieval times, all wealth was based on land ownership, and the king owned all the land. Below the king were feudal lords, or nobles, who were allowed to maintain estates on the king's land as long as they supplied him with a certain amount of knights to defend the kingdom. The estate was called a fief (FEEF), a word that, like *feudal,* is related to "fee." The nobles would in turn give knights title to small fiefs of their own, along with the authority to tax those who lived on the land.

The lowest-ranking people in feudal society were the serfs, or peasants, by far the largest group. They were the ones who worked the land, growing food—most of which they turned over to the lords—and paying taxes, which helped maintain knights. There were gradations of rank within the peasantry, with certain types of peasants who acted as foremen over other peasants, but they were all so far below the royalty and nobility that it hardly mattered. In return for their labors, they received protection from outside attack, itself a very real danger in the Middle Ages; but they also tied themselves and future generations to a life only slightly better than slavery.

In the medieval world, this arrangement did not seem unfair. People saw feudalism, if they considered it at all, as a system of mutual obligations in which everyone had a place— even the church. Lords provided their local church and monastery with protection; in return, priests and monks, who had great influence over the peasantry, supported the nobility and the king.

The Vikings (793–c. 1000)

Around the time of Charlemagne's coronation as emperor, just when it seemed that Europe was on the road to safety and unification, yet another great threat appeared from the north. They came from Scandinavia—now Sweden, Norway, and Denmark—where the land was rough and rocky, and people lived on the edge of the sea. With the population growing and the land ever more scarce, they began sweeping over Europe, killing and marauding as they went. Frightened Europeans called them Northmen, Norsemen, or—using a word from the invaders' own language—Vikings.

On January 8, 793, Viking raiders destroyed the church at Lindisfarne off the coast of England—ironically, one of the places where civilized learning had weathered the darkest years of the Middle Ages. In a further irony, Lindisfarne, Iona, and other scholarly centers now became bases for Viking raids throughout the British Isles. The marauders swept through Ireland, drawn by the gold and other wealth of its monasteries, and established colonies on the east coast. Among the latter was Dublin, which later became the Irish capital.

The Vikings were particularly savage in their attacks on Britain, so much so that the natives began unit-

This illustration of Duke Rollo of Normandy shows an example of chain mail armor. *Reproduced by permission of the Corbis Corporation.*

ing against them. This happened in Scotland, and again to the south, where attacks by the Danes helped produce the first true hero of English history. At first King Alfred (849–899) ruled only a small realm called Wessex; by 886, however, he had captured the city of London, and united all English lands that were not under Danish control. The Danes were pushed into the northeast of England, which came to be known as the Danelaw; thereafter, they became landowners and eventually melted into the population.

The Medieval Mind

Western Europeans during the Early Middle Ages were inclined to believe the most outlandish ideas, particularly where religious matters were concerned. For instance, they believed Satan was everywhere; thus one monk wrote that "the whole air is but a thick mass of devils." Another chronicler told of how a wicked priest tried to take sexual advantage of a woman. He kissed her with a Communion wafer in his mouth, hoping this would win her by affection; instead, the wafer caused him to suddenly grow so tall he could not leave the church building. He buried the wafer in a corner of the church, then later dug it up—only to find that it had turned into a blood-stained figure of Jesus on the cross. People who heard this story most likely gave it the same solemn respect that a modern person would for a nightly news report.

Superstition was an everyday part of life. Immediately after a death in the house, for instance, all bowls of water would have to be covered so that the loved one's spirit would not drown. Care also had to be taken to ensure that a cat or dog did not walk across the corpse in the coffin, lest the dear departed turn into a vampire. Some superstitions have survived from medieval times—for instance, saying "bless you" when someone sneezes, since sneezing was viewed as an opportunity for a demon to enter the body.

In place of scientific knowledge, people often relied on highly uneducated ideas about cause-and-effect relations. For example, people readily accepted an idea that has since come to be known as "spontaneous generation." If one were to leave food out in a room for long enough, it would of course draw rats; but medieval people, seeing a rat where a piece of cheese had been, reasoned that the cheese had actually turned into the rat. They also believed in what was later dubbed "acquired characteristics," another simple-minded fallacy. According to this notion, if a man lost his right arm in an accident, his children would be born missing their right arms as well.

The spread of the Vikings

In 860, Viking ships sailing westward found a relatively pleasant and fertile land far beyond England. Fearing the overpopulation that had driven them from Scandinavia, they gave it the discouraging-sounding name of Iceland. Beyond Iceland in 982, the Vikings found another land, one not nearly as hospitable. Because they were not worried about people overpopulating this area, they gave it an inviting name: Greenland.

Sailing still farther west, in about 1000 Leif Eriksson landed on what the Vikings called Vinland, probably Newfoundland. There they did battle with what they called "skraelings"—almost certainly the same people Columbus later mistakenly identified as Indians. Columbus's men had guns, whereas the Vikings' weapons were no more advanced than the war clubs and arrows of the "skraelings." Therefore the Viking colonization of the New World was shortlived, and soon forgotten except in legends of Vinland.

While some Vikings went west, others went south. From their homeland in Sweden, a group called Varangians in 862 sailed along rivers from the Baltic Sea deep into Eastern Europe. Drawn by myths of a rich, golden city—perhaps Constantinople—they founded a great city of their own, Novgorod, and also established their power in Kiev. The Slavs of the area called the Varangians "Rus," and eventually Russia became the name of the region.

Then there were the Vikings who came to be known as Normans, a corruption of "Norsemen." They began moving down the west coast of Europe in the mid-800s, and for the next two centuries battled throughout the western half of the Mediterranean. In 820, another group of Normans settled in an area of northwestern France that came to be known as Normandy. They adopted the French language and culture, and in 1066 would launch one of the most significant invasions in history when they conquered England.

Decline of the Vikings

By the time the Varangians and Normans were establishing themselves,

A Viking. *Reproduced by permission of the New York Public Library Picture Collection.*

Under the leadership of King Alfred, natives of Britain united in an attempt to defend themselves against attacks by Vikings.
Reproduced by permission of the Library of Congress.

(ruled 1016–35), they controlled England, Denmark, and Norway, but there is a legend about Canute that says something about these last Norsemen's attempts at conquest. Supposedly Canute ordered the tide not to wash in on the shoreline; of course it did anyway, thus proving that there are limits even to a king's power. As it turned out, his empire was shortlived, and the last Danes were pushed out of England by William of Normandy—himself a descendant of Vikings—in 1070.

The end of the Early Middle Ages (843– c. 1000)

The late 800s and 900s were a frightening time in Western Europe. Not only were the Vikings on the move, but the continent faced invasion by other forces from the south and east. The Muslims had already conquered Spain, and in the 800s they began menacing Italy. They drove out the Byzantines, who had held Sicily and southern Italy off and on for centuries, and even threatened Rome itself. At the same time, a group of nomads called the Magyars entered Eastern Europe from Ukraine, where they had been forced out by Central Asian nomads. This seemed like a repeat of events that had helped bring about the fall of the Roman Empire: indeed, the Magyars even took over the old stomping-grounds of Attila the Hun in Hungary, from which they launched attacks on various German states.

the Vikings as a group were dying out. By about 1000, they had accepted Christianity and become relatively civilized, meaning that they no longer had the same lust for raiding. In place of the old Scandinavian tribal lands, Norway, Denmark, and Sweden emerged as kingdoms, possessing formal governments with capitals and laws.

One last hurrah for the Norsemen came in the early 1000s, when the Danes briefly conquered England. At their high point under King Canute

Viking ships disembarking on the Normandy coast. *Reproduced by permission of the Corbis Corporation.*

The Vikings, or Norsemen, enjoyed great power under King Canute (ruled 1016–35). This illustration depicts the legend of Canute ordering the tide not to wash in. *Reproduced by permission of the New York Public Library Picture Collection.*

During this age, people who looked to the church for comfort were bound to be disappointed. The papacy had severely declined in the 800s and 900s, with murderers, thieves, and adulterers among the ranks of the popes during those years. An example was the man who became known as John XII in 955: among Pope John's many accomplishments were bribe-

Viking Mythology

According to Viking mythology, when soldiers died in battle they would be swept up by warrior maidens called Valkyries (vahl-KEER-uhz) and taken to a kind of heaven. The latter was called Valhalla (vahl-HAHL-uh), and was essentially a more perfect version of the Vikings' own feasting halls, where they dined on legs of mutton and drank an intoxicating honey malt beverage called *mead* (MEED).

Norse mythology became the basis for a number of great medieval epics: the Icelandic *Eddas* (c. 900–1241) and *Volsung Saga* (1200s), as well as the German *Niebelungenlied* (nee-buh-LOONG-en-leed; 1200s). In the nineteenth century, German composer Richard Wagner (REE-kard VAHG-nur) wrote a majestic series of operas, *The Ring,* based on the Nordic myths.

THOR.

Depiction of the Viking god Thor. *Reproduced by permission of the Corbis Corporation.*

One of the most memorable pieces from *The Ring* is called "Ride of the Valkyries."

taking and wild orgies in the papal palace. Yet this period also saw the beginnings of church reform, led by the Benedictine monks at Cluny in France in 910. The Cluniac (KLOO-nee-ak) movement stood for a new type of monasticism: instead of withdrawing from the world, the Cluniacs sought to strengthen the central authority of the pope as a way of reinvigorating the church, and thus society as a whole.

The 900s also experienced the rise of Western Europe's first great leader since Charlemagne, Otto the Great (912–973). In 955, he defeated the Magyars, who soon became Christianized and settled permanently in Hungary. He then marched into Italy, by then under threat from a variety of local kings. Otto defeated them, and in 962, the pope crowned him emperor, reviving the title held by Charlemagne. A year later, Otto had the crooked Pope John replaced, showing that though the bishop of Rome could crown him, he still held more power. The great struggle of kings and popes, a conflict that would dominate the eleventh century, had begun.

For More Information

Books

Clark, Kenneth. *Civilisation: A Personal View.* New York: Harper, 1969, pp. 1–32.

Dijkstra, Henk, editor. *History of the Ancient and Medieval World,* Volume 9: *The Middle Ages.* New York: Marshall Cavendish, 1996, pp. 1164–1224.

Hanawalt, Barbara A. *The Middle Ages: An Illustrated History.* New York: Oxford University Press, 1998.

Langley, Andrew. *Medieval Life.* New York: Knopf, 1996.

Severy, Merle, editor. *The Age of Chivalry.* Washington, D.C.: National Geographic Society, 1969, pp. 43–91.

Web Sites

Daily Life—Medieval History Net Links. [Online] Available http://historymedren. about.com/education/history/historymedren/msubmenudaily.htm (last accessed July 28, 2000).

Vikings and Scandinavian History. [Online] Available http://historymedren.about. com/education/history/historymedren/msubvik.htm (last accessed July 28, 2000).

Eastern Europe

5

In ancient times, Greece had built one of the world's greatest civilizations, a center of culture and science that reached its peak in the period 490–404 B.C. Even as Greece declined, its influence spread from Italy to Egypt to India, so that by the time the Roman Empire conquered Greece in 146 B.C., Rome had been thoroughly influenced by Greek civilization. Beginning in A.D. 330, the Roman Empire began to split into Greek, or Eastern, and Roman, or Western, halves. Divisions between the two lands widened after the West fell and the East became the Byzantine Empire. Ethnic differences further widened the gap: while Germans overran the western half of the continent, much of Eastern Europe came under the dominance of a people called the Slavs.

The Byzantine Empire

The Byzantine (BIZ-un-teen) Empire had its beginnings with Constantine, who in 330 founded a second Roman capital at a city overlooking the strait that separates Europe from Asia Minor (modern-day Turkey). The city became Con-

Words to Know: Eastern Europe

Civil service: The administrators and officials who run a government.

City-state: A city that is also a self-contained political unit, like a country.

Clergy: The priesthood, or all ministers.

Clerical: Relating to priests.

Deity: A god.

Diplomacy: The use of skillful negotiations with leaders of other nations to influence events.

Hagiography: An idealized biography, often of a saint.

Icon: In the Eastern Orthodox Church, an image of a saint.

Legal code: A system of laws.

Madonna and Child: Mary and the baby Jesus, as depicted in religious art.

Middle class: A group in between the rich and the poor, or the rich and the working class; usually considered the backbone of a growing economy.

Missionary: Someone who travels to other lands with the aim of converting others to his or her religion.

Nimbus: A halo-like cloud said to hover around a deity or exalted person.

Patriarch: A bishop in the Eastern Orthodox Church.

Plague: A disease that spreads quickly to a large population.

Protectorate: A state dependent on a larger, stronger state for military protection.

Siege: A sustained military attack against a city.

Strait: A narrow water passageway between two areas of land.

stantinople (kahn-stan-ti-NOH-pul), but later scholars used its old name of Byzantium (bi-ZAN-tee-um) to identify the entire Byzantine Empire. The Byzantine people, however, called themselves Romans, and their land the Roman Empire, which thus continued to exist in the East for another thousand years after the fall of the West.

In 500 Byzantium held most of the lands formerly controlled by the Eastern Roman Empire, including Greece and what is now Bulgaria, Asia Minor, a strip of land from Syria to Palestine, Egypt, and part of Libya. But Justinian (483–565; ruled 527–565), the greatest of Byzantine rulers, resolved to undertake the re-conquest of the Western Roman Empire from the barbarians. His brilliant general Belisarius (c. 505–565) won back North Africa from the Vandals in 534, and Italy from the Ostrogoths in 540. The Byzantines also took southern Spain from the Visigoths in 550.

A map of Eastern Europe in the eleventh century indicating the lands under the control of the Byzantine Empire as well as those controlled by Kievan Russia.
Illustration by XNR Productions. Reproduced by permission of the Gale Group.

These victories were costly, however, and except for a few parts of Sicily and southern Italy, the Byzantines did not hold their conquests for long. The empire soon had other troubles as well. Beginning in 541, a plague devastated Byzantium, and by the time it ended in the mid-700s, it had killed millions of people. Aside from everything else, this meant that the empire's tax revenues decreased dramatically, leaving it unable to pay for its armies. Enemies, including the Slavs, attacked from all sides, and the first successful rebellion in some three hundred years ended the life of the emperor Maurice (ruled 582–602). For more than a century, the empire was almost constantly at war with Persia, which conquered all Byzantine lands south of Asia Minor, and it was only with the help of the church that Heraclius (hair-uh-KLY-us; ruled 610–41) was able to hold on to Constantinople itself. It seemed that things could not get worse—but they did.

When the even more powerful Arab caliphate replaced the Persians, Byzantium seemed doomed. Yet thanks to reorganization of the military by Constans II (ruled 641–68), the Byzantines put up a strong defense of their homeland. They reached a turning point in 718, when the Arabs were forced to give up the siege of Constantinople. This had enormous significance for future history: if the Arabs had defeated the Byzantines, they would undoubtedly have conquered and forcibly converted Western Europe—which lacked unifying leadership at the time—to Islam.

By the 900s, Byzantium was on the offensive again, reconquering old territories and dealing severely with a tribe called the Bulgars, who had long posed a threat. These conquests reached their peak under Basil II (BAZ-ul; ruled 976–1025), nicknamed "The Bulgar-Slayer." Basil annexed Bulgaria in 1014, and by 1025 the empire had reached a second high point. Egypt, Palestine, and Lebanon were gone forever, but the Byzantine lands and protectorates stretched from southern Italy to Armenia, and from Croatia to Syria.

The Byzantine system

Justinian had laid the foundations for modern law with his legal code, or system of laws, completed in 535. Roman law dated back almost a thousand years, but Justinian's Code greatly simplified and organized it. Byzantium also had an excellent and highly organized civil service. Placed as they were between many lands in Europe and Asia, the Byzantines had to become skilled at diplomacy, or the art of negotiation. They also became mas-

ters at playing their enemies against one another; but when they had to go to war, they were a mighty force.

Having adapted to changing times, the Byzantines developed a strong cavalry, along with something the earlier Roman Empire had lacked: a powerful navy. In fact, the Byzantine fleet used the first modern-style chemical weapon, "Greek fire." The latter was a combination of petroleum, saltpeter, quicklime, and sulphur; when sprayed on an enemy's ship it would cause it to burn.

One of the most significant military-related developments, however, had nothing to do with actual fighting. This was the reorganization of the army by Constans II in the mid-600s, an act that may well have saved the empire. With funds running low, he gave soldiers plots of land called "themes" and made them self-supporting. This not only saved money, but also promoted good will with the troops and encouraged a stronger defense, since now the soldiers were defending their own land.

The economy

The "themes" bear some resemblance to aspects of Western European feudalism. Certainly both Byzantine and Carolingian society were made of similar elements: a tiny elite consisting of royalty, nobility, priests, and military; and a vast mass of toiling peasants. The lives of the peasants may not have been much better than those of their counterparts in Western Europe, but thanks to the efforts of

Mosaic of Justinian and his court from the Church of San Vitale. Justinian was the greatest of the Byzantine emperors. *Reproduced by permission of the Granger Collection Ltd.*

the Orthodox Church, literacy was much more widespread in Byzantium.

The Byzantine Empire even managed to create a middle class, something virtually unknown in the West until the 1000s. Typically these were merchants who profited from the extensive trade routes running through Byzantium, linking Europe and Asia. Thus Constantinople became known as a crossroads for the world and emerged as a most splendid city. At a time when Rome had perhaps 30,000 inhabitants, the Byzantine capital boasted a quarter-million people.

Byzantine culture

From an early time, it was clear that there was not really just one Christian church. The Catholic Church conducted its services in Latin, the Orthodox Church in Greek. Catholics looked to the pope for leadership, members of the Orthodox faith to the *patriarch* (PAY-tree-ark) or bishop of Constantinople. Gradually the Orthodox church came to have its own saints, its own holidays, and its own rules concerning marriage among the clergy.

At the heart of the division between churches was a debate about the identity of Jesus Christ: for Western

The Nika Revolt

Byzantine society in the 500s was dominated by two groups, the Blues and the Greens. The names came from the colors of their respective horse-racing teams, who competed regularly at the Hippodrome, or race track. Horse races in Byzantium were much more important than they are today: by cheering for the emperor's horse or that of a challenger, a citizen was making a political statement, and rivalries could often lead to violence.

It is not surprising, then, that a dispute that originated in the Hippodrome on January 13, 532, ended in massive bloodshed. This was the Nika Revolt, so named because *Nika!* or "Conquer!" was the favorite cheer of spectators at the races. In this particular instance, both the Greens and the Blues joined forces against the emperor Justinian, who had placed extraordinarily high taxes on his people and imprisoned members of both factions.

With an angry crowd gathering outside his palace, Justinian found himself unable to make a decision and began listening to advisors who suggested he should flee. It was then that the Empress Theodora (c. 500–548) stepped in and told him to act bravely: "For my own part," she said, "I hold to the old saying that the imperial purple makes the best burial sheet"—in other words, it is better to die defending the throne than to run away. Justinian listened to his wife's counsel and dispatched an army led by his general Belisarius to deal with the revolt. They trapped the rioters in the Hippodrome, where they massacred some 30,000 of them and reestablished order.

Christians, there could be no doubt that Christ *was* God, whereas most Eastern Christians maintained that the two were separate. In worldly matters, West and East also differed in their views on the relationship between church and state. In Western Europe, popes and kings vied for leadership, but in Byzantium the emperor's power was clear. He could even exercise final say in choosing the patriarch of Constantinople, and the Byzantines viewed the position of the emperor (though not necessarily any individual holding that position) as sacred.

In fact depictions of emperors and empresses in Byzantine art made use of an ancient pagan symbol called the *nimbus*, which was said to hover around a deity. Oddly, this was one of the few aspects of Byzantine culture that made an impact on the West, where artists began using a related symbol, the halo; but haloes were for Jesus, Mary, or the saints—not for rulers.

Iconoclasm

In the Byzantine world, the relationship between art, religion, and politics was a complicated one, and never more so than in the dispute over Iconoclasm (eye-KAHN-oh-klazm). The latter was the name for a movement, supported by Emperor Leo III (ruled 717–41), which held that all "icons," or images of religious figures, were idols, and hence went against Christian teachings. Under orders from Leo, icons were forbidden, and many existing ones were destroyed. A number of priests died trying to stop soldiers from tearing down statues, and under Constantine V (ruled 741–75) the persecution became even more vigorous.

Many medieval European rulers earned a title to distinguish them from others of the same name, a word or phrase that characterized the man, his reign, or his greatest achievement: thus Pepin III was known as "Pepin the Short," and Basil II became "the Bulgar-Slayer." Constantine's title—Copronymus, which means "name of dung"—says a great deal about the Byzantine reaction to Iconoclasm, which became more and more unpopular as the violence associated with it continued. Western church leaders meanwhile shared in the Byzantines' growing distaste for the Iconoclastic movement: indeed, Iconoclasm never had many supporters in the West, where few people could read. Images were an essential part of worship in Western Europe, and any attack on artwork was seen as an attack on Christianity itself.

Eventually the anti-Iconoclast movement—the Iconophiles (eye-KAHN-oh-fylz)—gained an important supporter on the throne, yet this did little to win favor with the pope in Rome. The new Byzantine ruler was a ruthless one; however, the real problem was that this emperor was an empress: Irene (ruled 780–802). It was considered bad enough that a woman ruled the empire, but she added insult to injury by using her authority to call the Second Council of Nicaea, which condemned Iconoclasm in 787.

The meeting was designated the seventh ecumenical council, implying that it brought together all Christians. In fact the split between East and West was only widening, and the pope's crowning of Charlemagne as Holy Roman Emperor in 800 was in part a reaction to Irene: since it was illegal for a woman to rule the Byzantine empire, the pope could claim that the Roman throne was vacant, and thereby crown Charlemagne. This in turn angered the Byzantines, who felt that the papacy had challenged their claim as the rightful heirs to the Roman Empire.

Byzantine art

As they became more cut off from "barbarian" Western Europe, the Byzantines became convinced that theirs was a superior culture that must be preserved unchanged. It is easy to understand how they believed this: there was their glorious Greek past, not to mention the fact that for many centuries, Byzantium was the only real civilization on the European continent. Thus the Byzantines developed a highly static, or unchanging, worldview.

This static quality translated to their art, which was brilliant if a bit

A mosaic depicting a Byzantine Madonna and Child. This mosaic is from the Hagia Sophia, the church completed under Justinian's orders in 537. *Reproduced by permission of the Corbis Corporation.*

proportion to head size than they really were. Babies looked like small adults, without the relatively large heads and "baby fat" that distinguishes real babies.

The Byzantines were masters in the form called *mosaic* (moh-ZAY-ik), usually created by arranging colored bits of glass or tile to form a picture. The most famous Byzantine mosaics are those depicting Justinian and Theodora in the Church of San Vitale at Ravenna, built during the brief Byzantine occupation of Italy. The greatest example of Byzantine architecture, however, was not the church in Ravenna but the Hagia (HAH-jah) Sophia in Constantinople. Built by Justinian, the Hagia Sophia was completed in 537 and quickly became recognized as one of the most magnificent structures in the world. It was dominated by a dome that, despite its enormous size—184 feet high and 102 feet wide—seemed to float over thin air. In fact it rests on four arches and the stone piers upholding them.

stiff. Iconoclasm caused Byzantine artists to develop a strong sense of abstract form—that is, designs and other non-representational shapes—but there was also a reaction to Iconoclasm; thus in the end, Byzantine art was more highly image-oriented than ever. Painting relied heavily on formal depictions of the Madonna and Child (Mary and the baby Jesus), as Western European art did later. The human figure in Byzantine art was elongated, with people's bodies much taller in

The Slavic peoples

Among the countless peoples inhabiting what is now western Russia during Roman times, later to be swept westward by the Huns, was a group called the Slavs. Twice they invaded the Byzantine Empire during its troubled years, but eventually they settled down and became mixed with the Avars, Bulgars, and Khazars, other nomadic groups in the region. Slavs and

The Hagia Sophia, built by Justinian, is the greatest example of Byzantine architecture. It was built in the Byzantine capital, Constantinople, which is now Istanbul, Turkey. *Reproduced by permission of Archive Photos, Inc.*

Bulgars founded the first Slavic kingdom, Bulgaria, whose independence Byzantium recognized in 716.

In the 800s, two Byzantine missionaries, the brothers Cyril (SEER-ul; c. 827–869) and Methodius (mi-THOH-dee-us; c. 825–885), began preaching the Christian message in what is now the Czech Republic. This ultimately led to the conversion of the Bulgarians, whose King Boris embraced Eastern Orthodoxy in 865. In a pattern that would be repeated throughout Slavic lands, conversion did not spread upward from the people; rather, it went from the top down, with the king ordering his subjects to convert. Around the same time, the Byzantine protectorate of Serbia accepted Orthodoxy as well. St. Cyril even developed an alphabet, based on Greek letters, which the newly converted peoples adopted, and which Slavic Orthodox nations use today: the Cyrillic alphabet.

Catholic nations

Some eastern European peoples, while linguistically and ethnically Slavic, embraced Roman Catholi-

Byzantine Literature: Tall Tales and Gossip

Byzantine literature is remembered for two opposing tendencies. On the one hand, there was the literature of *hagiography* (hay-jee-AHG-ruh-fee), official biographies of the Eastern Orthodox saints. These were a mixture of truth and legend, designed to provide readers both with entertainment and a moral lesson. Hagiography exaggerated the best qualities of the subject. On the other hand, Byzantium's gossipy historians (who also sometimes presented tall tales as fact) often tried to make people seem worse than they were, not better.

Such was the case with Procopius (pruh-KOH-pee-us), a historian of the 500s. Though he wrote a highly acclaimed account of Justinian's wars of conquest, Procopius secretly held deep grudges against the emperor, the empress Theodora, and

others. Therefore he wrote a work in which he told what he *really* thought. Procopius's *Secret History* was not published until many centuries after his death, and no wonder: had it been discovered, he would undoubtedly have been executed. Its chapters have titles such as "Proving That Justinian and Theodora Were Actually Fiends [i.e., demons] in Human Form."

The empress had been a prostitute in her younger days, and Procopius spared no detail regarding her shady past, his account at times verging on pornography. Other historians, by contrast, offer positive accounts of Theodora, and indeed it is hard to trust Procopius. He was a member of the Green faction, whereas Theodora supported the Blues, and this may explain some of his ill will.

---

cism. Instead of the Cyrillic alphabet, they adopted the Roman alphabet, used in virtually all Western nations (including the United States) today. Just to the north of Serbia was Croatia, whose people became a part of Charlemagne's empire, as did neighboring Slovenia. To the northeast was Hungary, one of the few nations in Eastern Europe that is neither Slavic nor Orthodox: its dominant Magyar population became Catholic after their defeat by Otto the Great in 955.

North of Hungary was Moravia, converted to Orthodoxy by Cyril and

Methodius. Later it would become Catholic after its conquest by Bohemia, itself converted during the 800s by German missionaries. Bohemia and Moravia, today part of the Czech Republic, would enjoy periods of great influence during the Middle Ages. Moravia briefly conquered a large area, including Slovakia to the east, in the late 800s; and during the 1200s Bohemia emerged as a great power.

Finally, there was the northernmost and most influential of the Slavic Catholic nations: Poland, whose king adopted Christianity in

This Bulgarian newspaper shows an example of the Cyrillic alphabet, which was developed by St. Cyril (c. 827–869). *Reproduced by permission of EPD Photos.*

966. Thus a large part of Slavic Eastern Europe was Catholic, yet to the east was a single Orthodox nation that became larger than all of Eastern Europe combined: Russia.

Kievan Russia

The region just north of the Black Sea has been inhabited since ancient times. All the tribes entering Europe from Asia, including not only the Huns and Turkic peoples but later the Mongols, passed through it; yet the Slavs remained. They were probably the founders of Kiev (kee-YEV), today the capital of Ukraine. Then in 862 the Vikings known as the Varangians arrived from Sweden and established the city of Novgorod (NAWV-guh-rud). Eventually one of the Vikings, whose name was Rurik (died c. 879), emerged as their leader, and founded a dynasty that would remain influential until 1598.

Rurik extended Slavic influence north, into the land of the Finns; but the real empire-building began with Oleg (died c. 912), who merged Kiev and Novgorod into a single entity called Kievan Rus or Kievan Russia. Oleg's daughter-in-law Olga accepted

St. Basil's Church, located in Moscow, Russia, is a magnificent example of an Eastern Orthodox church. *Photograph by Susan D. Rock. Reproduced by permission of Susan D. Rock.*

Eastern Orthodoxy; however, her son rejected it for fear that it would make him a subject of Byzantium. Conversion came during the reign of Vladimir the Great (VLAHD-i-meer; c. 956–1015), who in 987 agreed to marry Anne, the sister of the Byzantine Empire's mighty Basil II.

Vladimir set about forcibly converting Kiev and Novgorod while Basil occupied himself with the Bulgars. A power struggle followed the death of Vladimir, but Yaroslav the Wise (yuh-ruh-SLAHF; ruled 1019–54) restored order and began building a vast Russian empire that stretched the length of Eastern Europe, from the Gulf of Finland to the Black Sea.

The turning point for Eastern Europe

After 1054 and the death of Yaroslav, Kievan Russia began to decline, torn apart by rivalries between various city-states. Turkic nomads, by then a powerful force in Eastern Europe, became more involved in Russian affairs, and in 1097 a group of Russian nobles divided the empire with them. This would make Russia particularly vulnerable to the Mongol invasion about 150 years later.

The year 1054 also marked a turning point for Eastern Europe as a whole. It was then that the Eastern Orthodox Church formally broke with Rome over a number of issues, including clerical celibacy—that is, the question of whether priests could marry. Orthodox leaders held that they could and should; Rome, particularly after the split with the Orthodox Church, opposed marriage for priests.

Soon afterward, Byzantium experienced another, even more significant, turning point: its loss to the Turks at the Battle of Manzikert in Armenia in 1071. The Turks even took the Byzantine emperor prisoner, and soon afterward helped themselves to all of Asia Minor, thenceforth known as Turkey. Thus less than fifty years after the victories of Basil II, Byzantium lost everything it had gained, and though the empire would continue for three more centuries, Manzikert was a blow from which it would never recover.

For More Information

Books

Dijkstra, Henk, editor. *History of the Ancient and Medieval World,* Volume 8: *Christianity and Islam.* New York: Marshall Cavendish, 1996, pp. 1045–68.

Dijkstra, Henk, editor. *History of the Ancient and Medieval World,* Volume 9: *The Middle Ages.* New York: Marshall Cavendish, 1996, pp. 1243–66.

Dijkstra, Henk, editor. *History of the Ancient and Medieval World,* Volume 11: *Empires of the Ancient World.* New York: Marshall Cavendish, 1996, pp. 1513–18.

 How Basil Became the Bulgar-Slayer

In the 980s, Bulgaria's King Samuel (ruled 980–1014) began creating an empire to the north of Byzantium, one that ultimately included parts of Bulgaria, Macedonia, northern Greece, Serbia, and Albania. He even declared himself *czar* (ZAHR)—Slavic for "caesar."

The Byzantines' Basil II rightly saw this as a threat, and the two empires went to war. It took decades to subdue the Bulgarians, but Basil won the decisive Battle of Belasitsa on July 29, 1014. His army captured some 14,000 Bulgarian soldiers, and gouged their eyes out; every hundredth man, however, was allowed to keep one eye so he could lead the other ninety-nine home. It was said that when Czar Samuel saw his army limping home, he died of a heart attack.

Hanawalt, Barbara A. *The Middle Ages: An Illustrated History.* New York: Oxford University Press, 1998.

Roberts, J. M. *The Illustrated History of the World,* Volume 4: *The Age of Diverging Traditions.* New York: Oxford, 1998, pp. 48–95.

Periodicals

Treadgold, Warren. "The Persistence of Byzantium." *Wilson Quarterly,* Autumn 1998, pp. 66–91.

Web Sites

Byzantine Studies—Medieval History Net Links. [Online] Available http://historymedren.

about.com/education/history/histo-rymedren/msubbyz.htm (last accessed July 28, 2000).

Byzantium: The Byzantine Studies Page. [Online] Available http://www.bway.net/~halsall/byzantium.html (last accessed July 28, 2000).

"The Slavs." *Catholic Encyclopedia.* [Online] Available http://www.newadvent.org/ca-then/14042a.htm (last accessed July 28, 2000).

The Islamic World

6

In ancient times, the Middle East produced some of the most outstanding civilizations in the world. First there was Egypt, along with the Mesopotamian civilizations of Sumer, Babylonia, and Assyria; then there were Phoenicia, Israel, Syria, and—far to the east—Persia. During all this time, the least distinguished portion of the Middle East was the hot, dry Arabian Peninsula. The medieval era, however, would see a complete reversal of roles, as the deserts of Arabia produced a mighty faith that swept up the region in a surge of religious passion that remains strong in modern times.

Preparing the way for Islam (300s–632)

In the centuries preceding the birth of Islam (IZ-lahm; "submission to God"), two ancient powers dominated the Middle East. At one end was the Byzantine Empire, which controlled Egypt and, for many centuries, the strip of Mediterranean coastline between Egypt and Turkey. The other great power in the region was Persia, or more specifically the Sassanid (SAS-uh-nid) Empire, which first emerged in A.D. 226.

Words to Know: The Islamic World

Adultery: Voluntary sexual relations between a married person and someone other than his or her spouse.

Algebra: A type of mathematics used to determine the value of unknown quantities where these can be related to known numbers.

Arabesque: A type of ornamentation often used in Arab art, combining plant and sometimes animal figures to produce intricate, interlaced patterns.

Blasphemy: The act of insulting God.

Caliph: A successor to Muhammad as spiritual and political leader of Islam.

Caliphate: The domain ruled by a caliph.

Caravan: A train of pack animals and travelers journeying through an inhospitable region.

Dowry: The wealth that a bride brings to her marriage.

Emir: A military and political leader in Islamic countries, whose domain is called an emirate.

Fasting: Deliberately going without food, often but not always for religious reasons.

Hajj: A pilgrimage to Mecca, which is expected of all Muslims who can afford to make it.

Idol: A statue of a god that the god's followers worship.

Imam: The supreme spiritual leader in Shi'ite Islam.

Interest: In economics, a fee charged by a lender against a borrower—usually a percentage of the amount borrowed.

Indo-European languages: The languages of Europe, India, Iran, and surrounding areas, which share common roots.

Islam: A faith that teaches submission to the one god Allah and his word as given through his prophet Muhammad in the Koran.

Jihad: Islamic "holy war" to defend or extend the faith.

Judeo-Christian: Describes ideas common to the spiritual heritage of both Jews and Christians.

Persia had long been a great cultural center, and it produced a religion that influenced the development of Judaism, Christianity, and Islam: Zoroastrianism (zohr-oh-AS-tree-un-izm). Founded by the prophet Zoroaster (c. 628–c. 551 B.C.), Zoroas-trianism taught of a supreme deity representing ultimate good, who continually did battle with his satanic opposite. Not long after Zoroaster's time, Persian forces took Babylonia, which had a large population of Jews taken as captives from Israel. The

Koran: The holy book of Islam.

Lingua franca: A common language.

Minaret: A slender mosque tower with one or more balconies on which a muezzin stands to call the faithful to prayer.

Mosque: A Muslim temple.

Muezzin: A crier who calls worshipers to prayer five times a day in the Muslim world.

Muslim: A person who practices the Islamic religion.

Mysticism: The belief that one can attain direct knowledge of God or ultimate reality through some form of meditation or special insight.

Philosophy: An area of study concerned with subjects including values, meaning, and the nature of reality.

Pilgrimage: A journey to a site of religious significance.

Prophet: Someone who receives communications directly from God and passes these on to others.

Scientific method: A means of drawing accurate conclusions by collecting information, studying data, and forming theories or hypotheses.

Secular: Of the world; typically used in contrast to "spiritual."

Semitic: A term describing a number of linguistic and cultural groups in the Middle East, including the modern-day Arabs and Israelis.

Shi'ism: A branch of Islam that does not acknowledge the first three caliphs, and that holds that the true line of leadership is through a series of imams who came after Ali.

Sunni: An orthodox Muslim who acknowledges the first four caliphs.

Trigonometry: The mathematical study of triangles, angles, arcs, and their properties and applications.

Zoroastrianism: A religion, founded in Persia, that taught of an ongoing struggle between good and evil.

Jews were thus exposed to Zoroastrianism, by then the dominant religion of Persia, and the Zoroastrian idea of a devil entered the Jewish scriptures. (Parts of the Old Testament written prior to this time certainly contained references to evil itself, but there was little concept of a single entity as the source of that evil.) Thanks to the influence of Judaism on Christianity and Islam, the idea of a devil entered those faiths as well. In addition, Zoroastrianism also had an impact on an odd splinter religion known as

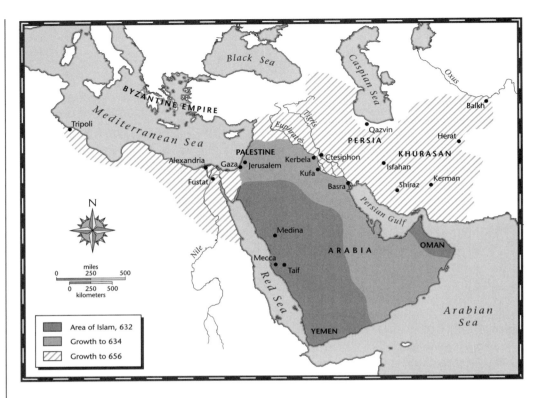

A map of the Middle East in the mid-600s shows the growth of Muslim territories in the years following Muhammad's death in 632. *Illustration by XNR Productions. Reproduced by permission of the Gale Group.*

Manichaeism (man-uh-KEE-izm; see box, "Manichaeism").

Arabia before Muhammad

In the early 600s, no one would have suspected that the Arabs would soon destroy the mighty Sassanid Empire and nearly destroy the Byzantines on their way to becoming the dominant power in the region—all within the space of one lifetime. Though coastal regions such as Oman (oh-MAHN) in the east and Yemen (yeh-MAHN) in the west enjoyed con-

siderable trade, and trade routes crossed the interior, Arabia was simply a place for goods to pass through on their way between Africa, Europe, and Asia. The hot, dry, center of the peninsula, an area about half the size of the United States, offered little to attract outsiders.

Arabia was a tribal society, divided between the nomadic (wandering) Bedouins (BED-oo-unz) of the desert and the settled peoples of the coastal areas. A dominant cultural center was Mecca, located halfway down the coast of the Red Sea that separated Arabia from Africa. Among Mecca's attractions was a shrine called the Kaaba (kuh-BAH), a cube-shaped building that housed a meteorite. According to the traditions of the Arabs, the meteorite had been hurled to Earth by a deity known as Allah (uh-LAH). In addition to Allah were some 300 other gods and goddesses, whose statues filled the Kaaba; yet Allah was supreme, like the God worshiped by Jews and Christians.

Muhammad

In the tribal environment of Arabia, loyalties were fiercely defended and family was essential. The leading tribe of Mecca was called the Quraish (koo-RESH), and it was into this tribe that one of the most influential figures of all time, Muhammad (moo-HAH-med; c. 570–632), was born. Orphaned at the age of six, he grew up poor and worked hard through his teen years, establishing himself as a thoughtful, trustworthy young man.

A wealthy widow named Khadijah hired him to act as her representative in a merchant business that took him to Syria, where Muhammad undoubtedly gained access to various ideas and traditions, including Judaism and Christianity. Khadijah was some fifteen years his senior, but Muhammad so impressed her that when he was twenty-five she made him an offer of marriage that he accepted. Of their many children, the only one who lived to bear him grand-

Manichaeism

One of the most interesting religious beliefs to emerge during the Middle Ages was Manichaeism, based on the teachings of the Persian prophet Mani (MAH-nee; c. 216–c. 276). Reflecting both Zoroastrian and Christian influences, Manichaeism taught that the universe was sharply divided between good and evil, and between the spiritual and physical worlds. Adherents to the Manichaean system believed that by practicing an ascetic lifestyle, they could help to defeat evil and open themselves up to great knowledge.

Fearing the new belief system, Zoroastrian priests had Mani skinned alive; however, the influence of Manichaeism grew after its founder's death. In his youth, Augustine was a Manichaean, and the religion continued to exert an influence in the East until the 1200s. The beliefs of the Albigenses, a sect that appeared in France about a millennium after Mani's death, mirrored those of the Manichaeans.

children was their daughter Fatima (FAT-uh-muh; c. 616–633), whose name means "Shining One."

For many years, Muhammad lived the ordinary life of a prosperous merchant; then in 610, when he was about forty years old, he had a vision in which an angel told him that Allah had called him to be his prophet. The vision frightened Muhammad, but gradually he accepted his destiny. During the twenty-two years of his life that remained, he would have some 650 of these revelations, which would become the basis for the Koran (kohr-AHN), Islam's holy book.

In 613, Muhammad began preaching his new faith, focusing on three principal themes: that Allah was the only god and all the other deities in the Kaaba were false idols; that the rich should share their wealth with the poor; and that all men would face a final judgment before Allah. The wealthy Quraish were not enthusiastic to hear this, and eventually their hostility forced Muhammad to leave Mecca along with his family (Khadijah died during this period) and his small band of followers. In 622, they settled in a town thenceforth known as Medina (muh-DEEN-uh; "The City"). Muslims (those who practice the Islamic religion) call Muhammad's flight from Mecca the *hegira* (heh-JY-ruh), and date their calendar from this event just as Christians date theirs from the birth of Jesus Christ.

Over the next few years, Muhammad led his followers on several raids against trading caravans from Mecca, and this eventually became outright warfare between Mecca and Medina. In one battle, a tiny Muslim force defeated a much larger Quraish army, which won the new religion many followers. In 630, Muhammad's army—by now more than 10,000 strong—took the city of Mecca, whereupon they destroyed the idols in the Kaaba. The latter, and Mecca as a whole, would thenceforth be the spiritual center of Islam, and non-Muslims were forbidden to enter the city.

The Islamic faith

Islam shares many features with Judaism and Christianity, including worship of a single god whose will is revealed in a holy book. East Asian religions such as Hinduism and Buddhism, by contrast, may have holy texts, but usually there is no one book supreme above all others. Islam also holds biblical figures, from Abraham to Jesus, in great esteem. In all, the Koran names twenty-eight true prophets who came before Muhammad; however, Muhammad is clearly understood as the greatest of the prophets. Whereas the Old and New testaments represent the work of many writers over a period of more than a thousand years, Muhammad alone wrote the Koran—or rather, in the belief of Muslims, he received the words of the Koran from Allah.

The Pillars of Islam

The Muslim faith has five central concepts, called "Pillars of Islam." First is the profession of faith, a recognition that "there is no god but Allah, and Muhammad is his prophet." Second is the institution of formal prayer at five set times during the day. Each city or town in the Muslim world has a large central mosque (MAHSK), or temple, crowned by a tall minaret—often the highest point in the town—from which a muezzin (moo-ZEEN) calls the faithful to prayer. Worshipers typically roll out prayer mats and bow in the direction of Mecca.

In line with Muhammad's message of charity, the third pillar of Islam is the giving of alms (money or food) to the poor. Fourth is the practice of fasting, or voluntarily going without food for religious purposes, during Ramadan (RAH-muh-dahn), the ninth month of the Islamic calendar. Finally, Muslims are encouraged to undertake a pilgrimage to Mecca, called a *hajj,* once in their lifetimes if they can afford to do so.

Islam as a political system

Though not one of the five pillars, there is one other concept central to the Islamic belief system: *jihad* (jee-HAHD), or "holy war." Muslims were expected to defend the faith against persecution or blasphemy, and if necessary to go to war for Islam. Obviously this aided in the spread of Muslim influence following Muhammad's death.

Islam was from the beginning intended both as a religious and a secular system, and eventually a whole system of law developed around it. Muslims were forbidden to loan money for interest, to eat pork, or to drink alcohol. Islamic law also gave women more rights than they had enjoyed under pre-Islamic society. The status of women in Islam has been a subject of particular significance, as some Muslim scholars interpreted Muhammad's teachings to mean that women should have few rights. Yet women played an important role in the foundation of Islam, and though men remained dominant under Muslim law, the Koran offered women a number of new legal protections.

No longer could men take as many wives as they wanted, for instance: now they could have only four, and they had to be able to provide financially for those four. Also significant was the fact that the bridal gift or dowry—that is, the money or holdings the groom received at marriage from the bride's family—now became the bride's property. If the husband divorced her, she got to keep the goods. Divorce remained much easier for a man than for a woman, but a man could no longer divorce his wife in anger and take her back the next day; once divorced, he had to wait three months before remarrying her. And whereas pre-Muslim Arabian society punished women more harshly than men for adultery, the Koranic penalty was the same for both participants: "flog each of them with a hundred stripes."

The Muslim emphasis on giving alms made Islam popular among the poor; so too did its teaching that all men were equal under Allah. Islam viewed other religions with toleration and gave Jews and Christians in captured territories special status. However, those who adhered to a faith other than Islam were not allowed to engage in religious activity outside their churches or synagogues, or to build new houses of worship. Furthermore, non-Muslims had to pay a special tax; to people who did not already feel strongly about their faith, this offered another incentive to convert.

The Sufis

In the late 900s and early 1000s, a movement known as Sufism (SOOF-izm) appeared in Persia, where it grew out of Shi'ite Islam. Incorporating ideas from Greek philosophy, Christianity, and even Buddhism, it stressed the mystical union of the soul with God. At its foundation were the ideas of Rabia al-Adawiyya (rah-BEE-ah al-ah-dah-WEE-ah; c. 713–801), a freed slave woman. In her poetry, Rabia presented an ideal love for Allah, which was tied neither to fear of Hell nor hope of Heaven.

The most influential Sufi thinker was al-Ghazali (1058–1111), who worked to reconcile traditional Islam with Sufi mysticism. The Sufis also had a strong influence on the poet Omar Khayyám, and in the present day they remain a small but significant group within the Islamic religion.

Islamic empires

The first wave of conquest (632–661)

Muhammad never clearly named a caliph (KAL-uhf), or successor; thus the first four caliphs—the term became a title for the spiritual and political leader of Islam—were men connected to the prophet through wives he married after Khadijah's death. His favorite wife was Aisha (ah-EE-shah; 614–678),

and therefore after Muhammad's death, the first caliph was her father, Abu Bakr (BAHK-ur; ruled 632–34). Next came Umar (ruled 634–44), the father of another wife, and then Uthman (ruled 644–56), who married one of Muhammad's childless daughters. Fourth was Ali (ruled 656–61), the prophet's cousin and husband of Fatima.

When Muhammad died, the Muslims held only the western portion of Arabia; less than thirty years later, the caliphate (KAL-uh-fet) stretched from Libya to Bactria (modern-day Afghanistan), and from the Caspian Sea to the Nile River. Problems over succession, however, threatened to undo these gains and created divisions in the Islamic world that exist even today. Umar was assassinated, and Uthman was killed during a rebellion; Ali, who had opposed the choice of Abu Bakr as first caliph, faced several rebellions himself, including one led by Aisha. He would ultimately be assassinated by members of a breakaway sect, and his assassination would in turn pave the way for a significant division among Muslims.

The Umayyads (661–750)

After Ali's death, Mu'awiya (moo-AH-wee-ah; ruled 661–80), a member of the powerful Umayyad (oo-MY-ahd) family, became caliph. Mu'awiya had opposed Ali vigorously during the latter's lifetime, and though he was not accused of the assassination, it was obvious that he had

Moorish Spain

Among the most notable of Islamic territories was Spain, which came under the control of the Moors in 711. The Moors were a nomadic people from North Africa, where the name of the nation of Morocco reflects the region's Moorish heritage. They were a group distinct from Arabs, but the name "Moor" eventually came to mean all Muslim peoples in Spain, both North Africans and Arabs. The latter arrived in 756, when Abd-ar-Rahman escaped Abbasid assassins to establish an Umayyad stronghold in Spain. There he founded what he called the emirate (IM-uh-ret) of Cordoba. An emir (i-MEER) is a type of commander in Islamic countries. Eventually the Umayyad leaders declared themselves caliphs, suggesting that they saw themselves as the legitimate leaders of the Islamic world.

Christian forces held the north of Spain, and scored a major victory when they retook the northern city of Toledo (toh-LAY-doh) in 1085. By then the Umayyad caliphate had fallen, replaced by more conquerors from Morocco: first the Almoravids (al-muh-RAH-vedz) in 1086, and later the Almohads (AL-moh-hahdz) in 1120. During the 1100s, the Christian reconquest of Spain was in full force, and after they conquered Cordoba in 1236, the Christians had the Almohads on the run. The Nasrid (NAHS-reed) dynasty, also from Morocco, ruled during a final period, beginning in 1238; then in 1492, the Spaniards expelled the last Moors from their country.

The Moors left a strong legacy in the form of architecture, the most notable example of which is a magnificent palace called the Alhambra. Thanks to the Arab influence, Spaniards enjoyed a highly civilized lifestyle while the rest of Western Europe remained mired in the ignorance and confusion that characterized the "Dark Ages."

profited from the death of his old foe. By taking power, he founded a new dynasty that would rule Islam during its period of greatest expansion.

In 680, Ali's son Husayn led a revolt against the Umayyads and was assassinated. His murder became a rallying cause for Shi'ite (SHEE-ight) Muslims, who broke away from the majority group, known as Sunni (SOO-nee) Muslims. The Shi'ites re- jected the first three caliphs, and maintained that Ali and the descendants of Fatima, starting with Husayn, constituted a line of infallible leaders or imams (i-MAHMZ). The Shi'ite interpretation of Islam spread among the poorer classes and among non-Arabs—particularly in Iran, where it remains the dominant faith today.

Meanwhile the center of power in the Islamic world shifted

The Alhambra is a magnificent palace built by the Moors in Spain during their control of the region in the Middle Ages. *Reproduced by permission of the Corbis Corporation.*

northward to the ancient Syrian city of Damascus, which became the capital of the Umayyad caliphate. The Umayyads soon expanded their boundaries to Spain and North Africa in the west, and India and the edge of China in the east. But this vast realm became difficult to govern; also, the Umayyads had a policy of only allowing Arabs to serve as leaders, and this made them many enemies. In 750 a descendant of Muhammad's uncle Abbas (uh-BAHS) led a revolt and began killing off all the Umayyad leaders. Only one escaped: Abd-ar-Rahman (AHB'd ar-ruh-MAHN; 731–788), who established a dynasty of long standing in Spain (see box, "Moorish Spain").

The Abbasids (750–1258)

One of the first steps taken by the Abbasids (uh-BAHS-idz) was to move the capital from Damascus to Baghdad in Iraq, many miles to the east. The Abbasids would flourish for about 150 years, then rapidly lose power; yet they formally held control for half a millennium. During that time, Islamic civilization had its brightest flowering, producing achievements

The Thousand and One Nights

The Thousand and One Nights, better known as *The Arabian Nights,* contains some of the world's favorite tales: Aladdin and his magic lamp, Ali Baba and the forty thieves, and Sinbad the Sailor. From these stories come such familiar concepts as "Open sesame" (the phrase used by Ali Baba to enter a cave filled with treasure), magic carpets, and the genie in the bottle. The collection's 264 tales, first assembled in the 900s, originated from a variety of Persian, Arabian, and Indian sources. From Persia came the "frame story" that ties all the tales together.

It seems that Sultan Shahriyar (SHAR-ee-yar) had decided all women were unfaithful, so he resolved to marry a new wife each evening, then put her to death the next morning. But his bride Shahrazad (SHAR-uh-zahd), or Sheherazade (shuh-HAIR-uh-zahd), managed to stay alive by beginning a new story each night and finishing it the next night—at which time she

Aladdin watches the genie emerge from the lamp in an illustration from *The Thousand and One Nights.* *Reproduced by permission of the Corbis Corporation.*

would begin a new tale, and buy herself another night. After 1,001 nights, during which she produced three sons, the sultan gave up his plans to kill off his wives.

beyond the imagination of most Western Europeans.

During this time, a number of great rulers, most notably Harun al-Rashid (hah-ROON al-rah-SHEED; ruled 786–809), led the caliphate. Harun was the subject of legend and is believed to be the model for the sultan in the *Thousand and One Nights* (see box); likewise the empire he ruled be-

came legendary throughout the world. At a time when the primitive buildings of the Merovingians constituted Western Europe's greatest architectural achievements, the Abbasids built great mosques noted for the intricacy of their design. While superstition took the place of medicine in Europe, the Arabs founded a school for doctors in Baghdad; and just as European monks were starting to use parchment, the

Arabs were learning paper-making from captured Chinese prisoners.

Islamic civilization

An explosion of knowledge

During the Middle Ages, the Muslim world underwent an explosion of knowledge like the one that occurred in ancient Greece during its golden age (490–404 B.C.) In fact, Arab Muslim scholars kept the Greek classics alive, particularly the works of the Greek philosopher Aristotle (AIR-uhs-taht-uhl; 384–322 B.C.). Aristotle may rightly be called the father of the scientific method and the leading proponent of logic, a system of reasoning for testing the accuracy of conclusions. During the period from the 700s to the 900s, at a time when Western Europe was almost wholly ignorant of ancient Greece, writings by Aristotle and other Greeks on everything from medicine to magic were translated into Arabic.

Learning flourished in the great cultural centers of Persia, Egypt, Syria, and Iraq, and the Middle Ages saw the emergence of many great scholars. Most notable among these were Avicenna (980–1137) and Averroës (uh-VEER-uh-weez; 1126–1198). Avicenna, a leading Islamic interpreter of Aristotle, wrote some two hundred works on science, religion, philosophy, and other subjects. Averroës, with his attempts to reconcile religious faith and Greek philosophy, would influence a number of Jewish and Christian thinkers.

Mathematics and science

Along with philosophy, science and mathematical knowledge expanded greatly during a two-century period beginning in about 900. Arab Muslims borrowed a system of numerals developed in India, but the Arabs became so famous as mathematicians that these came to be known as "Arabic" numerals. Arab mathematicians laid much of the groundwork for analytical geometry, algebra (itself an Arabic word), and particularly for trigonometry.

The Arabs put their mathematical knowledge to use in astronomy, greatly improving on the stargazing equipment available at the time. Through observatories along the breadth of the Islamic world, from Spain to Iraq, they charted the movement of the stars. Thus they were able to correct many mistakes of the ancients, mistakes accepted as fact by European astronomers until Arab learning trickled into Europe following the Crusades.

A citizen of Cairo, Baghdad, or Damascus was likely to receive the best medical treatment in the world from physicians who carefully observed the patient's condition before making a diagnosis. Muslim doctors were some of the first to prescribe drugs effectively, and many public hospitals were built in Islamic cities during medieval times.

The arts

As in Byzantium, the Islamic world had its own reaction to images

An Arabian astrolabe, an astronomical instrument, made in 1014. The Arabs made tremendous scientific advancements during the Middle Ages. *Reproduced by permission of the Corbis Corporation.*

in the 700s. Like the Bible, the Koran forbade the making of graven images or idols, but some took this to an extreme, demanding that no religious buildings include representations of human or animal forms. Outside the mosque, rules regarding representation of living creatures were more relaxed—with one exception. The face of Muhammad himself could not be

Arabic and Farsi

Most peoples of the Middle East today call themselves Arabs. In part this reflects an ethnic heritage, since Arabian tribes in the 600s and 700s intermarried with local populations and extended their influence throughout the region. More significant, however, is the common linguistic heritage of people who speak Arabic, a Semitic language related to Hebrew.

The people of Iran, on the other hand, are distinct from Arabs. Their language, Farsi or Persian, is an Indo-European tongue, meaning that it shares a common heritage with most languages of India and Europe—including English. Ethnically, Iranians are also more closely related to Indians and Europeans than they are to Arabs. Their distinction is reflected in the fact that Irani-

ans embrace the Shi'ite form of Islam rather than the majority Sunni interpretation.

During the Middle Ages, Arab culture and the Arabic language spread throughout the Middle East. Islamic law at that time prohibited translation of the Koran from the original Arabic, which furthered the spread of the language; but the cultural identity of Persia (as Iran was called at that time) was so strong that its people resisted the Arab influence. Persians adopted Arabic-style lettering, yet retained their own language and literature. Eventually Farsi and Arabic both became common languages in the Middle East, often used by people from different groups as a means of communicating.

shown; therefore it was usually represented either with a veil, or covered by a glowing fire.

During the Middle Ages, mosques took on the form that they would retain to the present day, including an open courtyard and "horseshoe" arches modeled on the rounded Roman arches of Byzantium. Minarets became a striking feature of mosque architecture, and the mosques themselves were beautifully decorated in a style of ornamentation known as arabesque (air-uh-BESK). Arabesque, which decorated virtually

every available surface, was characterized by graceful flourishes and ornate, flowery lines. Much of it was non-representational, but on secular buildings such as palaces, it might include plants, animals, and even human figures.

Arabian music, based on a five-note scale that gave it a distinctive, haunting sound, developed during medieval times. Early Islamic music grew out of oral poetry, with flutes, stringed instruments, and percussion complementing the poet's song. Sometimes professional female dancers also accompanied the performance.

The splintering of the Islamic world (c. 875–1258)

Beginning in about 900, the Abbasid caliphate began to lose power, and the Islamic world gradually broke into a confusing array of competing dynasties. Of these, only a few—in particular, two Egyptian ruling houses—would go on to assume great significance. Gradually the cultural center of Islam moved away from Baghdad to Egypt, the oldest civilization of all. Even today, Egypt is among the leaders of the Islamic world.

Members of the Shi'ite Ismaili (iz-MY-ah-lee) sect founded a dynasty called the Fatimids, named after Muhammad's daughter, that ruled Egypt from 909 to 1171. They established the city of Cairo, maintained a prosperous economy, and flourished for many years before being overtaken by the Ayyubids (uh-YÜ-bidz).

The Ayyubid dynasty came to power under Saladin (SAL-uh-dun; c. 1137–1198). Europeans who fought against him in the Crusades came to admire Saladin as the greatest of Muslim heroes; yet he was not an Arab but a Kurd, a member of a nation closely related to Iranians. The Ayyubid dynasty ruled Egypt from 1169 to 1252, when they were replaced by Turkish slave soldiers called Mamluks.

The rise of the Mamluks (Turkish rulers) would nearly coincide with the destruction of Abbasid power in Baghdad in 1258. By then, Islamic civilization had spread far beyond the Middle East. Word of Muhammad and the Koran had reached India and Southeast Asia, the rocky coastline of Spain, and desert kingdoms in the heart of Africa. Meanwhile, leadership among Islamic peoples had passed to a nation virtually unknown during Muhammad's lifetime: the Turks.

For More Information

Books

Bacharach, Jere L. *A Middle East Studies Handbook.* Seattle: University of Washington Press, 1984.

Dijkstra, Henk, editor. *History of the Ancient and Medieval World,* Volume 8: *Christianity and Islam.* New York: Marshall Cavendish, 1996, pp. 1069–1134.

Dijkstra, Henk, editor. *History of the Ancient and Medieval World,* Volume 9: *The Middle Ages.* New York: Marshall Cavendish, 1996, pp. 1225–42.

Hanawalt, Barbara A. *The Middle Ages: An Illustrated History.* New York: Oxford University Press, 1998.

Roberts, J. M. *The Illustrated History of the World,* Volume 4: *The Age of Diverging Traditions.* New York: Oxford, 1998, pp. 8–47.

Stewart, Desmond, and The Editors of Time-Life Books. *Early Islam.* New York: Time-Life Books, 1967.

Web Sites

IslamiCity in Cyberspace. [Online] Available http://www.islam.org/ (last accessed July 28, 2000).

Muslim Scientists and Islamic Civilization. [Online] Available http://users.erols.com/zenithco/ (last accessed July 28, 2000).

The Turks | 7

The name of Turkey, a country that forms a land bridge between Europe and Asia, reflects the Turkish heritage of its majority population. Yet the region was inhabited for thousands of years before the Turks arrived, during which time it was known variously as Asia Minor or Anatolia. Its ancient civilization and culture were much more closely tied to Greece than they were to the Turks, a Central Asian people who arrived only in the Middle Ages. Once they arrived, however, they soon made their influence known, establishing a distinctive culture and several mighty empires.

Early Turkish empires (500s–900s)

As with most ethnic groups, the Turks can be defined not so much on the basis of race or appearance, but according to language. Because of their nomadic (wandering) lifestyle and lack of written records, it is difficult to know much about their movements; nonetheless, it appears that in the 500s a group who spoke a Turkic language were enslaved by a nation known as the Juan-Juan in what is now Mongolia. In about

Words to Know: The Turks

Diplomat: Someone who negotiates with other countries on behalf of his own.

Divan: A council of state in the Ottoman Empire.

Islamize: To convert to Islam.

Khan: A Central Asian chieftain.

Shi'ism: A branch of Islam that does not acknowledge the first three caliphs, and that holds that the true line of leadership is through a series of imams who came after Ali.

Sultan: A type of king in the Muslim world.

Sultanate: An area ruled by a Sultan.

Sunni: An orthodox Muslim who acknowledges the first four caliphs.

Terrorist: Frightening (and usually harming) a group of people in order to achieve a specific political goal.

Vizier: A chief minister.

550, these Turks overthrew the Juan-Juan, who moved westward and became known as the Avars.

Avars, Khazars, Bulgars, and Oghuz

The Avars would remain a threat to the Byzantine Empire for two centuries beginning in the late 500s, but in so doing, they had to face an old enemy. Tribes of Turks had also moved westward, to what is now southern Russia, where they established an empire called the Khazar Khanate (kuh-ZAHR KAHN-et). *Khan* is a title of leadership among Central Asian peoples, and though the khanate was loosely organized as befit a nomadic tribe, the Khazars viewed themselves as enough of a nation to send an ambassador to Byzantium in 568. Later the region came to be known simply as Khazaria, and in the 700s its people converted to Judaism (see box, "The Jewish Kingdom of Khazaria," chapter 8).

In the 600s, another Turkic group moved westward, where they became identified as Bulgars. As they intermarried with Slavs to found the nation of Bulgaria, their Turkish identity vanished. Also during this time, various groups of Turks controlled an enormous expanse of land from China to the Black Sea, and some historians view this as a single, ill-defined "empire." Whatever the case, its impact on history was minor, particularly in the face of the rapid Arab expansion that followed the establishment of the Islamic faith.

Among the Turkish groups in the "empire" to become Islamized (IZ-lum-ized) were the Oghuz (oh-GÜZ), converted by missionaries from Persia in 960. Their Islamic faith had enormous significance for the Turks' future history, as did the fact that many Turks had served the Abbasid caliphate as slave soldiers. The use of slave soldiers, males raised and trained from childhood to serve a military commander, would become a common practice in Turkish-dominated states throughout

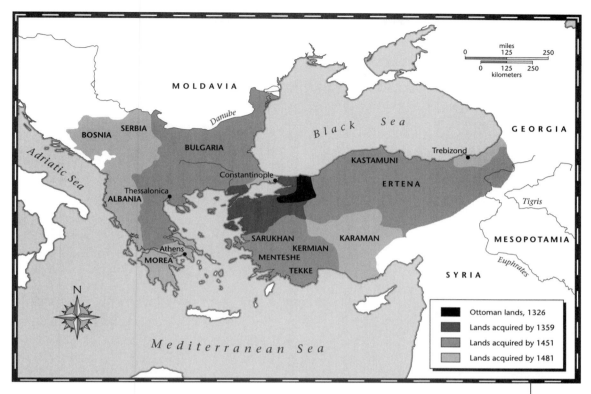

A map showing the expansion of the Ottoman Empire in the fourteenth and fifteenth centuries. *Illustration by XNR Productions. Reproduced by permission of the Gale Group.*

the medieval world. Slave soldiers often gained their freedom, and many went on to become leaders: a slave soldier established the Delhi Sultanate in India in 1206, and a group of slave soldiers called Mamluks won control of Egypt in 1252.

The Seljuks (900s–1243)

In the late 900s, the Oghuz split into several groups, among them the Cumans, who moved into the Black Sea area of southern Russia and would remain there for two centuries. Another tribe of Oghuz, the Seljuks,

began migrating southward and westward into Iran, causing their fellow Turks the Ghaznavids to spread into India. By then the Abbasids controlled their caliphate (the region they ruled) in name only; the Buwayhids (boo-WY-edz), a Shi'ite dynasty, actually ruled in Baghdad—that is, until 1055, when the Seljuks seized control. The fact that the Seljuks were Sunni Muslims, like the majority of people in the area, probably helped them win the allegiance of the conquered.

In 1060, the founder of the principal Seljuk dynasty, Toghril Beg (tawg-REEL; c. 990–1063) declared

City walls of Istanbul, Turkey, formerly Constantinople. The walls were built by the emperor Constantine in A.D. 324. *Reproduced by permission of the Corbis Corporation.*

himself sultan. His successor, Alp Arslan (ruled 1063–72), dealt the Byzantines a near-fatal blow at Manzikert in 1071, and soon afterward the Seljuks gained control of Asia Minor, which they called the Sultanate of Rum—that is, Rome. At this point, they constituted a tiny ethnic minority in the region, but they had established a foothold.

The Seljuks reached the height of their power under Alp Arslan's son Malik Shah (mah-LEEK; 1055–1092), controlling a large portion of the Middle East. After that, they began to de-

cline, partly due to a lack of organization typical among nomadic-style rulers. The Crusades also played a role. The Seljuks had a less tolerant attitude than the Arabs toward Christians visiting the Holy Land, and their harassment of pilgrims—combined with their use of the name "Rome," which implied that they viewed themselves as inheritors of the Roman Empire—angered Europeans.

The Seljuks, finally defeated by the Mongols in 1243, left several important legacies. One was an informal power structure based on loyalty to

The Assassins

Today the word "assassin" refers to anyone who kills for a political purpose; originally, however, the name referred to a group of fanatical killers whose primary targets were the Seljuk Turks.

A terrorist organization associated with the Ismaili sect of Islam, the Assassins were established in 1090 by Hasan-e Sabbah, an Iranian religious leader. Hasan was known as the "Old Man of the Mountain," a title that passed to each successive Assassin leader. Operating from a castle in a valley stronghold, the Assassins conducted acts of terrorism and political killing throughout the Muslim world, but particularly in Iran and Iraq. Because the Seljuks happened to be in power at that time, they were the principal target, and all attempts to uproot the Assassins proved fruitless.

During the Crusades, Assassins in Syria terrorized both Turks and Christians, but combined attacks by the Mongols and Mamluks in the mid-1200s brought about the end of the terrorist group.

Crusaders brought the word "assassin" home with them, and eventually it entered the languages of Europe. It is thought that the name derives from the Assassins' use of the drug hashish. According to Venetian traveler Marco Polo, Assassin leaders would ensure their men's loyalty by drugging them and taking them to a garden where they could enjoy all manner of earthly delights—pleasures that, they were told, would await them in the afterlife if they died on the field of battle. Contemporary Ismaili sources, however, contain no mention of this "Garden of Paradise."

local religious leaders, who in turn gave their allegiance to political leaders. This made it possible for conquerors to easily replace one another, because the religious leaders served as a buffer between the people and their rulers, who were often foreigners. Another important feature of Seljuk rule was the use of slave soldiers, a group of whom would soon rise to prominence in Egypt.

The Mamluks (1252–1517)

From the time of the Fatimids (909–1171), Egyptian rulers had used the services of Turkish slave soldiers who came to be known as Mamluks (MAM-lükz). In 1252, the Mamluks come to power, and they would maintain control of Egypt for more than 250 years. During that time, the elite Mamluk troops typically chose their rulers, rather than simply passing leadership from father to son.

One of the Mamluks' most astounding achievements came in 1260, when they dealt the Mongols the first defeat in their long campaign of conquest. Their control spread to Syria,

The Janissaries

Around the time he conquered Bulgaria in 1388, the Ottoman sultan Murad established a force similar to the Mamluks, an elite military group called the Janissaries (JAN-uh-sair-eez). The latter was composed of non-Turkish captives who had been converted to Islam and subjected to strict discipline.

In time the Janissaries became so influential that they had the power to make or break sultans. The institution continued to exist for more than 400 years, until 1826, when Sultan Mahmud II (ruled 1808–39) ordered the execution of all Janissaries.

and the Mamluks' capital at Cairo in Egypt flourished. The late 1200s constituted a golden age for the Mamluks, and this was followed by a long, slow decline. In 1517 they were removed from power by yet another group of Turks, the Ottomans.

The Ottomans

In the aftermath of the Seljuks' defeat by the Mongols, various Turkish principalities came to power in Anatolia. Among the most prominent was one controlled by the Osman (ahs-MAHN) family. Around 1300, Osman Gazi (GAH-zee; 1258–c. 1326) founded what came to be known as the Ottoman dynasty.

The rise of the Ottomans (c. 1300–1389)

Osman's son Orkhan (OHR-kahn; ruled 1326–62) greatly expanded Ottoman control, partly by military action but even more so by skillful maneuvering. Orkhan introduced the offices of vizier and divan (di-VAHN), or council of state, and proved his ability as a diplomat in his relations with the Byzantine emperor John VI Cantacuzenus (kan-tuh-kyoo-ZEE-nuhs; ruled 1347–54).

Orkhan supported John militarily in a struggle against another claimant on the Byzantine throne, and in return the Ottomans received the Gallipoli (gah-LIP-oh-lee) Peninsula. A narrow strip of land some sixty-three miles long, Gallipoli happened to lie on the other side of the strait separating Europe from Asia.

Beginning with this small territory, Orkhan's son Murad (moo-RAHD; ruled 1362–89) was able to greatly expand Ottoman territories in Europe. Following his defeat of Serbian and Bulgarian forces in 1371, Murad moved his capital from Bursa in Anatolia to Edirne (ay-DEER-nuh) or Adrianople in Europe, thus showing his determination to keep moving deeper into the continent.

Murad went on to conquer Bulgaria in 1388, and on June 28, 1389, his armies defeated a combined force of Serbians and others at Kosovo (KOH-suh-voh) Field in southern Serbia. The battle established Ottoman power over the southeastern portion of Europe—all except for the remnants of the Byzantine Empire—but Murad himself did not get to enjoy it for long. Soon after Kosovo, he was assassinated by a Serbian officer.

Troubled times and recovery (1389–1481)

In 1396, on a battlefield in what is now Bulgaria, an army led by Murad's son Bajazed (by-yuh-ZEED; ruled 1389–1402) defeated a combined Hungarian and Venetian force, organized by the pope to protect Europe from an Islamic invasion. The Ottomans seemed poised to begin absorbing more and more of Europe; then from the east came the Mongol armies of Tamerlane, who in 1402 captured Bajazed himself.

As it turned out, Mongol power was as shortlived in Anatolia as in most parts of the world, and upon Tamerlane's death in 1405, the sons of Bajazed began vying for power. The restored line of Ottoman rulers faced numerous military challenges: from Venice in the Aegean Sea; from Hungary in the Balkans; and from rebel forces in Anatolia and Albania. The leader of the Albanian revolt, Skanderbeg or George Kastrioti (1405–1468), was celebrated throughout the Western world for his brave resistance to the Turkish armies, and Albanians remember him as their national hero.

Had the Ottoman Empire kept going the way it was, it would not have lasted much longer, but in fact it continued until 1922. Its recovery began under Mehmed (meh-MET) the Conqueror, who ruled from 1451 to 1481. It was Mehmed who finally brought down the Byzantine Empire in 1453, after which Constantinople became the new Ottoman capital, Istanbul. Mehmed added Bosnia and Herzegovina (hurt-ze-GOH-vi-nuh) to the empire, and by the end of his reign Turkish power extended from the coast of the Adriatic (ay-dree-AT-ik) Sea, which faces Italy, to the region known as the Caucasus (KAW-kuh-sus) in southern Russia.

For More Information

Books

Dijkstra, Henk, editor. *History of the Ancient and Medieval World,* Volume 11: *Empires of the Ancient World.* New York: Marshall Cavendish, 1996, pp. 1555–65.

Roberts, J. M. *The Illustrated History of the World,* Volume 4: *The Age of Diverging Traditions.* New York: Oxford, 1998, pp. 97–102, 122–23.

Stewart, Desmond, and The Editors of Time-Life Books. *Early Islam.* New York: Time-Life Books, 1967.

Web Sites

"End of Europe's Middle Ages—Ottoman Turks." [Online] Available http://www.ucalgary.ca/HIST/tutor/endmiddle/ottoman.html (last accessed July 28, 2000).

"The Seljuk Civilization." *Explore Turkey.* [Online] Available http://www.exploreturkey.com/selcuklu.htm (last accessed July 28, 2000).

"The Turkish Dynasties: The Seljuks." *Art Arena.* [Online] Available http://www.artarena.force9.co.uk/seljuk.html (last accessed July 28, 2000).

The Jewish World 8

Because it is written in the most famous of all books, the Bible, the story of the Jews is more well known than that of almost any other nation. The Old Testament tells that they were "God's chosen people," for whom he had selected a special land in Palestine. The Jewish nation of Israel, with its capital in Jerusalem, maintained control of that land for centuries; after 586 B.C., however, a succession of empires ruled. In A.D. 70, about forty years after the crucifixion of Jesus Christ, the Romans destroyed Jerusalem, and in 135, banished all Jews from the city. Over the years that followed, the Jews tried unsuccessfully several times to reestablish at least partial control over the area; by the beginning of the Middle Ages, however, many had moved on to find what they hoped would be a better life.

Jews, Judaism, and anti-Semitism

The term "Jew," strictly speaking, refers simply to someone who practices Judaism, the Jewish religion. A faith rich in symbolism and ritual, Judaism provided the founda-

Words to Know: The Jewish World

Anti-Semitism: Hatred of, or discrimination against, Jews.

Ashkenazim: Jews who settled in Central or Eastern Europe during the Middle Ages, along with their descendants.

Cabala: A Jewish mystical system for interpreting the Scriptures.

Diaspora: The settlement of the Jews outside their homeland in Palestine.

Ethnic group: People who share a common racial, cultural, national, linguistic, or tribal origin.

Holy Land: Palestine.

Judaism: The Jewish religion, whose sacred text is the Old Testament.

Ladino: A dialect spoken by Sephardic Jews, combining Hebrew and Spanish.

Messiah: The promised savior of Israel, foretold in the Old Testament.

Rabbi: A Jewish teacher or religious leader.

Ritual: A type of religious ceremony that is governed by very specific rules.

Scriptures: Holy texts.

Sephardim: Jews who settled in Spain during the early Middle Ages and later spread to other parts of the world, along with their descendants.

Synagogue: A Jewish temple.

Theology: The study of religious faith.

Usury: Loaning money for a high rate of interest; during the Middle Ages, however, it meant simply loaning money for interest.

Yiddish: A language spoken by Ashkenazim, combining German and Hebrew.

tion on which both Christianity and Islam developed. The Old Testament, the principal Jewish scripture, contains a number of themes familiar to believers in all three religions: sin and redemption, faith, sacrifice, obedience, and charity. At the center of all these concepts is the idea of law, and Jewish rabbis were trained in the religious law that originated with the prophet Moses in about 1300 B.C.

In practice, "Jew" is often used—and certainly was used in the

Middle Ages—to describe an ethnic group whose ancestors belonged to the nation of Israel during ancient times. As a nation, the Jews believed that they had a special relationship with God; therefore the many misfortunes they faced as a people were a punishment from God for disobedience.

After they were taken into captivity by the Babylonians in 586 B.C., the Jews gradually came to believe that God would send them a Messiah, a savior who would liberate them. Many

A page from a Torah scroll. The Torah, which is written in the Hebrew language, comprises the five books of Moses, part of the Jewish scripture. *Reproduced by permission of the Corbis Corporation.*

people believed that Jesus Christ (c. 6 B.C.–c. A.D. 30) was the promised Messiah, and this was the foundation of Christianity. However, most Jews rejected the idea that Jesus was the Messiah, and a group of Jewish leaders called the Pharisees (FAIR-uh-seez) had even arranged for him to be put on trial by the Romans, who controlled the region at the time. As a result, Jesus was crucified, or nailed to a wooden cross and forced to hang on it until he died. Not all Jews called for his crucifixion, of course, but the fact that some did would later be used as an excuse for anti-Semitism during the

Middle Ages. This was more than a little ironic: not only was Jesus Christ a Jew, but the Bible makes clear that all of humanity—not just the Jews or even the Roman soldiers who actually nailed him to the cross—shares the blame for killing the man Christians believe was God in human form.

Jews in the Middle East and North Africa

The settlement of the Jews throughout the world is known as the Diaspora, but in fact many Jews stayed in Palestine or nearby Syria. After 638, when the Muslims conquered Jerusalem, Jews were allowed to reenter the city, and in general, they lived much better under Muslim than under Christian rule. Jews in southern Arabia fared particularly well: for many centuries, the region that is now Yemen was a wealthy community of Arab merchants who embraced the Jewish faith.

The center of Jewish life during the Middle Ages lay in Mesopotamia and Persia—modern-day Iraq and Iran. Again, the establishment of Islamic rule benefited the Jews. They had suffered some persecution under the Sassanid rulers of Persia, but after Muslims replaced the Sassanids in the 600s, Jews began to hold positions of influence in Persia. Jews gravitated into positions as merchants and bankers, and enjoyed considerable control over the Islamic government's purse strings. The greatest contribution of Jews in Iraq, however, was the Talmud (see box), along with other works of literature and philosophy.

North Africa represented extremes of good and bad for Jewish communities under Islam. During the late 900s in what is now Tunisia, the town of al-Qayrawan (AL ky-rah-WAHN) became the biggest center of Jewish life outside of Iraq. The experience of Jews was also relatively good in Egypt at around the same time, with the tolerant Fatimids in power; but Jewish communities there declined after the 1000s, along with the power of the Fatimids themselves. On the other hand, the rule of the Almo-

hads in Morocco from the mid-1100s to the mid-1200s was particularly harsh. Jews were forcibly converted, and those who refused to accept Islam were slaughtered. As was the case in Europe at about the same time, the Almohads began forcing Jews to wear special clothing to set them apart from the rest of society.

Jews in Spain

During much of the Middle Ages, Spain—or rather the Iberian (eye-BEER-ee-un) Peninsula that includes both modern Spain and Portugal—was a special case in many regards. Geographically and historically it was part of Europe, but culturally it was part of the Islamic world. Likewise Jews in Spain were a distinct group, called Sephardim (suh-FAHR-dim). They even developed their own language, a mixture of Spanish and Hebrew called Ladino (luh-DEE-noh).

The Visigoths had persecuted Jews, who therefore welcomed the Muslim conquest in 711. As in most other Muslim countries, Jews found themselves tolerated, but they began to flourish in the 900s, thanks in large part to one Jewish man: Hisdai ibn Shaprut (kis-DY ib'n shahp-RÜT; c. 915–c. 975). Court physician to Caliph Abd ar-Rahman III, Hisdai acted in the capacity of vizier or chief minister, and often went on important diplomatic missions for the caliph. He also used his influence to encourage Hebrew scholarship in general, and study of the Talmud in particular.

The Talmud

First compiled in the 500s, the Talmud brings together Jewish oral law as a complement or supplement to the written law, the Old Testament. It consists of two major parts, the Mishnah and the Gemara.

Later scholars produced commentaries on the Talmud. Rashi (Shlomo Yitzhaqi; 1040–1105), a rabbi in France, added insights drawn from the Jewish experience in Christian Europe during the Middle Ages. Even more important were the Talmudic commentaries of Moses Maimonides a century later.

A rabbi reading the Talmud. *Reproduced by permission of the Corbis Corporation.*

Jewish culture in Spain reached a high point during the eleventh century. Following Hisdai's example, a number of Jews attained positions of influence in the Muslim government, none of them more prominent than Samuel ha-Nagid (hah-NAH-geed; 993–c. 1055). A Talmudic scholar and military commander, Samuel was the actual power behind the caliph, handling all political and military matters himself. He also found time to write several classics of medieval Jewish scholarship.

Conditions for Spanish Jews began to decline after the Almoravids took power in 1086. Not only were the new rulers less tolerant than the Umayyads (Muslim rulers) had been, but Christians were beginning to reconquer the northern part of the country. The takeover by the Almohads in the 1100s signaled an even further decline in the Jews' situation, yet it was during this period that Spain produced the greatest Jewish thinker of the Middle Ages: Moses Maimonides (my-MAHN-uh-deez; 1135–1204). As Muslim philosophers before him had done, Maimonides attempted to strike a balance between the philosophy of the ancient Greeks on the one hand, and religious faith on the other.

With the Almohads conducting massacres and forced conversions as they had done in Africa, many Jews fled

Moses Maimonides, a great Jewish thinker from the Middle Ages, attempted to blend religious faith with ancient philosophy.

to other parts of Europe. Muslim power in Spain dwindled and conditions worsened in the 1200s, yet Jewish intellectual life continued to bear fruit. During this era, many talented minds embraced the cabala (kuh-BAH-luh), a mystical system for interpreting the Scriptures based on the belief that every word and punctuation mark in the holy texts contains a secret message.

Jews in Europe

European Jews outside of Spain were called Ashkenazim (ash-kuh-NAHZ-im), and in contrast to the Sephardim, they followed worship rituals established in Palestine rather than in Iraq. Beginning in the 800s, Jews in Central Europe began developing their own language, a mixture of Hebrew and German called Yiddish.

It is sad but true that during the Middle Ages, persons acting in the name of Christianity—a religion rooted in Judaism and based on compassion, charity, and love—typically treated Jews with cruelty and brutality. Thus the Jews fared better under pagan rulers in Rome and among the barbarians than they did later, when the Romans and barbarians converted to Christianity.

This is not to say that all Christian peoples treated them badly: in the 500s, the Ostrogoths and later the Lombards in Italy, both Christianized tribes, accorded Jews a high degree of respect. Even in the Carolingian Empire, where all other non-Christian religions were forbidden, Jews were allowed to continue holding services in their synagogues or temples.

Anti-Semitism gathers force

In fact the situation for Jews in Western Europe did not really deteriorate until the Crusades in the 1000s. The timing is ironic, since the purpose of the Crusades was supposedly to recapture the Holy Land—that is, Palestine—from the Muslims; but the Crusaders had no intention of returning it to the Jews. Instead, Jews were seen as enemies because they had rejected Christ, and the fact that they had lost their nation and were forced to wander seemed like a clear-cut judgment from God.

In the frenzy that attended the First Crusade in 1096, people in a number of German towns slaughtered Jews as enemies of Christ. Thereafter, anti-Semitism would periodically die down, then reemerge in new forms. In 1215, the pope ordered that Jews had to wear special clothing so that Christians would not accidentally associate with them. During the Black Death of the 1300s, a rumor spread that Jews had caused the plague by poisoning wells. Economic problems, too, were blamed on Jews.

The economic explanation

Economic motivation certainly explains some of Europeans' hatred. Jews had long been dominant in the business world, in part because a Jewish businessman traveling to a faraway city knew that he could count on the finances and connections of the Jewish community there. Therefore some, though far from all, Jews were wealthy, a fact that enraged many of Europe's poor.

Furthermore, Jewish skill in business, combined with a growing attitude of anti-Semitism, had forced Jews into positions such as pawnbroker, moneylender, and banker. At that time those professions were viewed with disdain. The Catholic Church had condemned usury (YOO-zhur-ee), which today means lending money at an extremely high rate of interest; in the Middle Ages, however, it meant

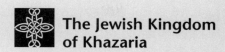

The Jewish Kingdom of Khazaria

Though Israel ceased to be a nation in 586 B.C. and would not be reestablished until A.D. 1948, a Jewish kingdom did flourish during the Middle Ages. It was ruled not by descendants of the ancient Israelites, however, but by Turks.

This was Khazaria, the kingdom that emerged from the Khazar Khanate in southern Russia. Accounts vary, but it appears that in the 700s, the Khazars converted to Judaism, and thereafter followed all Jewish rituals. The kingdom flourished until the 1000s, when it was conquered by Kievan Russia.

lending money and charging interest, no matter how low the rate.

In fact, when lenders are able to charge a reasonable rate of interest, this helps the entire economy to grow and benefits the poor as well as the rich. People in medieval times, however, had no notion of such concepts: rejecting reason in favor of emotion, they found it easy to blame the Jews for the problems in their lives.

Expulsion and forced conversion

Eventually many nations worked themselves into such a fever of anti-Semitism that they forced all Jews to leave. It happened first in France in 1182, when King Philip II Augustus expelled all the Jews in order to seize their assets. Over the following years, France pursued an erratic policy toward its Jews, repeatedly inviting them back long enough to grab more wealth, then expelling them again.

England took a much simpler approach to the Jews, who first appeared in Britain following the Norman Invasion of 1066. English nobles had managed to profit off of the Jewish community for some time before King Edward I sent them away in 1290. Jews would not be readmitted to England again until the 1600s.

But the most disastrous situation for European Jews was on the Iberian Peninsula, where Jews had once been tolerated. Beginning in 1391, as the Christian re-conquest of Spain gathered momentum, Jews were offered the option of conversion or expulsion. Some chose conversion—and were dubbed Marranos (muh-RAH-nawz; "pigs") by disdainful Christians. In 1492, Spain ordered all Jews out, and five years later, Portugal did the same. Thereafter the Sephardim spread throughout North Africa and the Middle East.

For More Information

Books

Abrahams, Israel. *Jewish Life in the Middle Ages*. Philadelphia: Jewish Publication Society, 1993.

Cohen, Mark R. *Under Crescent and Cross: The Jews in the Middle Ages*. Princeton, NJ: Princeton University Press, 1994.

Dijkstra, Henk, editor. *History of the Ancient and Medieval World,* Volume 10: *Medieval Politics and Life.* New York: Marshall Cavendish, 1996, pp. 1369–74.

Luchs, Alvin Schanfarber. *Torchbearers of the Middle Ages.* Illustrated by Stanley Maxwell. Freeport, NY: Books for Libraries Press, 1971.

Web Sites

"Beyond the Pale: The Middle Ages." [Online] Available http://www.friends-partners. org/partners/beyond-the-pale/english/ 06.html (last accessed July 28, 2000).

The Khazaria Info Center. [Online] Available http://www.khazaria.com/ (last accessed July 28, 2000).

The Eleventh Century

9

A central theme of the eleventh century (the 1000s) in Europe was the struggle between church and state, or between popes and kings. From the mid-800s to the early eleventh century, a series of corrupt popes succeeded in nearly destroying the reputation of the papacy, just as emperors such as Otto the Great were enhancing their own power. In the 1000s, however, church reformers would bring Rome greater authority than it had ever enjoyed and would eventually launch Europe on an ambitious campaign of military and religious conquest called the Crusades.

Europe on the eve of the Crusades

Just as Charles Martel had established the Carolingian throne on the ruins of the Merovingian dynasty (see Chapter 3: The Merovingian Age), so medieval France grew from the ruins of Charlemagne's empire. In 987, the Carolingian ruler of the West Frankish Empire died without an heir; therefore French nobles and church leaders gathered to choose a successor. They elected a member of France's most powerful family,

Words to Know: The Eleventh Century

Abbess: The head of a convent.

Abbey: A monastery or convent.

Abbot: The head of a monastery.

Absolution: Forgiveness of sins, particularly by a priest.

Antipope: A priest proclaimed pope by one group or another, but not officially recognized by the church.

Cardinal: An office in the Catholic Church higher than that of bishop or archbishop; the seventy cardinals in the "College of Cardinals" participate in electing the pope.

Cleric: A priest.

County: In the Middle Ages, an area ruled by a relatively low-ranking type of nobleman called a count.

Duchy: An area ruled by a duke, the highest rank of European noble below a prince.

Eucharist: Communion, or the Lord's Supper service.

Habit: The clothing worn by a monk or nun.

Infidel: An unbeliever.

Indulgence: The granting of forgiveness of sins in exchange for an act of service for, or payment to, the church.

Investiture: The power of a feudal lord to grant lands or offices.

Mass: A Catholic church service.

Ordination: Formal appointment as a priest or minister.

Principality: An area ruled by a prince, the highest-ranking form of noble below a king.

Saracen: A negative term used in medieval Europe to describe Muslims.

Simony: The practice of buying and selling church offices.

Tonsure: A rite in which a candidate for priesthood had part of his hair removed; later this became the name for the hairstyle of monks and other clerics.

Vassal: A noble or king who is subject to a more powerful noble or king.

Hugh Capet (kuh-PAY; ruled 987–96), whose Capetian (kuh-PEE-shun) dynasty would rule the country until 1328. As his capital, Hugh Capet chose a city along the River Seine (SEHN), a town that had existed long before the Romans captured it in 52 B.C.: Paris.

Outside of a small region controlled by the Capetians, however, France was divided into a number of principalities, one of the most significant of which belonged to the Normans. Descendants of the Vikings, the Normans had first sailed up the Seine

Scene of William the Conqueror and his army on the attack; this image is part of the Bayeux Tapestry, which provides a visual account of the Norman Invasion. *Reproduced by permission of the Corbis Corporation.*

in 820, and by 911 the Carolingian king had been forced to make a treaty recognizing their right to occupy a large area of northwestern France. The Normans agreed to convert to Christianity and to protect France from other invaders; in exchange, they received the region between the English Channel and Paris, which became known as Normandy.

In 1002, the English king Ethelred the Unready—so named for his inability to resist the invasions of Canute—married Emma, daughter of Duke Richard I of Normandy. From then on, the Normans had their eye on the English throne, and in 1042, Ethelred's and Emma's son Edward the Confessor became king. During his reign, many Normans settled in England; then in 1066, the Normans launched a full-scale invasion of England. On October 14, they dealt the English a decisive blow on a beach near the town of Hastings. The leader of this victorious force, the new king of England, was William the Conqueror (c. 1028–1087; ruled 1066–1087).

As it turned out, the Norman Conquest would have wide-ranging effects felt even today (see box, "Chickens, Churches, and Normans"); more immediately, however, it posed a challenge for France. Kings of England after William held the title "duke of Normandy"; and after 1154, an English king was also count of Anjou (ahn-ZHOO), a French province. France began reconquering French lands in 1254, and by 1450 would place all of Normandy under the rule of Paris; along the way, however, English claims to French lands would spawn a series of conflicts.

Germany

Germany was formally under the control of the Holy Roman Empire, though that name did not actually appear until 1254. In any case, the Holy Roman Empire was—to quote a joke almost as old as the Middle Ages—neither holy, nor Roman, nor an empire. In fact it was a mask for the German empire, itself a loose collection of duchies such as Saxony and Bavaria. Each had its ruling nobles, and with the end of Carolingian power in 911, these began electing kings to lead the various German states.

The election of Saxony's king Henry, father of Otto the Great, in 918 led to a century of Saxon domination. Otto vastly expanded Germany, transforming the kingdom into a true empire. His victories over the Slavs to the northeast added lands that would become Prussia, or eastern Germany, and the conquest of the Magyars in the southeast led to the establishment of the "eastern kingdom"—Österreich, or Austria. To the southwest, Otto reconquered territories formerly controlled by Charlemagne, including Lorraine and Burgundy, today in eastern France.

With Otto's conquest of Italy and the reviving of the Holy Roman Empire, German kings thenceforth claimed the title of emperor, which they usually received in a coronation ceremony overseen by the pope. Otto's grandson Otto III (ruled 983–1002), whose mother was a Byzantine princess, grew up nourished on grand dreams of an empire. He believed that the empire could become more than just a name. As emperor, he presented a crown to his counterpart in Byzantium, proclaiming him ruler of the East as Otto was of the West. The Byzantines, however, had no interest in an alliance, and Otto's magnificent visions of an empire died with him.

Italy

Italy had revived in the 700s, thanks to its increased contact with the highly civilized Arab world; but by the late 900s, it had become mired in a state of near-constant warfare that would not lift for more than three centuries. During this time, a force for stability was the port of Venice in northeastern Italy. Built on lagoons, islands, and mud flats, the city had existed since the 300s and had flourished as a province of the Byzantine Empire. By the 1000s, Venice remained one of the few Byzantine colonies on the Italian mainland, and

Otto III standing at the tomb of Charlemagne, finding the body of the dead emperor undecayed. Otto III had dreams of leading a great empire as Charlemagne had done almost two hundred years earlier. *Reproduced by permission of Archive Photos, Inc.*

Chickens, Churches, and Normans

The Norman Conquest of 1066 was the central "before and after" in English history, and in the history of the English language. The Anglo-Saxon invasion of the 400s had established the Germanic roots of English, but the invasion by the French-speaking Normans added a whole new Latin-based (or Romance) layer. It is for this reason that English is perhaps the richest and most varied of languages.

To use an everyday example, there is the German word for chicken, *Hünchen* (HÜN-ken), which sounds much like its English counterpart. In French, this is *poulet* (poo-LAY), a close relative of the English word "poultry." Thus English has two words, where German and French each have just one. Another example involves the English words "church" and "ecclesiastical" (ee-klee-zee-AS-ti-kul), an adjective meaning "church-related." The first word is close to the German *Kirke* (KEER-kuh), the second to the French *eglise* (ay-GLEEZ).

An English-speaker who studies German will be pleasantly surprised at all the familiar-sound words such as *Buch, Auto,* and *Freund* (FROIND)—respectively "book," "auto," and "friend." German grammar, however, is much more of a challenge to English speakers, since English primarily took on Romance, rather than German, sentence structure.

it would soon become clear that Byzantium lacked the power to control the city.

At the south end of the peninsula was the triangle-shaped island of Sicily, which had fallen under Muslim control in 827. Therefore the church was inclined to view the Normans who conquered it as heroes for Christ, though the truth was not so glorious. These Normans had first come south in the early 1000s, when the duke of Naples used them to subdue Lombard princes eager to reassert their power. In return, the Normans had received a county in Italy, thus establishing a foothold in the area.

The church and the German empire each wanted to oust the Byzantines, Lombards, and others, then establish full control over Italy. Their biggest rivals (besides one another) were the Normans, and specifically Robert and Roger Guiscard (gee-SKARD), sometimes known as the de Hauteville (DOHT-veel) brothers. At first the papacy attempted to stop the de Hautevilles with military force, but by 1059 the pope realized they were too powerful.

So Rome tried a different strategy, much like the one used by French kings with the Normans' ancestors nearly 150 years before: in return for a promise that they would defend the Papal States against all *other* invaders, it conferred the title of duke on both brothers. The de Hautevilles also agreed to drive the Muslims out of Sicily, and Roger began conquering the island in 1061. Meanwhile Robert drove the Byzantines from southern Italy in 1071.

Eastern Europe

In Eastern Europe, Catholic nations prospered: Poland briefly flourished under the Piast (PYAHST) dynasty, and in 1085 Bohemia emerged as an independent kingdom. At the same time, Orthodox lands experienced a severe decline.

After the decline of Kiev, the only significant principality in Russia was Vladimir, an area to the northeast first settled in the 900s. Its people were originally Finnish in origin, but as Kievan Russia fell apart, more Slavs moved into the towns of Vladimir and Rostov, where they intermarried with the Finns to form a stable local population. Around 1147, the Russians established a fortress in the area, and named it Moscow. One day it would become the center of a great empire; but that day was long in the future.

In 1071, the same year they were driven from Italy, the Byzantines had suffered a devastating defeat by the Turks at Manzikert. Fearing Muslim conquest, Emperor Alexis I Comnenus (kahm-NEEN-us; ruled 1081–1118) appealed to the pope for military help. Despite the relatively recent break between the Greek Orthodox and Roman Catholic churches, Alexis had reason to believe that his Christian brothers would aid him in the fight against the infidels. He had no idea of the forces he was unleashing, however. Over the next two centuries, Byzantium would get more "help" than it could stand as Europeans unleashed a series of wars called the Crusades, which would have a devastating effect on the Byzantine Empire.

A gondola approaches the Bridge of Sighs in Venice, Italy. Venice flourished as a province of the Byzantine Empire during the early Middle Ages. *Photograph by Susan D. Rock. Reproduced by permission of Susan D. Rock.*

The recovery of the church

The church had declined during the 800s and 900s, a period in which many church leaders obtained their posts not through great devotion to God but in return for money. The practice of buying and selling church offices was called simony, and the church took no specific measures against it until the 1000s. Another issue of concern was that of clerical marriage, which in the view of many church leaders would only encourage priests to think about sex. Therefore the church officially prohibited clerical marriage in 1059.

The pope who put the ailing church on the road to recovery was Gregory VII (ruled 1073–85). Gregory started as a Benedictine monk, and under his leadership the monasteries or abbeys became an important instrument of reform. Gregory's new activist monasticism would later find its fullest expression with the establishment of the Cistercian (sis-TUR-shun) order in France. Cistercian monks, who typically lived in isolated areas, worked hard clearing land for agricultural use, growing crops, making wine, keeping bees for honey, and even mining.

The organization of the church

By the eleventh century, the church had a well-established system of organization for monks and nuns. They were usually led by an abbot or abbess, and they wore simple garments of rough, loose-fitting material called a habit. Monks were a part of the priesthood, and all priests were distinguished by the tonsure (TAHN-shoor), a type of hairstyle in which the top of the head was shaven. After meeting certain obligations, a candidate for priesthood joined the church, then progressed through a series of "minor orders." A man could leave the minor orders if he chose, but ordination—the act of formal appointment as a priest—was irreversible, and leaving the priesthood was a grave sin.

Given its size, the organizational system of the church was exceedingly simple. For a long time, the only level above a priest was a bishop, with the bishop of Rome occupying the leading position as pope. By 1059, however, the church came to recognize certain "cardinal"—most important—bishops, eventually known simply as cardinals. Like bishops, the cardinals represented given regions, though their regions were larger, and there were fewer of them. Originally there were only seven, but in time this number grew to seventy, a group known as the College of Cardinals. Distinguished by their red caps, cardinals were the men who gathered to elect a new pope upon the death of the old one.

Another key instrument of church organization was the ecumenical councils. Actually, the last truly ecumenical one—joining both Eastern and Western churches—was the Fourth Council of Constantinople in 869, or eighth ecumenical council. Then, more than 250 years later, Catholic bishops in 1123 met at Rome's Lateran (LAT-ur-un) Palace, the papal residence. Whereas the first eight councils had focused on issues of belief and heresy, the four Lateran councils and others that followed centered on matters relating to church discipline.

The church-state struggle: round one

With the church on the rise after a period of decline, and with

German emperors seeking to establish their power, the two forces were bound to collide. The showdown came in 1075, when Gregory faced off with Emperor Henry IV (ruled 1056–1106) in a bitter struggle called the Investiture Controversy. The term *investiture* referred to a king's authority to give property to appoint or "invest" local church leaders, a right Henry claimed on the grounds that bishops and abbots held political as well as spiritual power.

On December 8, 1075, Gregory sent Henry orders to stop appointing bishops and abbots, and Henry responded by calling Gregory a "false monk." Gregory then brought the full power of his papal authority to bear: not only was Henry excommunicated (1076) and his rulership of Germany declared null and void, he was condemned to eternal damnation. Henry quickly lost the support of his nobles, so in January 1077, in a symbolic act of humility and submission, he appeared at the castle of Canossa (kuh-NAH-suh) in northern Italy, where the pope was temporarily residing, and waited barefoot outside in the snow for days until the pope granted him absolution.

But the story did not end with Henry in the snow at Canossa. Seven years later, Henry marched into Rome and had Gregory removed, to be replaced by the antipope Clement III (c. 1025–1100). Only the help of Robert Guiscard returned Gregory to power, but in the process Robert's troops so badly devastated the city that the people turned against Gregory. He lived

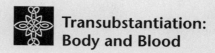

Transubstantiation: Body and Blood

A central aspect of worship during the Middle Ages was ritual, and nowhere was this tendency more apparent than in the Eucharist (YOO-kuh-rist), or Communion service. The Eucharist had originated with the Last Supper of Jesus and his disciples. There Jesus stated that the bread they ate was his body, which would soon be broken on the cross, and the wine they drank was his blood, which would soon be shed. In the future, he told them, they should eat bread and drink wine together "in remembrance of me."

Originally it was understood that the bread and wine were symbols of Christ's body and blood, but by the 1000s, the church had come to embrace the idea of transubstantiation (trans-sub-stan-shee-AY-shun). According to transubstantiation, the bread became Christ's literal body, and the wine his actual blood. This did not mean it was physically the same as actual flesh and blood, but it was Christ's body and blood all the same. In 1215, the Fourth Lateran Council confirmed the doctrine of transubstantiation.

out his days under the protection of the de Hautevilles. Yet Gregory passed his fervor for reform and papal authority on to Urban II (ruled 1088–99), who would prove the ability of the church to make emperors and kings do its bidding.

Santiago de Compostela, in northwestern Spain, was a favorite destination for pilgrims because it was said to be the burial place of the apostle James. *Reproduced by permission of the Corbis Corporation.*

The First Crusade (1095–99)

During the Middle Ages pilgrimages became popular both as an act of devotion to God and as a form of retribution for sins or even crimes (see box, "Punishment, Prison, and Pilgrimage"). A favorite site for pilgrims from France was Santiago de Compostela in northwestern Spain, where the apostle James had supposedly been buried. In Europe as a whole, the lead-

ing spot was Rome, not only as the center of the papacy, but also because of its association with the saints and martyrs of the early Church. Yet one place exceeded the glory even of Rome. This was the place where Jesus himself had walked, and where many events from the Bible had occurred: the Holy Land, or Palestine, specifically the city of Jerusalem.

For centuries, the Holy Land had belonged to the Muslims, or Saracens (SAR-uh-sunz) as many Europeans called them. The Arab caliphate had respected the right of Christian pilgrims to visit Jerusalem, a city holy to Islam as well; yet the Seljuks had proven less tolerant than the Arabs and had begun harassing pilgrims visiting the Holy Land. Therefore when Alexis I Comnenus sent a request to Urban II for military help against the Turks, Urban saw it as something much bigger: a chance to reclaim the Holy Land for Christ, to bring the Orthodox Church back within the Catholic fold—and to make the pope the most powerful man in the world. Furthermore, he needed a foreign war to occupy the energies of the Normans.

Launching of the crusade

Like Gregory before him, Urban had found himself dependent on the de Hautevilles, in his case Robert's son Bohemond I (BOH-ay-maw; c. 1050–1111). Bohemond took Rome from Henry IV in 1094, and thus allowed Urban to take control of the Lateran. Certainly Urban was grateful for the assistance, but he was also aware that the Normans were interested primarily in conquest and treasure, not the church. Therefore they could easily become dangerous foes, and Urban was only too happy to send them far, far away to attack someone else. In so doing, he claimed, that would be performing God's work.

There were other, equally ungodly, forces motivating the "wars of the cross," or Crusades, that followed. Kings and nobles were eager for a chance to prove the strength of their armies. Later crusades would involve commercial powers such as Venice, whose interest was expansion of trade. Among the common people, plenty were drawn by the desire for riches, or even worse by a lust for killing. Certainly some genuinely believed that they were fighting to rescue God's holy city from the hands of unbelievers—but many of these same people believed that this gave them justification to kill every Muslim or Jew they found.

In the speech that began the First Crusade, Urban promised that participants would enjoy the protection of the church over their homes and loved ones while they were away, and that they would earn complete forgiveness for their sins. This was an early example of an indulgence, the granting of forgiveness for sins in exchange for some act of service to the church. Many powerful men heeded his call, and in turn mobilized their armies, setting a pattern for crusades to come. Aside from Bohemond, there was his nephew Tancred; the French noble Godfrey of Bouillon (boo-

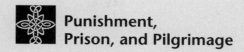

Punishment, Prison, and Pilgrimage

Medieval justice had severe punishments, such as branding or mutilation, for serious crimes. For less serious offenses, however, or for crimes committed by persons of high social rank, fines were generally imposed. Later, the practice of judicial pilgrimage replaced fines as a punishment.

First introduced in Ireland during the 500s, judicial pilgrimage might seem like an easy sentence. But this was a time when travel in any form was highly uncomfortable—especially if one had to walk barefoot and in chains, as most criminals did. Persons accused of murder often had to walk with their murder weapons chained to them, and these might come in handy, since the roads of Europe were teeming with bandits and cutthroats.

YAWn) in France, later to be idealized as the perfect knight; Godfrey's brother Baldwin of Boulogne (boo-LAWN); and Raymond IV, count of Toulouse (tuh-LOOS).

The Peasants' Crusade

Alongside these figures were men who possessed neither wealth nor official power, but who could command masses of followers. Most notable among the latter was Peter the Hermit (c. 1050–1115), a French ascetic who mobilized thousands with his speeches; and Gautier Sans Avoir

Byzantine territory at the city of Belgrade, the frightened Byzantines tried to turn them back, so the peasants began looting and pillaging. They were attacked by troops in Bulgaria, and by the time they reached Constantinople, their numbers had been reduced by one-quarter. They began conducting raids against Byzantine homes and churches, so Emperor Alexis wisely offered to ferry the entire peasant army across the strait called the Bosporus (BAHS-pur-us) and into Anatolia. They never got much farther: a local Turkish leader led the "Franks"—the Turks' name for the Europeans—into a trap, and most of them died. Peter himself, away in Constantinople to seek aid from Alexis, survived.

Pope Urban II launched the First Crusade in 1095 as an attempt to seize the Holy Land from the Muslims. *Reproduced by permission of the Corbis Corporation.*

(GOH-tee-ay SAWNZ a-VWAH, "Walter the Penniless"), a French knight. These two led the disastrous Peasants' Crusade (1096–97), which shadowed the official First Crusade.

The armies of peasants first made a shameful name for themselves in 1096, when they massacred countless German Jews as "enemies of Christ," then helped themselves to the Jews' possessions. From there they headed southeastward in a traditional pilgrims' route that took them through Hungary. When they entered

Spoils for the victors

Meanwhile the official crusade was just getting started. Unlike the peasants, the nobles had taken time to organize and prepare their armies, which reached the Holy Land in early 1097. They scored their first major victory at Nicaea in June—but only with the help of Alexis, who claimed the city for Byzantium. A few months later, Baldwin took Edessa in eastern Asia Minor and established the County of Edessa, the first of several "crusader states"; but he seized it from Armenian Christians, not Turks. Meanwhile the main body of crusaders besieged Antioch (AN-tee-ahk), an ancient city on the border between Turkey and Syria that had been an important center of the early church. An-

A Crusader. *Reproduced by permission of the New York Public Library Picture Collection.*

tioch became another crusader state, under the rule of Bohemond.

Then in July 1099, forces under Tancred and others conducted a brutal assault on Jerusalem, and seized the city after slaughtering thousands of Muslims. Ironically, Jerusalem was no longer in the hands of the Turks; a year earlier, it had fallen under the control of the Egyptians, who despised the Turks almost as much as the Europeans did. The Egyptians had promised that once they controlled Jerusalem, the Christians would have full access to all holy sites. But the original purpose of the Crusades had already been lost: the Europeans wanted land and treasure, and they could only get those by stealing. In the end, Godfrey of Bouillon emerged as the ruler of the new Latin Kingdom of Jerusalem.

With the establishment of a fourth crusader state, the County of Tripoli, the crusaders controlled the entire Mediterranean coast of what is now Syria, Lebanon, and Israel. Though the Crusades would continue for centuries, this was the high point from the Europeans' perspective; from then on, they would mostly be fighting to hold on to what they had gained in the 1090s. Eventually the Muslims, caught off guard by the First Crusade, would begin to react in a spirit of jihad. One of the most negative outcomes of the Crusades—a deep hatred of Christians among many Muslims—had been set into motion.

For More Information

Books

Dijkstra, Henk, editor. *History of the Ancient and Medieval World,* Volume 9: *The Middle Ages.* New York: Marshall Cavendish, 1996, pp. 1213–24.

Hanawalt, Barbara A. *The Middle Ages: An Illustrated History.* New York: Oxford University Press, 1998.

Jones, Terry, and Alan Ereira. *Crusades.* New York: Facts on File, 1995, pp. 11–80.

Langley, Andrew. *Medieval Life.* New York: Knopf, 1996.

Severy, Merle, editor. *The Age of Chivalry.* Washington, D.C.: National Geographic Society, 1969, pp. 92–130.

Web Sites

"The Cistercians." [Online] Available http://www2.csbsju.edu/osb/cist/intro.html (last accessed July 28, 2000).

"The First Crusade." [Online] Available http://history.idbsu.edu/westciv/crusades/01.htm (last accessed July 28, 2000).

Medieval Sourcebook: Empire and Papacy. [Online] Available http://www.fordham.edu/halsall/sbook11.html (last accessed July 28, 2000).

The Norman Conquest. [Online] Available http://historymedren.about.com/education/history/historymedren/msubnorm.htm (last accessed July 28, 2000).

The Twelfth Century

10

Though the Crusades would continue in some form until 1464, the crusading movement reached its peak during the twelfth century, as Europeans fought to maintain what they had gained in the First Crusade. The Crusades were the heart of the Middle Ages, source of the ideas and images most closely associated with the medieval period; but they were also the turning point, the beginning of the end. Conceived in ignorance, greed, and superstition, these so-called "holy wars" would have the unexpected effect of exposing Europeans to new ideas; as a result, the Europeans and their world were forever changed. From 1100, the reawakening of Europe began to pick up speed, and soon there was no turning back.

A changing world

Early in the twelfth century, England had its own Investiture Controversy. William the Conqueror's son William II (ruled 1087–1106), though he proved greedy and foolish as a king, was smart enough to appoint an outstanding man as archbishop of Canterbury, the leader of England's church.

Words to Know: The Twelfth Century

Allegory: A type of narrative, popular throughout the Middle Ages, in which characters represent ideas.

Artillery: Cannons and other heavy firepower.

Archbishop: The leading bishop in an area or nation.

Buttress: An exterior supporting structure.

Chateau: Originally a type of feudal castle in France, but later a name for a large country house.

Classical: Referring to ancient Greece and Rome.

Coat of arms: A heraldic emblem representing a family or nation.

Courtly love: An idealized form of romantic love, usually of a knight or poet for a noble lady.

Heraldry: The practice of creating and studying coats of arms and other insignia.

Intellectual: A person whose profession or lifestyle centers around study and ideas.

Moat: A large deep trench, filled with water, that surrounds a castle.

Page: The first step in training for knighthood, usually undertaken by young boys who performed menial tasks for a knight or feudal lord.

Penance: An act ordered by the church to obtain forgiveness for sin.

Reason: The use of the mind to figure things out; usually contrasted with emotion, intuition, or faith.

Squire: The middle stage in training for knighthood, usually undertaken by teenaged boys who became a knight's personal assistant.

Troubadour: A type of poet in Provence who composed in French rather than Latin, and whose work chiefly concerned courtly love.

Trinity: The three persons of God—Father, Son, and Holy Spirit—which according to Christian theology are also a single entity.

This was Anselm (c. 1034–1109), who quarreled first with William and later with his younger brother Henry I (ruled 1100–1135)—a much more competent ruler—over the powers of the church versus those of the king. Finally Henry and Anselm reached a compromise in 1105.

Anselm and Abelard (c. 1079–1144), two of the medieval world's greatest philosophers, worked to reconcile reason with religious faith. Like Anselm, Abelard was a cleric; indeed, there was simply no other place for an intellectual. His position in the church, however, had not stopped him from engaging in a celebrated love affair with his young student Héloïse (EL-uh-eez; c. 1098–1164). They conceived a child and were secretly married, but their relationship angered her uncle, a powerful church official, who arranged to have Abelard castrated. Abelard entered a monastery, while Héloïse joined a convent, and they became a symbol of enduring, if tragic, love. During this time he wrote a work in which he questioned established teachings about the Trinity, or the three-part nature of God.

Abelard was an early proponent of Scholasticism, a philosophical movement that attempted to bring together Christian faith, classical learning, and knowledge of the world. It marked the first stirrings of an intellectual reawakening in Europe. More typical of the medieval mind, however, was Bernard of Clairvaux (klair-VOH; 1090–1153), a Cistercian who perceived reason as a threat to religion. This made him an outspoken critic of Scholasticism in general, and of Abelard in particular.

Héloïse and Abelard. Abelard was one of the greatest philosophers of the Middle Ages, but he is also remembered for his tragic love affair with Héloïse. *Reproduced by permission of the Library of Congress.*

The Second Crusade (1147–49)

Bernard was also a passionate speaker, and in the Second Crusade, he combined the roles formerly played by Urban II and Peter the Hermit. After the Muslims captured Edessa in 1144, Pope Eugenius III, a former student of Bernard, called on his help. On March 31, 1146, Bernard made his first crusade sermon in France, and as was the custom, he handed out wooden crosses to those who volunteered to go. So many men "took up the cross" that he

ran out of wooden ones, and in an extremely dramatic move, he began cutting his own garments into crosses and passing them out to the crowd.

Among the royal leaders of the crusade were Conrad III, founder of the Hohenstaufen dynasty (hoh-un-SHTOW-fun), which was destined to rule Germany for a century, and Louis VII of France. This Crusade even included a woman, one of the most extraordinary figures of the Middle Ages:

Bernard of Clairvaux, a powerful church leader, called for the Second Crusade in a famous sermon on March 31, 1146.
Reproduced by permission of Archive Photos, Inc.

Louis's wife, Eleanor of Aquitaine (c. 1122–1204).

The Crusade itself was a devastating failure, largely due to the treachery of the crusaders' supposed allies in the Holy Land. On their way through Anatolia, the crusaders suffered heavy losses, but they were determined to take Edessa. Then the Europeans controlling Jerusalem convinced them to attack Damascus—one of the only Muslim cities in the area still on good terms with the Christians—instead. In Damascus, the Muslims dealt the crusaders a heavy blow; meanwhile the Latin Kingdom of Jerusalem negotiated a separate peace with the enemy and withdrew from the fight.

Castles and arms

The Crusades exposed Europeans to the Middle Eastern art of castle-building. Since the fall of the Western Roman Empire, when invasions by barbarian tribes had made it necessary to build forts, castles had existed in a crude form, as earthen mounds surrounded by ditches. Usually the mound had a high wall and perhaps a tower made of wood. In Palestine, however, wood was far from plentiful, and in any case, stone made for more sturdy fortifications. Impressed by the defensive architecture of the Byzantines and Muslims—not to mention their considerably more sophisticated military technology—the Europeans began imitating their fortresses. Some of the greatest castles were built in the Holy Land, to defend the crusader states, and later they appeared in Europe itself (see box).

The Crusades would transform the entire structure of knighthood, beginning with the knight's appearance. The heat in Palestine made chain mail uncomfortable, and to deflect the Sun's rays, crusaders began wearing sleeveless coats, decorated with crosses and other designs, over their armor. Only knights were allowed to wear these "coats of arms," as they came to be called. The exact appearance of

When a Castle Was a Castle

Castles changed dramatically during the Middle Ages, and with each new offensive technique developed by invading forces, castle-builders added new defensive technology. For instance, because castles were vulnerable to attack by sappers, men who dug under the walls and caused the foundations to collapse, builders surrounded castles with moats, or large deep trenches.

To make it easy for troops to retreat into the castle without the enemy pursuing them, builders added drawbridges, which were lowered and raised by a series of cranks. Eventually they also added an outer gate house, a fortified tower that stood in front of the drawbridge and provided an additional line of defense. In place of the single tower that had dominated early castles, later structures included a number of defensive towers, linked by walkways from which defenders could fire.

Within the castle walls was a courtyard where troops could assemble and regroup, and beneath ground level was the dreaded dungeon for prisoners. There were also stables and storerooms just inside the walls, and the main building housed sleeping quarters, a kitchen, the great hall (for dining and meeting), and a chapel.

Castle defenses became increasingly elaborate, but the development of cannons and other new forms of artillery in the late 1300s began to render the medieval castle obsolete. Eventually the chateau (sha-TOH), a massive but delicate structure with real windows instead of small slits from which to fire at attackers, took the place of the castle as a residence for kings and noblemen.

---

their insignia, which they also carried on their shields, was important because it identified them on the field of battle. Therefore men known as heralds were charged with keeping track of the knights' symbols, and they developed the art of heraldry, which survives today in many a family's or country's coat of arms.

Romanesque turns to Gothic

The world was changing, and so were Europeans' perceptions of it as reflected in art and architecture. From about 1000 onward, a style termed Romanesque (roh-mun-ESK) had dominated; but in about 1150, this gave way to the Gothic, which originated in France and spread throughout the continent during the next four centuries. The names appeared later, and "Romanesque," at least, is accurate, since aspects of this style resembled Roman architecture—particularly its use of vaults and round arches. But there is little in the delicate beauty of Gothic architecture to suggest the

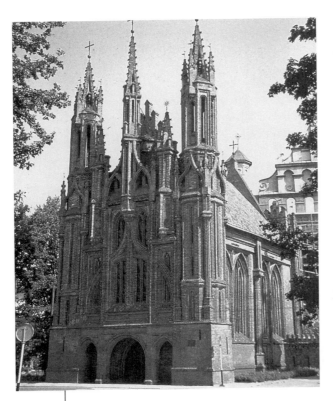

This church, located in Lithuania, is a fine example of Romanesque architecture, which dominated in Europe from about 1000 to about 1150. *Photograph by Cory Langley. Reproduced by permission of Cory Langley.*

Gothic tribes that destroyed the Roman Empire; in fact later art historians used the deceptive name as a way of identifying the entire medieval period with barbarism.

Gothic became the style for cathedrals, which were not simply large churches but the centers of their communities, the place where the bishop had his throne, or *cathedra*. Among Europe's finest Gothic cathedrals are Notre Dame (NOH-truh

DAHM; "Our Lady") in Paris, started in 1163; and Chartres (SHART), southwest of Paris, built after the old Romanesque cathedral there burned down in 1194. These two became models for the Gothic style, imitated throughout Catholic Europe, from northern Spain to Poland.

The cathedral's spire was always the highest point in any medieval city. Not only was the building a symbol of man's yearning to reach heavenward, but the height emphasized the power of the church above all other forces in medieval society. In order to achieve this height, Romanesque architects developed buttresses, or exterior supporting structures. These not only made it possible to build higher towers, but also gave buildings a distinctive appearance. What Romanesque churches lacked, however, was light: fearful that windows would weaken the structures, designers allowed only narrow slats.

Architects of the Gothic era solved this problem with a number of innovations. First was the pointed arch, which not only looked more striking than the curved arch, but was also more sound structurally. This allowed more windows and a higher roof. In place of Romanesque-style buttresses, Gothic designers used a flying buttress, a stone support connected to the building by an arch.

The building of a cathedral took place over decades, and there was never a single architect who received credit for the design; instead, a team of architects (typically former stone-

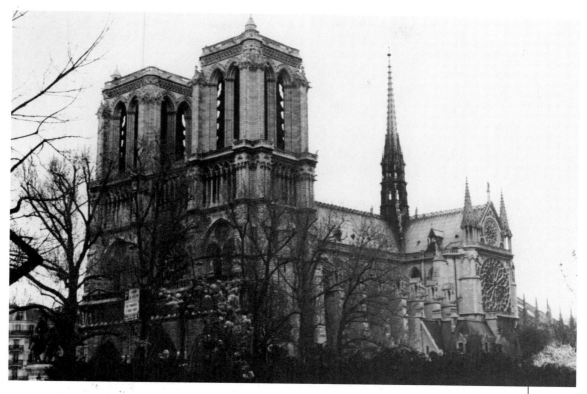

Notre Dame, located in Paris, France, is a magnificent example of a Gothic cathedral.
Photograph by Jeffrey Hill. Reproduced by permission of Jeffrey Hill.

masons) worked under a master architect. Yet even the names of the master architects are lost to history, in part due to the medieval world's lack of emphasis on individual achievement.

The same is true of the many sculptors whose work filled Chartres and other sites. In an age when few people could read and write, the intricate sculptural work decorating virtually every surface provided clearly understandable "sermons in stone" depicting events from the Bible. Stained glass served the same purpose in a particularly striking way. Since the 800s, artists had known how to use melted glass with metallic oxides of various colors; but in the century after 1150, the art of stained glass reached a high point. When sunlight entered a church window and illuminated scenes of Jesus Christ and the saints, it filled believers with the sense that the light of God was shining down upon the world.

The cross and the sword

A new struggle between pope and king, sparked by the efforts of Emperor Frederick I Barbarossa (bar-buh-ROH-suh; "Red Beard"; ruled 1152–90) to forge a single German state, began in the 1150s. Frederick set out to subdue all rival princes, and initially allied himself with Adrian IV, history's only English pope. Soon afterward, however, Frederick broke off the alliance.

He invaded northern Italy in 1154, and after twenty years of fighting, he succeeded only in making himself more and more unpopular with the Italians. One of his most bitter foes was Pope Alexander III (ruled 1159–81), against whom Frederick supported an antipope. Alexander countered by helping to organize the Lombard League, an alliance of cities opposed to Frederick. In 1175 Frederick also had a falling-out with Henry the Lion, Duke of Saxony and a member of the powerful Welf family. Soon Frederick's Italian opponents began calling themselves Guelphs (GWELFZ), and joined forces with the church against the emperor and his supporters, the Ghibellines (GIB-uh-leenz; see box, "Church vs. State vs. People").

Frederick suffered a major military defeat in 1176 and made a truce with Alexander a year later. The Peace of Constance in 1183 gave Lombard League cities their freedom. Frederick had meanwhile turned his attention to his homeland, where he adopted an entirely new strategy, supporting the German noblemen he had once opposed. To give the nobles more power, he adopted feudalism, which had long since taken hold in France and England. The resulting peace and unity among the Germans made him one of his nation's greatest heroes.

England's own struggle

As with the Investiture Controversy, events in England reflected the church-state struggle in Central Europe. In 1152, Eleanor of Aquitaine had divorced Louis VII of France to marry Henry II of England (ruled 1154–89), which gave England title to new French lands and further heightened tensions between the two countries. Meanwhile, Henry became involved in a heated dispute with Thomas à Becket (uh BEK-et; 1118–1170), the archbishop of Canterbury.

The conflict centered around the question of whether a church official charged with a crime such as rape or murder should be tried by the church, as Thomas maintained, or the state. Knights loyal to Henry attempted to settle the issue on December 29, 1170, when they murdered Thomas inside his cathedral. This only made Thomas a martyr: he was canonized just three years after his death (a *very* short interval), and Henry had to do penance at Thomas's shrine in Canterbury. Eventually, however, Henry persuaded the pope to make a series of compromises that gave the English king greater power over church affairs.

The Third Crusade (1189–92)

Henry's and Eleanor's son Richard I, the Lion-Hearted (ruled 1189–99), became one of the leading figures in the Third Crusade. He was joined by Frederick I Barbarossa and Philip II Augustus of France (ruled 1179–1223), who is remembered for turning his nation into a great power.

Church vs. State vs. People

Americans typically guard against encroachments on their freedom by church authorities, citing "separation of church and state" as one of the bedrock principles of the U.S. government. Thus it is easy for them to sympathize with the Ghibellines, supporters of the Holy Roman emperor, in their long struggle against the pro-papacy Guelphs. Yet upon closer investigation, one finds that the Guelph-Ghibelline rivalry was really about power and not principle; thus by the 1300s, two centuries after the conflict began, it had become little more than a struggle between various Italian families.

As opposed to government by church or state, America's system is based on a third force, the people, who exercise authority through elected representatives. One of the most important milestones in the development of government by the people occurred during the Middle Ages, when a group of English nobles forced King John to sign the Magna Carta, or "Great Charter," in 1215. Thenceforth England's government would take quite a different course from that of France and other nations on the European continent, which continued to be dominated both by priests *and* kings.

Later, English settlers in the New World brought with them advanced notions about the idea of freedom, and these would find their greatest expression in the U.S. Constitution (1787). In fact the latter does not contain the phrase "separation of church and state": what it does say, in the First Amendment, is that the government may not favor one religious group over another.

To complete this assembly of great personalities was their brilliant opponent: Saladin.

Saladin had united Egypt with Syria and Mesopotamia, then conquered a number of cities in Palestine. On July 4, 1187, he dealt the crusaders a devastating blow in the Battle of Hittin, where the Europeans found themselves on a dry, desolate plain, overcome by thirst. Saladin's forces set fire to the dry grass around them, nearly wiping out the European forces, and went on to capture Jerusalem on October 2.

On his way to the crusade, Frederick drowned in Anatolia. Richard arrived late in Palestine, having stopped to conquer the strategically located island of Cyprus (SY-prus) in the Mediterranean. (Cyprus would remain a crusader state until 1384, and briefly emerged as an imperial power during the mid-1300s.) Arriving in what is now Israel, Richard joined Philip outside Acre (AH-kruh), an important trading center for the Italian city-states of Genoa (JEN-oh-uh) and Pisa (PEE-zuh). Their use of the siege engine, a recently developed catapult for hurling stones

Thomas à Becket was murdered as a result of his conflict with King Henry II of England.

Richard and Saladin, two of the most romantic figures of the Middle Ages, squared off against one another. Though their conflict inspired many legends, in fact it ended in a stalemate—and the two men never even met. Richard needed to get back to England, where his brother John (ruled 1199–1216) had been making trouble for him, so in September 1192, he signed an agreement with Saladin. The Muslims still held Jerusalem, but the crusaders had regained a number of areas along the coast.

The age of chivalry

Prior to about 1200, knights had been mere soldiers employed by the nobility; after that time, however, they were recognized as nobles in their own right. During this period, knights began to adopt a code of honor known as chivalry (SHIV-ul-ree; from *chevalier,* the French word for *knight*). In modern times, chivalry is understood chiefly in terms of male courtesy toward women, but in fact this was only part of the larger code, which included offering protection for the weak and defenseless and performing service for God. As with much about medieval times, of course, the truth is rather more complex than the myth: even under the code of chivalry, knights were often brutal creatures. But before the church began its attempts to civilize them in the 900s, introducing concepts that developed into chivalry over the centuries, they were *truly* brutal.

over castle walls, helped the Europeans gain victory at Acre.

In 1191, Philip learned that his only heir had taken ill, so he rushed back to France. This left just

A young boy who wanted to become a knight went to work as a page, waiting table for a knight or lord and performing other menial tasks. In his late teens, a page who had proved himself became a squire, who cared for the knight's horse—his most trusted companion—and carried the knight's shield and armor into battle. Then in his early twenties, a squire who had received the blessings of his lord was chosen for knighthood. A royal, noble, or priestly figure conferred the title of knight by the ceremony of dubbing, touching a young man's shoulders with a sword.

The orders of knights

Eventually, knights began to see themselves as soldiers for Jesus Christ. Just like monks, these knights formed themselves into orders, their stated purpose being to protect pilgrims. First of the three great orders was the Knights Hospitalers, or Knights of St. John of Jerusalem, formed in 1113. They wore distinctive colors and insignia, including the eight-pointed Maltese cross, and built one of the medieval world's greatest castles, Krak des Chevaliers (DAY shuh-VAHL-yay), in Syria. After the end of the Crusades, they occupied a series of Mediterranean strongholds, and in 1530 ended up on the island of Malta, where they became known as the Knights of Malta.

The Knights Templars, or Poor Knights of Christ, were formed in 1119 to defend one of the most sacred spots in Palestine, the Holy Sepulchre (SEP-ul-kur), where it was believed

Richard I, also known as Richard the Lion-Hearted, was a leading figure of the Third Crusade, which ended in a stalemate when Richard had to return to England to protect his throne. *Reproduced by permission of the Corbis Corporation.*

that Christ had been buried before his resurrection. Their name came from that of another holy site, where the temple of King Solomon had stood. In contrast to the Hospitalers' black cloaks with white crosses, the Templars wore white cloaks with red crosses. They developed so much military and economic power, and thus aroused so much hostility in England, France, and Spain, that in 1312 the pope disbanded the order.

King Arthur: Fact and Legend

Such a great legend has developed around King Arthur that it may come as a surprise to learn that the character is based on a real person: a Christian general named Ambrosius Aurelianus, who led the Britons to victory over the invading Anglo-Saxons at the Battle of Mount Badon in 516. This figure became associated with Arthur, and as the centuries passed, legend obscured fact.

There are literally hundreds, perhaps thousands, of Arthurian tales, but most depict Arthur as king over a realm centered in western England and Wales, where he had his castle at Camelot. There he held council with his Knights of the Round Table, among whom the greatest was Sir Lancelot. A pure Christian sworn to defend his king, Lancelot fell in love with Arthur's beautiful queen, Guinevere (GWIN-uh-veer), and was torn by conflicting loyalties. In the end, he gave in to his passion and thus helped usher in the end of Camelot.

The legend of Camelot included numerous mystical elements. There was, for instance, the figure of Merlin, a magician with amazing powers who seemed to live forever. There was the knights' quest for the Holy Grail, said to be the cup from which Christ had drunk at the Last Supper.

This medieval French manuscript illustration shows Lancelot, the greatest of King Arthur's knights, embracing a lady. *Reproduced by permission of the Corbis Corporation.*

And there was the account of Arthur's death, after which fairies whisked him away to a magical land called Avalon, where he was restored to life and would one day return to save England.

All in all, it is one of the most intriguing tales in Western literature, though in fact it is not purely English in origin. During the Middle Ages, an extensive body of French, German, Italian, Spanish, and even Hebrew Arthurian legends developed.

The last of the great orders was formed in 1191, and consisted primarily of Germans: hence its name, the Teutonic (too-TAHN-ik; German) Knights, or the Teutonic Order. In 1225, they set out to conquer the last two non-Christian European tribes: the Prussians of eastern Germany, and the Lithuanians farther east. They tamed the wilds of Prussia, destined to become the most powerful of German states, and built Europe's largest castle at Marienburg in 1309.

The literature of chivalry

In addition to the three spiritual orders of knights, there were numerous secular orders throughout Europe—among them the Order of the Garter, which exists today as an honor conferred on Englishmen of merit. Chivalry itself assumed a non-religious character, and became much more concerned with things of this world than with matters of the spirit. In fact chivalry spawned some of the world's first self-help literature, "courtesy books," or manuals that taught people how to behave politely—a rare skill in the Middle Ages. Most popular were courtesy books for pages, squires, and knights. Books for pages taught them how to act like little men rather than boys, whereas squires' courtesy books dealt with more adult issues, such as how to be a brave soldier, a loyal servant of a lord—and a discreet lover of a lady.

A more well-known type of literature associated with chivalry was courtly love poetry, popularized by a new breed of poets called troubadours (TROO-buh-dohrz). The latter, who came from Provence (pruh-VAWNts) in southern France, took the revolutionary step of composing not in Latin, but in the local language, French. Courtly love poetry drew on stories from the past, such as the Celtic legend of Tristan and Isolde (TREES-tahn; ee-SOHld), whose love was doomed because Isolde was married to Tristan's uncle, a powerful king.

One notable type of courtly love poetry was the *aubade* (oh-BAHD), or "dawn song." This was a song of parting, or to put it more bluntly, of a knight who has to beat a hasty retreat from his lady's bedroom in the morning. The aubade was meant to be taken seriously; by contrast, the *Romance of the Rose*, written by two French poets in the mid-1200s, was a biting work of satire demonstrating what its authors perceived as the fickleness of women. It was an example of allegory, a type of narrative popular throughout the Middle Ages in which characters represent ideas.

The great poetic narratives of the High Middle Ages were often called "romances," and they typically concerned one of three basic subjects: the classical world (ancient Greece and Rome); France, or specifically Charlemagne; and Britain's great hero Arthur. An example of the first type was the *Romance of Troy*, written by a French clerk in the court of England's Henry II. The greatest of the Charlemagne epics was the *Song of Roland*, set during the emperor's otherwise uneventful campaign against the Muslims of Spain in 778. Then there was the legend of Arthur, which gained popularity in the 1100s and later found expression in one of the first printed books produced in England, Sir Thomas Malory's *Le Morte D'Arthur* ("The Death of Arthur"; 1470). A thousand years before Malory, however, there really was a King Arthur—perhaps (see box, "King Arthur: Fact and Legend").

For More Information

Books

Dijkstra, Henk, editor. *History of the Ancient and Medieval World,* Volume 9: *The Middle Ages.* New York: Marshall Cavendish, 1996, pp. 1267–78.

Jones, Terry, and Alan Ereira. *Crusades.* New York: Facts on File, 1995, pp. 81–180.

Langley, Andrew. *Medieval Life.* New York: Knopf, 1996.

Severy, Merle, editor. *The Age of Chivalry.* Washington, D.C.: National Geographic Society, 1969, pp. 131–271.

Web Sites

Armor. [Online] Available http://www.geo cities.com/Vienna/9604/armor.html (last accessed July 28, 2000).

Castles Are Rubbish. [Online] Available http://www.castlewales.com/rubbish.html (last accessed July 28, 2000).

"The Chivalry FAQ Sheet." [Online] Available http://members.tripod.com/~Baron91/Chivalry_FAQ.html (last accessed July 28, 2000).

The Crusades. [Online] Available http://historymedren.about.com/education/history/historymedren/msubcrus.htm (last accessed July 28, 2000).

Knighthood, Chivalry & Tournament Glossary of Terms. [Online] Available http://www.chronique.com/Library/Glossaries/glossary-KCT/glssindx.htm (last accessed July 28, 2000).

Knight Life. [Online] Available http://history medren.about.com/education/history/historymedren/library/blknighttoc.htm (last accessed July 28, 2000).

Medieval Sourcebook: The Crusades. [Online] Available http://www.fordham.edu/halsall/sbook1k.html (last accessed July 28, 2000).

The Thirteenth Century

11

If the twelfth century was the peak of the Middle Ages in Western Europe, the thirteenth century (or the 1200s) offered clear signs that the medieval period was drawing to a close. The Crusades continued, but the crusading spirit lost force; and though the church reached the pinnacle of its powers in the mid-1200s, other elements were gaining influence. Among these competing forces were kings and emerging nation-states such as France and England. But kings and popes were far from the only influential figures in thirteenth-century life: merchants and scholars, though they had little in common, threatened to tear down the power of both church and state.

The end of the Crusades

By the time of the Fourth Crusade (1202–04), Europeans had begun to lose faith in the whole crusading enterprise. Only a figure as strong as Innocent III (ruled 1198–1216), who controlled the papacy at the time of its greatest power, could even have mobilized the people for an-

Words to Know: The Thirteenth Century

Alchemy: A semi-scientific discipline that holds that through the application of certain chemical processes, ordinary metals can be turned into gold.

Apprentice: A first stage in the training of a craftsman, in which a young boy went to work, for no wages, in the shop of a master.

Astrology: The study of the stars and planets with the belief that their movement has an effect on personal events.

Friar: A type of cleric, neither a priest nor a monk, who both preaches and teaches.

Guild: An association to promote, and set standards for, a particular profession or business.

Journeyman: A middle stage in the training of a craftsman, in which a teenaged boy worked for wages; if he proved himself as a journeyman, the guild would declare him a master craftsman.

Mendicant: Dependent on charity for a living.

Minstrel: A wandering musician.

Nation-state: A geographical area composed largely of a single nationality, in which a single national government clearly holds power.

Working class: A group between the middle class and the poor, who typically earn a living with their hands.

other crusade; even so, his initial call for troops in 1198 raised little interest. It took four years to pull together a big enough army.

Other than Innocent, this Crusade lacked the strong figures who had driven the first three ventures; this time the guiding force was Venice, which provided five hundred ships and expected to make a profit. The crusaders set off for Egypt, which they intended to conquer before going on to win back Jerusalem, but they never got past Constantinople. There they became involved in a power struggle in which they helped the Byzantine prince Alexis seize the throne from his father. In the meantime, they had to pay off their Venetian sponsors, so they captured one of the Byzantines' port cities, Zara, in October 1202. When the Byzantines overthrew Alexis in 1204, the crusaders took over Constantinople.

Thus the Byzantine capital became the center of yet another crusader state, the so-called Latin Empire, which consisted of little more than a portion of Greece. The Byzantines retreated to Trebizond in Turkey until the recapture of Constantinople in 1261 by Michael VIII Palaeologus (pay-lee-AHL-uh-gus; ruled 1259–82). Michael founded a dynasty under which Byzantium enjoyed its last gasp of power, but the damage done by the crusaders was irreparable. This probably bothered the Western Europeans little, however: they despised the Greeks even more than they did the Muslims and were happy to participate in Byzantium's destruction—even though to do so was to erode an empire that had long served as a buffer between Western Europe and its enemies to the east.

The Albigenses and the Inquisition

The next "crusade" did not even take place in the East, and its target was not Muslims but a religious group called the Cathars. Based in Albi, France, they were also called Albigenses (al-buh-JIN-seez), and they practiced a faith similar to Manichaeism. Like the Manichees long before, the Albigenses believed that all of existence was a battle between evil and good, and that they alone were capable of understanding the terms of this battle.

The church considered this heresy, and at first it dealt with the Albigenses by sending them missionaries such as St. Dominic (c. 1170–1221). Dominic later founded the Dominicans, a mendicant (that is, dependent on charity for a living) order of friars—neither monks nor priests, but preachers and teachers. Another mendicant order was the Franciscans, founded by St. Francis of Assisi (uh-SEE-see; c. 1182–1226).

St. Dominic founded the Dominicans, an order of friars who depend on charitable donations. *Reproduced by permission of the Corbis Corporation.*

Innocent III ultimately decided to deal harshly with the Albigenses, and in 1208 launched the so-called Albigensian Crusade. Invaders eager for land and treasure swarmed over southern France, seizing the estates of the nobility and replacing bishops who had sympathized with the Cathars.

The Albigensian Crusade, which ended in 1229, had a powerful effect on history. By displacing much of France's nobility, it greatly strengthened the French king, and from then on France would have a powerful central government in contrast to the looser system that had prevailed under feudalism. This in turn tied the French royal house close to the church, and eventually the two would become inseparable. The Albigensian Crusade also led to the establishment of the Inquisition by Pope Gregory IX in 1231.

The Inquisition, which lasted until the 1300s, was the name for a court through which the church investigated, tried, and punished cases of heresy. Many inquisitors, Church officials appointed to oversee investigations, were excessive in their methods, but generally the Inquisition was not as harsh as is popularly believed. During the 1200s in France, for instance, only about one percent of accused heretics were burned at the stake; some ten percent were imprisoned, and the rest received lesser sentences. When modern people talk about the horrors of the Inquisition, what they are actually referring to is the *Spanish* Inquisition, an entirely separate system (see box, "The Iberian Peninsula," chapter 19).

Later Crusades

The year 1212 saw the pathetic "Children's Crusade." Some historians believe that the participants in this crusade were not children, but poor people from the countryside who were viewed as childlike innocents by medieval society. Perhaps, many believed, these "children" could achieve what kings and knights had not. In fact they never made it to the Holy Land, and though some returned home safely, many were captured and sold into slavery in the Arab world.

There were other such crusades by the downtrodden; meanwhile, formal Crusades continued with ever-diminishing success. The Fifth Crusade (1217–21), also ordered by Innocent III, included leaders from England, Germany, Hungary, and Austria, and took place entirely in Egypt, which the crusaders tried unsuccessfully to conquer. The Sixth Crusade (1228–29) is significant not so much for its outcome as for its leader: Holy Roman Emperor Frederick II (ruled 1212–50), a figure of many and varied talents whose interest in literature and science made his court an exciting place. He and Gregory IX also quarreled openly, as other emperors and popes before them had, and during his reign the Guelph-Ghibelline conflict turned into open warfare.

As for the crusade itself, it was chiefly a matter of diplomacy and not warfare. Though Frederick worked out an agreement with the Muslims regarding possession of Jerusalem and visits to holy sites, neither side was happy with the arrangement. Gregory also organized the Seventh Crusade (1239–40), another failure. The last two numbered Crusades, the Eighth (1248–54) and Ninth (1270–72), were led by France's King Louis IX (ruled 1226–70), better known as St. Louis. By then the Seljuks' power had faded, and the Mamluks were the enemy; but the results were the same.

The Mamluks conquered the last Christian stronghold at Acre in

The Children's Crusade was a failure—the crusaders never even reached the Holy Land, and many were captured and enslaved along the way. *Reproduced by permission of the Corbis Corporation.*

Frederick II, leader of the Holy Roman Empire, led the Sixth Crusade (1228–29).

1291, thus ending two centuries of European presence in the Holy Land. There were still crusades of a limited nature in later years, but the targets were usually in Asia Minor or Egypt. In addition, there were crusades against heretics or rebellious emperors, not to mention the Reconquista (ray-kawn-KEES-tah), or reconquest, of Spain from the Muslims (see box, "The Iberian Peninsula," chapter 19). The last crusade of any kind came in 1464, in response to the Ottoman capture of Constantinople in May 1453. Pope Pius II (ruled 1458–64) led the Crusade himself; but he died en route,

and the crusading movement died with him.

The new Europe

In about 1100, Western Europe began changing rapidly, a change characterized by the reemergence of large towns and cities. The largest ones were Paris, with a population of some 200,000; London, somewhat smaller but still a great city; and Rome, struggling to return to its former glory. Then there were the great Italian cities, each with a population of about 100,000: Venice, Genoa, Pisa, and Florence.

Driving this growth was an economic boom, itself a partial result of the Crusades. The latter had exposed Europeans to the idea of international trade, which grew rapidly in the twelfth and thirteen centuries. The largest component of international trade, however, was not commerce with lands outside of Europe, but between European states. Such activity took place at large annual trading fairs that sprang up during the 1100s in two great centers: Champagne, a county in northwestern France; and Flanders, a coastal region in the area of modern-day Belgium and Holland.

Not only did merchants from all over Europe present their wares at these gatherings, but the fairs also facilitated cultural exchanges; and for peasants and poor people, they broke up the monotony of daily life. Soon the fairs became great celebrations

The Positive Side of the Crusades

In the modern view, the Crusades were a shameful episode in European history, a time when savagery in the name of God reached a low point. The truth, however, is far more complex: though the Crusades were unquestionably a brutal act of invasion—not to mention a massive failure—they were crucial to the opening of trade routes to the East and to the reawakening of Europe. Through these vicious, misguided "holy wars," Western Europeans gained exposure to Byzantium and the Arab world, civilizations in which learning had never faded.

Arab figures such as Avicenna and Averroës helped reintroduce Greek learning to the West. In fact, contact with Arab civilization led to nothing short of a full-scale reintroduction of scientific learning in Europe. At that point, neither the Arabs nor the Europeans knew the difference between real science and false science: thus the Arabs passed on both scientific astronomy and the hocus-pocus of astrology, not to mention the "science" most closely associated with the Middle Ages, alchemy. From the latter, however, would come the serious scientific discipline of chemistry.

There are other legacies of the Crusades in almost every aspect of life—for instance, chess. The game originated in India during the 500s, and later spread throughout the Muslim world, where it reached the crusaders. Originally the figures on the chess board were based on ranks within the Indian army; later they took on a specifically European character that reflected the power of the church: hence the most useful piece, after the queen, is the bishop. Of course the king is not a particularly useful piece, but his loss marks the end of the game—checkmate, a term that comes from a Persian expression, *shah mat.*

with all sorts of entertainment provided by acrobats, minstrels, or wandering musicians, and others.

The growth of trade led to greater increases in knowledge. When Marco Polo (1254–1324) of Venice embarked in 1271 on his celebrated journey to China, his immediate purpose was commercial. Yet his later writings would give Europeans their first glimpses of the Far East and would establish geography as a science rather than a collection of fantastic stories about other lands.

International commerce also forced an improvement in European travel conditions. New roads were built for the first time since the fall of Rome, and civil authorities sought to make travel safe by providing protection against highway robbers. This in turn led to the strengthening of national governments: as in the modern United States, maintenance of large

Marco Polo and his brother Nicolo, shown here on horseback behind a caravan of camels, journeyed to China in 1271. *Reproduced by permission of the Corbis Corporation.*

"interstate highways" was more practical at a national than at a local level.

Guilds and classes

In Germany, which lacked a national government, cities began banding together in 1160 to form the Hanseatic (han-see-AT-ik) League, designed to help them secure greater trade privileges in international markets. The Hanseatic League was itself an outgrowth of another change in commercial life, the reemergence of guilds, or associations, to promote a particular profession or business.

Guilds had existed in ancient times, but had disappeared until the 1000s, and thereafter they became much more organized than their ancient counterparts. There were merchant guilds such as those that made up the Hanseatic League, and there were craft guilds. The latter represented specific crafts, such as that of stonemason, and protected their economic interests while establishing standards for their members. A young man rising through the ranks of the guilds went through stages akin to those of a prospective knight, working first as an apprentice, then as a journeyman in his teens before finally emerging as a master—and thus as a full member of the guild.

The growth of commerce in general, and the guilds in particular, led to the expansion of the middle class and working class, both of which separated the very rich from the very poor. As for the poor, they had plenty of incentive to move to the cities, where they stood a chance of rising to one of the more fortunate classes; all that awaited them in the country, by contrast, was a lifetime of toil on a feudal lord's manor. The resulting desertion of the countryside, combined with the growth of new classes, signaled the end of feudalism as an economic system—though not yet as a political system. Peasants no longer needed the protection of feudal lords, but the latter retained considerable power and wealth, and would continue to do so for several centuries.

Thomas Aquinas was a philosopher and theologian who felt that reason and faith were not incompatible, though he always placed primary importance on faith.

New ideas

An increase in learning accompanied the expansion of trade. The first real colleges made their appearance in France and Italy during the late 1100s; then in 1221, a French scholar first used the term "university" to describe a type of college that offered students a broader range of studies and greater freedom in which to pursue them. For the first time, education was open to young men outside the priesthood, and this led to an explosion of learning as profound as the economic boom then taking place.

Of course the church itself was still the home of many intellectuals, among them Thomas Aquinas (uh-KWYN-us; 1226–1274). Thomas, who replaced Averroës as the leading interpreter of Aristotle, represents the fullest development of Scholasticism. His contemporary, Roger Bacon (c. 1220–1292), another priest, was a forerunner of modern thought who insisted that a scientific approach to the natural world was not inconsistent with Christian belief. The church, on

Romantic Love—A Matter of Economics?

Unlike marriage, sex, and procreation, romantic love has not always been a part of life; even today, the concept is virtually unknown in traditional societies. In order for romantic love to take root in a society, there has to be a certain amount of wealth and leisure. There also has to be a period between the first manifestations of sexual desire, which typically happen in puberty, and their fulfillment. In societies where most people are poor and live off the land, there is a great incentive to marry at puberty and start having offspring so that children can help on the farm. There is simply no time to fall in love.

The idea of romantic love had existed in ancient Greece and Rome and parts of the Middle East—the Bible's Song of Solomon is clear evidence of this—but had largely faded from Western Europe with the fall of the Western Roman Empire. Then, in the High Middle Ages (1100–1300), it took hold among the upper classes, as the popularity of courtly love illustrates. During the thirteenth century and later, the concept spread to the middle class. Marriage prior to that time had been chiefly a business arrangement, with the young man's family offering some advantage to the young woman's family, and the latter providing a dowry (the wealth that a bride brings to a marriage) in exchange. Perhaps the couple might grow to love one another, but this was only a happy accident, and not considered a vital part of marriage.

With the emergence of the middle class, however, it became possible for a young man and woman to marry for love, and not primarily for money. Ironically, the people who were least free to marry for love were the most wealthy and powerful: the motivation behind the vast majority of royal or noble marriages remained political or economic, not romantic.

the other hand, considered science a threat to its dominant position in European intellectual life.

Nations and non-nations

Across the European continent, nations were coming together and empires falling apart. In Eastern Europe, Byzantium—permanently crippled by the Crusades—limped along, while the city-states of Russia, led by Novgorod, gradually gathered strength. Greatest of Novgorod's leaders was Alexander Nevsky (c. 1220–1263), a prince who repelled invasions by the Swedes in 1240 and the Teutonic knights in 1242. His defeat of the knights, in a battle on a frozen lake, is one of the most celebrated events of Russian history.

Alexander did not act so decisively against a new breed of invaders

Filmmaker Sergei Eisenstein immortalized Russian ruler Alexander Nevsky in his movie of the same name, made in 1938. *Reproduced by permission of the Kobal Collection.*

from the east, the nomadic Mongols of Central Asia. By 1241, they had swarmed over Russia, the Ukraine, Poland, and Hungary, and had reached the gates of Vienna, Austria's capital. Alexander saw the Mongols as protection from enemies to the west, and submitted to their rule. Upon his death, he made his son Daniel ruler over Moscow, which thenceforth became known as the principality of Muscovy. During the centuries that followed, the Mongols would rule Russia until Muscovy became powerful enough to overthrow them; in the process, the Russian system would become characterized by highly centralized authority, with a prince whose subjects did not dare question his power.

Quite the opposite thing was happening in England, where the signing of the Magna Carta in 1215 led to greater power for the nobility over the king—and ultimately to greater power for the people over both. In other countries, too, the central authority lost power, but not by such orderly means as in England. Italy remained a confused collection of warring states, and Germany began to fall apart when the Hohenstaufens lost the imperial throne in 1254. In 1273, however, the election of Rudolf I (ruled 1273–91) as emperor established the powerful Hapsburg dynasty, destined to remain a factor in European politics until 1918.

The strongest nation in Western Europe was France, where a series of powerful kings increased the dominance of the royalty over all other forces in French life. Philip IV (the Fair; ruled 1285–1314) proved just how strong a French king could be when he went up against Pope Boniface VIII (BAHN-i-fus; ruled 1294–1303) and won. The conflict began when Philip's government established a tax to pay for a series of wars with England, and a group of Cistercians protested the tax. They appealed to Boniface for support, and Boniface ordered all French bishops to Rome so that he could review Philip's policies. Philip responded by supporting a group who kidnapped the pope.

Though Boniface was only held prisoner for a few days, the incident marked the end of the papal dominance over kings. Philip later arranged to have a pope who would do his bidding, Clement V (ruled 1305–14), placed on the throne. In 1309, Clement moved the papal seat from Rome to Avignon (AV-in-yawn) in southern France. This in turn sparked one of the greatest crises in the history of the Catholic Church, as Western Europe was divided between supporters of the Avignon papacy and those who submitted to a rival pope in Rome. The church would recover from this rift, but its power would never again be as great.

For More Information

Books

Dijkstra, Henk, editor. *History of the Ancient and Medieval World,* Volume 10: *Medieval Politics and Life.* New York: Marshall Cavendish, 1996, pp. 1303–44.

Jones, Terry, and Alan Ereira. *Crusades.* New York: Facts on File, 1995, pp. 181–241.

Langley, Andrew. *Medieval Life.* New York: Knopf, 1996.

Severy, Merle, editor. *The Age of Chivalry.* Washington, D.C.: National Geographic Society, 1969, pp. 272–89.

Web Sites

The Catholic Encyclopedia. [Online] Available http://www.newadvent.org/cathen/ (last accessed July 28, 2000).

The Mongols | 12

The Middle Ages in Europe and the Middle East were marked by three invasions of nomads from Central Asia: first the Huns, then the Turks, and finally the Mongols. The Mongols would conquer the largest empire of all, a vast realm that stretched from the Korean Peninsula to the outskirts of Vienna; but the Mongols' empire would fall apart almost as quickly as it came together. For a brief time, however, the Mongols—a people with no written language, and thus no real past history—would dominate much of the known world and hold many nations in terror.

Genghis Khan (c. 1162–1227)

For centuries, the Mongols had lived on the steppes (pronounced "steps") or plains of Central Asia, herding sheep and occasionally raiding other tribes. There was little to distinguish them from any number of other nomads—that is, until the appearance of an extraordinary young chieftain. His name was Temujin (TIM-yuh-jin); but in 1187, a group of clans declared him their "rightful ruler," and it was by this title—

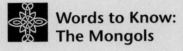
Genghis Khan (JING-us)—that his name would resound through history.

After a series of battles, Genghis united the Mongols for the first time in 1206. Soon after he took power, the government of the Sung Dynasty in China sent an ambassador to him, demanding an oath of loyalty. Genghis's response was to sweep into China in 1211 at the head of his army, which like other Central Asian invaders before them was filled with extraordinary horsemen and skilled archers. They were also quite well organized, being divided into groups of 10,000, called a horde, which were further subdivided all the way down to groups of ten men, the basic unit in the Mongol army.

Despite the fact that the Chinese had long despised the Mongols and other nomadic tribes as "barbarians," a number of Chinese generals and government officials were so impressed by Genghis's power that they changed sides. This gave the Mongols the benefit of Chinese knowledge, not only of warfare and technology, but also of another mystery: reading and writing. By 1215, Genghis had taken the city that is today China's capital, Beijing (bay-ZHEENG); the Mongols named it Khanbalik (kahn-bah-LEEK).

Genghis conquered the Manchus, a people of northeastern China related to the Mongols, and in 1218 a Mongol force launched a war on the Korean Peninsula. Meanwhile their leader moved westward, and between 1219 and 1225 he conquered a Turkic khanate that controlled a huge region in Central Asia. Other Mongol forces moved deep into Russia in 1223, but in 1226 Genghis himself turned back toward China to deal with a rebellious group there. He died on August 18, 1227, having conquered more land than any ruler since Alexander the Great fifteen hundred years before.

Conquests in Eastern Europe (1227–41)

In tribal fashion, Genghis had divided his lands between his three sons, who elected the youngest among them, Ogodai, as their leader. But Ogodai lacked his father's vision, or perhaps his ruthlessness, and though the Mongol realms would grow under his leadership, the driving force was gone.

Poor timing, motivated by concerns over succession, characterized Mongol actions in Eastern Europe. Juchi Khan, the son who had led

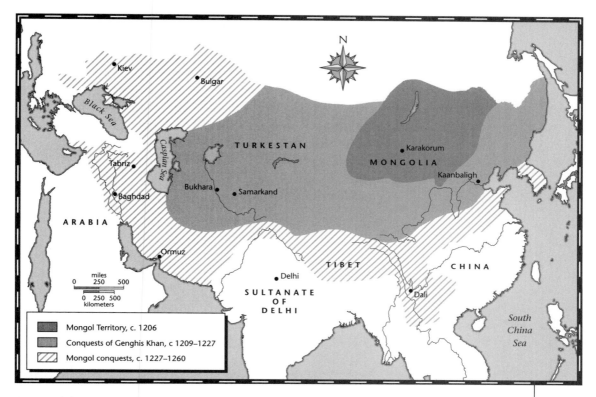

A map of the Mongol Empire before, during, and after the lifetime of Genghis Khan (c. 1162–1227), when the Mongols were unified and ruled a massive empire. *Illustration by XNR Productions. Reproduced by permission of the Gale Group.*

the attack on Russia in 1223, had returned to the homeland following the death of Genghis; but in 1235 Ogodai sent Juchi's son Batu Khan to resume the attack. Batu's army was composed mainly of Tatars (TAT-arz), another nomadic nation of Central Asia, and by 1236 it had entered the heartland of Russia. The army sacked Moscow and Kiev in 1240, and in 1241 devastated Poland and neighboring Silesia (sy-LEE-zhuh). They poured into Hungary, and by July 1241 were prepared to take Vienna. Then suddenly they were gone: Batu had received word that Ogodai was dead, and he has-

tened back to Karakorum (kar-uh-KOHR-um), the Mongol capital, to participate in choosing a successor.

If Batu had kept on going westward, it could have changed the whole course of history, with the Mongols perhaps leaving an imprint on Western Europe as they did on Russia. There the Mongol-Tatar force, which came to be known as the Golden Horde, maintained control for several centuries. Though Mongol rule in Russia was not extraordinarily harsh, and the conquerors interfered little with the affairs of the locals, they did ex-

Genghis Khan was a powerful Mongol ruler who united his people and conquered vast amounts of land. *Reproduced by permission of the Corbis Corporation.*

pect hefty payments of tribute. They also kept Russia isolated from the changes taking place in Europe, and this would have an effect on that land for centuries to come.

A shift to Southwest Asia (1241–60)

The Mongols did not choose the new khan (chieftain), Kuyuk, until 1246, and when they finally renewed their efforts in the west, they shifted their focus from Europe to the Arab lands. This, combined with the fact that Kuyuk had taken an interest in Nestorian Christianity, convinced many Western Europeans that he was doing God's work. (Nestorian Christians believed that Jesus Christ had two separate identities, one human and one divine.) Some even suggested that Kuyuk might be linked with Prester John, a fabled Christian king in the East whose existence had been rumored since the 1100s (see box, "Prester John," chapter 18).

But Kuyuk died in 1248, and it took the Mongols three more years to choose another khan, his cousin Mangu. Mangu sent Hulagu, yet another cousin, into Persia and Mesopotamia (modern-day Iran and Iraq). Hulagu destroyed the Assassins, a terrorist group associated with the Ismaili sect of Islam, in 1256 before sweeping into Baghdad and killing the last Abbasid caliph in 1258. Upon Mangu's death, Hulagu gave himself the title Il-khan, and thenceforth all of southwestern Asia would be a separate khanate under his rule.

The Mongols had already destroyed what was left of the Seljuks in 1243, and when Hulagu invaded Syria, it appeared they were about to destroy the last remaining Muslim power, the Mamluks. This inspired great hope in Western Europe; but in a battle at Goliath Spring in Nazareth on September 3, 1260, it was the Mamluks who defeated the Mongols. Mongol conquests in the west thus came to an end.

The Mongols in battle in Eastern Europe. *Reproduced by permission of Archive Photos, Inc.*

Kublai Khan (1215–1294)

In the years after Genghis's death, four separate khanates emerged. Aside from the Golden Horde in Russia and the realm of the Il-Khan in southwest Asia, the Chagatai (chah-guh-TY) khanate, named after one of Genghis's sons, covered the area that today includes Kazakhstan and other former Soviet republics in Central Asia. To the east, in an area that comprised the Mongolian homeland and the Mongols' most prized possession, China, was the realm of the Great Khan, Genghis's successor and the leader of the Mongols. Since Genghis's death, the Great Khans had been minor figures, but in 1260, leadership fell to the greatest of Genghis's descendants: Mangu's and Hulagu's brother Kublai Khan (KOO-bluh).

Kublai and his brothers conquered southern China, all the way to the borders of Tibet, and in 1264 Kublai established his capital at Khanbalik. By 1279 he controlled all of China, and founded the Yüan (yee-WAHN) Dynasty, the first foreign dynasty to rule that country. Kublai extended Mongol conquests deep into eastern Asia, subduing Korea in the north and Burma in the south, but invasion attempts failed in Japan in 1274 and 1281, and in Java in 1293.

THE EMPEROR KUBLAI,
GRAND KHAN OF THE MONGOLS AND TARTARS:

Commanding in a battle fought
between Pekin & Siberia in which were

Kublai Khan and soldiers traveling on the backs of elephants. Kublai Khan conquered China, and in 1279 founded the first foreign dynasty to rule that country. *Reproduced by permission of the Corbis Corporation.*

He is best remembered for the splendor of his court in Khanbalik, and for his interaction with the great Euro-pean explorer Marco Polo, who lived in China from 1275 to 1292.

Tamerlane and the end of the Mongols (1294–c. 1500)

The Yüan Dynasty lasted until 1368, but none of its later rulers possessed Kublai's strength, and the Chinese eventually overcame them. Yet the Mongols had one last moment of glory under Timur Lenk (tee-MOOR; 1336–1405), or "Timur the Lame," who became known to Europeans as Tamerlane. Though he was not related to Genghis Khan, Tamerlane saw himself as a successor to the great conqueror, and he set out to build an empire of his own.

First he established his capital at Samarkand (sah-mur-KAHND), an ancient city in what is now Uzbekistan, in 1370, and in the years from 1383 to 1385 he conquered Khorasan (kohr-ah-SAHN) on the Iran-Afghanistan border, as well as eastern Persia. Conquests between 1386 and 1394 won him Armenia, Mesopotamia, and Georgia (see box, "Georgia and the Mongols"), and in the process he destroyed the power of the Golden Horde in Russia. In 1398 he sacked the Indian city of Delhi, but by 1401 he was moving westward again, attacking first Damascus and then Baghdad. A year later, he defeated the Turks in a major battle, and captured their sultan, Bajazed, who committed suicide. Soon he was heading east once more, intent on conquering China; but he died on the way.

Tamerlane would be remembered for his cruelty as a conqueror and for his establishment of Samarkand as a great cultural center. His descendant Babur founded the Mogul dynasty in India, and Babur's grandson Akbar would prove to be one of the most enlightened rulers in history.

Such contrasts were typical of the Mongols' history: from Genghis's time onward, they had been feared as bloodthirsty conquerors who cooked their enemies in pots of hot water, yet they were also known as patrons of culture who could be fair rulers. Genghis had declared that all Mongols were equal, and in administering many of their conquered lands, the Mongols had likewise treated subject peoples as equals.

Recognizing their own lack of civilization, the Mongols had adopted the civilizations of the lands they ruled and often the religions as well. Ironically, this fact aided in their downfall: too small in numbers to overwhelm any population for long, the Mongols simply faded into the local landscape, and those who remained in Mongolia went back to the simple herding lifestyle they had practiced before Genghis's time.

For More Information

Books

Dijkstra, Henk, editor. *History of the Ancient and Medieval World*, Volume 11: *Empires of the Ancient World*. New York: Marshall Cavendish, 1996, pp. 1531–42.

 Georgia and the Mongols

Like many other countries that made up the former Soviet Union, Georgia received its independence in the early 1990s; yet it had a history that went back to ancient times. Located in the area called the Caucasus (KAW-kuh-sus), a region between the Black Sea and the Caspian Sea, Georgia's history was long tied with that of the Eastern Roman Empire, and the majority of its people were Orthodox Christians. Nonetheless, Muslims conquered it in the 640s, and ruled through the Bagratid (bahg-RAH-teed) family, a powerful Georgian dynasty. Yet when the Abbasid caliphate began to fade, Bagrat III (978–1014) took the opportunity to unite Georgia for the first time.

In 1122, Bagratid rulers seized the Georgian capital of Tbilisi (tuh-BLEE-see), which the Arabs had held for half a millennium, and Georgian power reached its peak under Queen Tamara (tuh-MAR-uh; ruled 1184–1212). The Mongol invasion in 1220, however, spelled the end of independent Georgia, and the country dissolved into a number of competing states. During the 1300s, Georgian rulers tried to reassert their authority, and in 1327 they drove out the Mongols. Tamerlane's invasion in 1386, however, broke the remaining power of the Georgian monarchs.

Roberts, J. M. *The Illustrated History of the World*, Volume 4: *The Age of Diverging Traditions*. New York: Oxford, 1998, pp. 104–114.

Web Sites

"Genghis Khan: Timeline." *National Geographic*. [Online] Available http://www.nationalgeographic.com/features/97/genghis/timeline/index.html (last accessed July 28, 2000).

The Mongols. [Online] Available http://historymedren.about.com/education/history/historymedren/msubmong.htm (last accessed July 28, 2000).

India

The religions of India are as vital a part of that country's history as Catholicism was in the story of medieval Europe. First among those religions was Hinduism, which grew out of the beliefs brought by Indo-European invaders. Later, India became home to a second great faith, Buddhism, which became the religion of the Mauryan Empire (324–184 B.C.). However, the other great Indian dynasty of ancient times, the Gupta Empire (c. A.D. 320–c. 540), embraced Hinduism. In the Middle Ages, India became the battleground of a third religion as invaders poured in from the Muslim world.

A land of divisions

India is a vast land, with a variety of climatic zones, but its enormous population has long been concentrated in a fertile strip of land created by the Indus River in the west and the Ganges (GAN-geez) in the east. This was the center of both Mauryan and Gupta power, and mountain ranges to the north—the world's highest—had long protected the land. Only once had India been successfully invaded, when the

Words to Know: India

Anarchy: Breakdown of political order.

Caste system: A means of ranking people into very rigid social groups, closely tied to Hindu concepts of reincarnation.

Karma: According to Hinduism and Buddhism, the force generated by a person's actions, which influences the circumstances of their future reincarnation.

Monotheism: Worship of one god.

Polytheism: Worship of many gods.

Refugee: Someone fleeing political violence.

Reincarnation: The idea that people are born on Earth to live and die, again and again.

Indo-Europeans, a group with roots in what is now southern Russia, entered in about 1500 B.C.

The Indo-Europeans had completely transformed Indian society, but no more invaders came for a full two thousand years. Then in about A.D. 500, the Gupta Empire—which had brought about a golden age, a time of advancements in learning seldom equaled in the ancient world—faced another invasion from the north. Their attackers were the same force that had helped bring down the Western Roman Empire: the Huns, or Hunas as they were called in this part of the world.

North and south

Though northern India fell into a state of anarchy after 540, the south remained relatively protected. Geography made the difference: south of the lush Indus-Ganges region was the Thar Desert, and below that the enormous Deccan Plateau, an extremely dry, hot region. Because of these barriers, southern India had developed along different lines than the north.

In their Sanskrit language and their Caucasian features, the people of the north showed that they were descendants of the Indo-Europeans. The people of the south, by contrast, were much darker-skinned, and the dominant language, Tamil (TAH-meel), bore no relation to the languages of Europe or Iran. After about 300, the Pallava (PAH-luh-vuh) dynasty of Hindu kings, who possibly had northern origins, ruled the south.

The Pallavas reached their peak in the two centuries following 550, a period that saw outstanding achievements in art and architecture as well as settlements in the islands off Southeast Asia. During the Pallava high point, central India remained splintered into a number of small states; but order returned to the north, for a time at least, under the rule of the Buddhist king Harsha (ruled 606–47).

Buddhism and Hinduism

Harsha's court was a place of great artistic refinement, and he was himself a poet and playwright. A vivid account of his reign lives in the writ-

A map of the present-day Indian sub-continent, including the nations of India, Pakistan, and Bangladesh. *Illustration by XNR Productions. Reproduced by permission of the Gale Group.*

ings of the Chinese traveler Hsüan-tsang (shooy-AHND ZAHNG; 602–664). Hsüan-tsang had come as a pilgrim to visit the many holy sites associated with the founder of Buddhism, an Indian prince named Siddhartha Gautama (si-DAR-tuh GOW-tuh-muh; c. 563–c. 483 B.C.), whose followers called him the Buddha or "Enlightened One." Yet Buddhism never

A statue of Buddha, or Siddhartha Gautama, the founder of Buddhism. *Reproduced by permission of Archive Photos, Inc.*

gained a lasting hold on the nation of its birth, even though it shared many common roots with Hinduism.

Both religions accepted reincarnation, the idea that human beings are reborn many times as a way of working out their karma, or the results of their actions. To Hindus, this meant that a person would be reincarnated as a member of a higher or lower caste (KAST; social group), depending on their actions in a past life. People of the higher castes enjoyed great wealth and privilege while the bottom rungs of so-

ciety were condemned as "Untouchables." Whereas most modern Americans would consider this situation as unjust, Hindus considered this a completely fair result of karmic forces.

Buddhism, by contrast, offered the possibility that one could escape the endless cycles of reincarnation by achieving enlightenment. This gave it great appeal among the lower castes and with descendants of the land's original inhabitants, many of whom had spread southward into southern India and the island of Ceylon (seh-LAHN; now Sri Lanka) after the Indo-European invasion. Buddhism also rejected the Hindu gods and the rituals associated with them.

Hinduism and Islam

There may have been disagreement over religious issues between adherents of Hinduism and Buddhism, but the two had much in common; it would be hard, however, to imagine two faiths more different than Hinduism and Islam. Hinduism is polytheistic, meaning that it has many gods, with statues of each; Islam, with its prohibition of religious images and its declaration that "there is no god but Allah," is completely iconoclastic and monotheistic. Hinduism places people in castes; Islam treats all Muslim men (if not women) as equals. Hindus believe that people die many times, whereas Muslims believe they die only once.

The two worlds had been in contact since ancient times, with extensive trade links between ports in India and Yemen. In fact, it was this relationship that would bring Indians and Arabs into conflict after a group of Arab sailors were shipwrecked on Ceylon. Some of the sailors died, and the local ruler put their widows and children on a boat along with gifts and letters of goodwill to Hajjaj (hah-ZHAZH; 661–714), ruler over the eastern lands of the Caliphate (the domain ruled by the Muslim leader). However, pirates near the Sind, in what is now Pakistan, attacked the boat, captured the wives and children, and stole the gifts. Hajjaj demanded that the ruler of the Sind help him obtain the release of the prisoners and their possessions, and when the nobleman refused, Hajjaj sent an invading force under his son-in-law Qasim (kah-SEEM).

Qasim gained control over the entire Sind in 712, then conquered the neighboring Punjab (POON-jahb) region in the following year. The Muslims proved themselves able administrators, quickly making peace with local officials, who they placed in administrative positions to help them run the government. With the exception of taxes imposed to pay for their military and government, the Arabs interfered little with local affairs, and as they had done with Christians and Jews in other lands, they allowed the Hindus to continue practicing their religion in a limited form.

Muslim empires and Hindu kingdoms

With the overthrow of the Umayyads (Muslim rulers) in 750 (see

A Hindu statue. In the Middle Ages, India was divided by three major religions: Hinduism, Buddhism, and Islam. *Reproduced by permission of the Corbis Corporation.*

Chapter 6: The Islamic World), the Arabs were unable to retain control over the Sind and Punjab, and during the next 250 years, numerous dynasties competed to control parts of India. In the 800s, a dynasty called the Palas ruled in the east, but in the 900s they were replaced by the Rajputs (RAHZH-pootz). The Rajputs' name means "sons of kings," and they claimed descent from the gods. In fact they apparently descended from the intermarriage of Indians and invaders, particularly Huns and

A Touch of India

The Arab and Muslim worlds would have a great influence on India during the Middle Ages, but the influence went both ways. During the glory days of the Gupta Empire, Indian medicine had been the most advanced in the world, and in the early Middle Ages, numerous doctors from India were invited to work in Baghdad. A number of them served as chief physicians in hospitals, while others translated works of medicine, science, and philosophy from Sanskrit into Arabic.

Indians also shared their advances in the realm of mathematics. One of their greatest achievements was the numeral zero, and this made possible the decimal system and other benefits of the highly practical "base-10" system in use through-

out the world today. Indeed, the numbers 0 through 9 are themselves a gift of Indian mathematicians, who taught their system to the Arabs. Europeans adopted it during the Crusades, replacing the hopelessly cumbersome Roman numeral system, but they incorrectly called the numerals "Arabic"—a name that stuck.

Not all Indian contributions to the Arab world were quite so serious in nature. The game of chess first originated in India, then spread to the Arab world, as did a number of stories that went into the *Thousand and One Nights*. Indian music also influenced its Arabic counterpart. Both use five-note scales: for Westerners accustomed to the eight-note octave scale, this gives Indian and Arabic music an exotic sound.

Scythians (SITH-ee-unz), a group from what is now Ukraine who entered India in about A.D. 100. The local Hindu princes considered them barbarians, but submitted to their leadership in a mysterious "fire ceremony" atop Mount Abu in northwestern India.

In the south, the Cholas (KOH-lahz), a Tamil dynasty, replaced the Pallavas as the dominant power in about 850. They conquered the Deccan Plateau and Ceylon, and engaged in trade with China. In the early 1000s, they would even extend their rule into the Ganges valley, becoming

the first kingdom of southern India to expand so far northward. Though they maintained power until 1279, their impact was limited from the standpoint of world history.

The Ghaznavids and Ghurids

When the next Muslim invasion of India came in 1001, the driving force was Turkish rather than Arab. These were the Ghaznavids (GAHZ-nuh-vidz), displaced by their cousins the Seljuks. Their leader was Mahmud of Ghazni (mah-MOOD; ruled 997–1030), who subdued a large re-

A mazelike assembly of sandstone buildings survive from medieval times in the Indian city Jaisalmer. *Reproduced by permission of the Corbis Corporation.*

gion in what is now Afghanistan, Pakistan, and western India. Strong Hindu resistance, however, prevented him from establishing Muslim rule in most of the Indian regions he conquered.

As the Ghaznavids declined, another dynasty called the Ghurids (GÜR-idz) took their place in the region. The greatest of the Ghurid rulers was Muhammad Ghuri, who destroyed the power of the Rajput kings in 1192 and built an empire based in the cities of Lahore (now in Pakistan) and Delhi (DEL-ee). Though he was assassinated in 1206, he managed to establish Mus-

lim control over much of northern India. Adopting a practice common among the Turks, Muhammad Ghuri made use of slave soldiers, and one of these, Qutb-ud-Din Aybak (küt-büd-DEEN eye-BAHK; ruled 1206–10), became his successor. Aybak was the first independent Muslim ruler of northern India, with no ties to an outside realm, and is thus acknowledged as the founder of the Delhi Sultanate.

The Delhi Sultanate

The Delhi Sultanate marked a high point for Muslim rule in India up to that point, and the Delhi sultans made their capital city a great cultural center. They founded an outstanding library, acknowledged as the greatest establishment of Islamic learning in the East, and Muslim mosques and other buildings—often built from the ruins of Hindu temples—sprouted up throughout their realm. Ironically, the sultanate owed some of its success to the Mongol invasions threatening the Muslim lands to the west, which brought an influx of wealthy and talented refugees.

A number of able rulers followed Aybak, among them his son-in-law Iltutmish (il-TÜT-mush), who consolidated the power of the sultanate and built a number of impressive structures around Delhi. A power struggle followed his death in 1236, and eventually the former slave Balban took control, even though Iltutmish's son actually occupied the throne. Facing a Mongol threat from the west, Balban built up India's military.

Yet another scramble followed Balban's death, with the Khalji (kal-JEE) family assuming control in 1290. The most outstanding figure of this dynasty was the ruthless Ala-ud-din (uh-LAH-ood-deen; ruled 1296–1316), who seized the throne after having his uncle assassinated. He greatly expanded the sultanate's realms, conquering the Deccan and much of southern India, and might have kept going had his advisors not urged him to consolidate his power. Instead he contented himself with the vast wealth he had acquired in his conquests of the south. Like Indian rulers of ancient

times, he built a vast and efficient spy network. Ala-ud-din's conquests in the south became the stuff of legend (see box, "The Face That Launched a Siege"), and indirectly influenced the founding of Vijayanagar (vi-juh-yah-NAH-gar), the most powerful kingdom in southern India. Founded in 1336 by Hindus who had become united by their opposition to Ala-ud-din, Vijayanagar would withstand Muslim onslaughts for some two centuries.

In 1320, four years after the death of Ala-ud-din, the Tughluq (tug-LUK) family assumed the throne. Muhammad ibn Tughluq (ruled 1325–51) made Ala-ud-din seem mild by comparison. It was said, for instance, that he punished a rebellious noble by having the man skinned alive and cooked with rice, and then he sent the remains to the wife and children— and the noble happened to be his cousin. His successor, Firuz (fee-ROOZ; ruled 1351–88), was much more evenhanded and became noted for his many building projects. After his death, however, the sultanate dissolved into civil war, which left it ripe for attack by Mongol leader Tamerlane in 1398.

Later invaders

Tamerlane sacked Delhi, but as was his practice, he did not stay long. The Tughluqs managed to hold on for another fifteen years until 1413; then other powers rushed into the vacuum. Afghanistan emerged for the first time as an independent nation in 1451, and Vijayanagar gained strength in the south while smaller Muslim king-

The Face That Launched a Siege

In 1303, the Muslim conqueror Ala-ud-din took the city of Chitor (chi-TOOR) in southeastern India, one of many conquests during his southern campaign. He besieged the city for the usual reason conquerors do such things: as a military, political, or even economic objective. However, a fanciful book called the *Annals of Rajasthan* (RAH-jus-tahn) put a much more romantic spin on it. According to this work of "history," it was because he wanted the lovely princess Pudmini (POOD-mi-nee).

The name Pudmini, readers of the *Annals* were assured, is "a title bestowed only on the superlatively [exceptionally] fair." According to this legend, Ala-ud-din promised to spare the city if they would give him the princess; but when that offer was refused, he said he would call off the attack if they only let him see her. This, too, seemed too great a request for those who knew of Pudmini's beauty, so Ala-ud-din—according to the legend—asked merely to look at her reflection in a mirror. The people of the city again denied his request, and instead its women fought alongside the men to defend the Hindu stronghold. In the end, it was said, all the men died in battle, and the women who were not killed committed suicide rather than surrender.

doms divided northern and central India. By the end of the 1400s, Muslim life in India had shifted to the city of Agra, and away from Delhi.

It was in Agra that Babur (BAH-boor, "Lion"; 1483–1530) established his capital when he invaded India in 1526. His bloodline included Turkish and Persian strains, but as a descendant of Tamerlane, he was technically a Mongol. Hence the name for his dynasty was the Persian word for Mongol: Mogul (MOH-gul). The Moguls were Muslims, but Babur's grandson Akbar (ruled 1556–1605) would be noted for his open-mindedness regarding religion. For the half-century of Akbar's reign, at least, India's competing faiths were in harmony with one another.

For More Information

Books

Dijkstra, Henk, editor. *History of the Ancient and Medieval World,* Volume 11: *Empires of the Ancient World.* New York: Marshall Cavendish, 1996, pp. 1489–1500.

Kalman, Bobbie. *India: The Culture.* New York: Crabtree Publishing Company, 1990.

Kalman, Bobbie. *India: The Land.* New York: Crabtree Publishing Company, 1990.

Kalman, Bobbie. *India: The People.* New York: Crabtree Publishing Company, 1990.

Schulberg, Lucille. *Historic India.* New York: Time-Life Books, 1968.

Web Sites

Discover India. [Online] Available http://www. meadev.gov.in (last accessed July 28, 2000).

Southeast Asia | 14

The mainland of Southeast Asia is tucked between India in the west and China to the north; hence the name "Indochina," applied to much of the region. India and China were also Southeast Asia's primary cultural influences. But with the spread of Islam to the region during the Middle Ages, a third influence made itself known, primarily in the adjoining Malay Archipelago.

Indochina

China's first imperial dynasty in the 200s B.C. claimed three loosely defined provinces along the South China Sea coast in what is now Vietnam. As powerful as the Chinese emperor was, however, he could hardly control such distant lands. Thus it was easy enough for one of his generals to break away and establish his own kingdom, which came to be known as Van Lang (VAHN LAHNG), an early version of Vietnam.

China later reclaimed the province, then lost it again until finally another powerful Chinese general subdued the

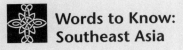

Words to Know: Southeast Asia

Archipelago: A string of islands.

Indigenous: Local; not from outside.

Pagoda: A type of tower monument in the Far East.

Province: A political unit, like a state, that is part of a larger country.

Relief sculpture: A carved picture, distinguished from regular sculpture because it is primarily two-dimensional but textured.

area in about A.D. 40. To the south of the conquered lands he set up two bronze pillars, marking the edge of the civilized world: below that line, he declared, lived ghosts and demons.

Funan and Champa

In fact there were two kingdoms to the south: Funan, which straddled an area that is now part of both Vietnam and Cambodia; and Champa along the coast. Funan controlled a lesser state called Chenla, yet by the 500s, Chenla had become strong enough to absorb Funan.

A century later a new nation emerged in the region to the west and north of Funan and Champa. These were the Khmers (k'MEERZ) of Cambodia, soon to develop one of the most powerful empires in the region.

Meanwhile the people of northern Vietnam became culturally and politically tied with China, while southern Vietnam continued an independent existence as Champa.

The Khmer Empire

The Khmers had a close trading relationship with India, and this led to the adoption of Hinduism by their first powerful king, Jayavarman II (jah-yah-VAR-mun; ruled c. 790–850). Jayavarman founded the Khmer Empire, which also became known as the Angkor Empire after two extraordinary creations.

The first of these was Angkor Thom (TOHM), which began to emerge as a city after 900. Angkor Thom covered some five square miles, quite impressive for any medieval city—but particularly one carved out of a jungle. With its moat and walls, its temples, palaces, and tower—all carved in detail with images of Hindu gods—Angkor Thom would have put contemporary London or even Paris to shame. Then there was Angkor Wat (see box), a temple almost big enough to be considered a city in its own right.

The builder of Angkor Wat was Suryavarman II (soor-yah-VAR-mun; ruled 1113–50), who went on to expand his empire into what is now Thailand, Burma, Vietnam, and Malaysia. He also established formal diplomatic relations with China in 1119. A war with the Vietnamese, however, did not prove so successful.

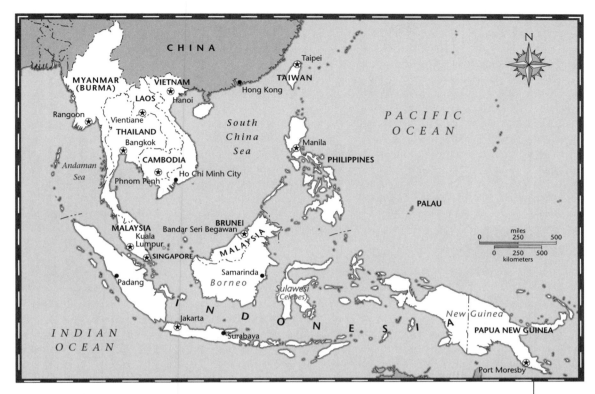

A map of Southeast Asia in the twenty-first century. *Illustration by XNR Productions. Reproduced by permission of the Gale Group.*

The northern Vietnamese had revolted against Chinese rule in 939 and established an empire of their own. Burma, too, had established its independence under Anawrahta (ahn-ow-RAHT-uh; ruled 1044–77). A Buddhist, Anawrahta built many pagodas (puh-GOH-duhz), or tall shrines, in his capital of Pagan (puh-GAHN).

The Khmer Empire remained the dominant power in the region, but in 1176 Champa invaded. Its forces even occupied Angkor Wat until Jayavarman VII (ruled 1181–c. 1215), the Khmer's greatest ruler, drove them

out in 1181. He conquered the Champa kingdoms and other neighboring territories and set about rebuilding and improving Angkor Wat.

Competing powers

After Jayavarman, the Khmer Empire declined quickly. Indeed, in the densely packed lands of Indochina, it was always difficult for one kingdom to hold power for very long, and at the first sign of weakness others were more than willing to step in. Under the Tran dynasty (1225–1400), northern Vietnam annexed the Cham-

Workers in the rice fields of present-day Vietnam. *Photograph by Cory Langley. Reproduced by permission of Cory Langley.*

pa lands as Khmer influence faded. But an even greater force was pushing in from the north: the Mongol Yüan dynasty of China.

The Mongols forced a group called the Nan-chao (nahn-ZHOW), ancestors of the Thais, into the region in 1253. The Nan-chao swept into the power vacuum created by the decline of the Khmer, and conquered the Angkor Empire in 1431. Thereafter the Nan-chao and the Vietnamese alternately controlled Khmer lands. Vietnam itself came under Chinese rule in the early 1400s, but reemerged more powerful

than ever under the Le dynasty (1428–1788), which fully conquered the southern part of the land.

Farther west, the Mongols brought an end to the Burmese kingdom in 1287, and for the next five centuries anarchy reigned in that country. Between Burma, Thailand, Vietnam, and Cambodia, the tiny, landlocked kingdom of Laos unified under the Buddhist monarch Fa Ngum (fahng-OOM; 1316–73). Educated at Angkor, Fa Ngum returned to his homeland with a Khmer army in 1353, and brought Laotian power to the greatest extent it would ever reach. Within a few years, however, the Thais had absorbed much of Laos.

The Malay Peninsula and Archipelago

Technically the Malay Peninsula is part of Indochina, but its history was much more closely linked with that of the Malay Archipelago (ar-ki-PEL-uh-goh). An archipelago is a group of islands, and the Malay complex is the world's largest. It forms a huge triangle, with the northern Philippines at the "top"; the Indonesian island of Sumatra (soo-MAH-truh) at the southwest corner, where the Indian Ocean joins the Pacific; and New Guinea on the far southeastern corner. In addition to their shared geography, the people of these islands (and of the Malay Peninsula) speak languages from the same family, Malay.

During the Middle Ages, this region would undergo an experience similar to that of India, where Hindu, Buddhist, and Muslim states vied for control. Buddhism and Hinduism came first, and each established strongholds in parts of what is now Indonesia. The Hindu Pallavas of southeastern India had colonized the area from an early time, but by the 600s the dominant faith had become Buddhism.

Buddhism was the religion of the Srivijaya (shree-vi-JY-yuh) Empire, based in Sumatra, which ruled parts of the region from the 600s onward. At its peak in the 1100s, it controlled much of the Philippines, Borneo, western Java, and even the Moluccas

An entrance to the temple of Angkor Thom, a medieval city carved out of the jungle during the Khmer Empire in what is now Cambodia. *Reproduced by permission of the Corbis Corporation.*

(muh-LUK-uz), an island group far to the east. Another Buddhist dynasty, the Sailendras, controlled eastern Java during the 700s and 800s. There they built a great temple complex at Borobudur (boh-roh-bü-DOOR), Asia's largest Buddhist monument, with hundreds of relief sculptures depicting scenes from the life of the Buddha.

Hindus dominated the island of Bali (BAH-lee), and Hinduism spread into eastern Java after the Sailendras lost power in 856. There

Angkor Wat

Of all the monuments built during the Middle Ages, few can equal the great Khmer temple complex of Angkor Wat for sheer scope, mysterious beauty, and eery charm. The surrounding moat alone was a vast engineering feat, 600 feet wide and 2.5 miles long. Inside its walls was an enormous temple complex of towers guarding a central enclosure, an architectural symbol of Hindu beliefs concerning the outer and inner worlds.

Like the Gothic cathedrals in France around the same time, Angkor Wat was a gigantic "sermon in stone," with carvings on virtually every surface showing Hindu gods and other aspects of the Khmer culture and religion. But this was a world utterly foreign to the European mind. For one thing, Angkor Wat was not a place where the common people were invited to enter and worship, as they were at Notre Dame or Chartres; it was set aside purely for the royal house. Furthermore, one can only imagine what a European priest would have made of the many sculptures showing bare-chested beauties. Yet this was an everyday sight in the humid jungles of Southeast Asia, where Khmer women wore wraparound skirts with nothing covering their breasts.

Despite these and other scenes depicting ordinary life—planting and harvesting rice, trading goods such as spices and rhinoceros horns with Chinese merchants—Angkor Wat can justly be described as a spooky place. Its abandonment after the Thai conquest in the mid-1400s added greatly to this quality: in the centuries that followed, this gargantuan temple city was forgotten, its towers choked by vines while its inner courts became home to snakes and other creatures of the jungle. It was only rediscovered in the 1860s—by the French, who then controlled Indochina.

the powerful Hindu kingdom of Majapahit (mah-jah-PAH-hit), founded in about 1263, began to extend its influence, taking control of Sumatra as the Srivijayas declined. In 1292, Marco Polo visited the Majapahit kingdom and also noted the existence of a Muslim community on Sumatra.

This was the first proof by an outside observer of the Muslim presence in the region, though in fact Islam had probably arrived two or three centuries earlier. In the two centuries following Marco Polo's visit, Islamic forces would bring down the Majapahits and convert many peoples on neighboring islands. The Balinese, however, remained predominantly Hindu.

Muslim sultanates

The most significant area of Muslim influence was in Melaka, or

Angkor Wat is a massive Hindu temple complex built by the Khmer Empire in the Middle Ages.
Reproduced by permission of the Corbis Corporation.

what is now Malaysia. That area became so heavily Muslim during the 1400s that people used the expression "to become a Malay" to mean converting to Islam. Melaka had been under the control of the Srivijaya through the 1300s, when a king from Singapore, a tiny city-state at the tip of the Malay Peninsula, founded the independent state of Melaka.

The origins of Singapore itself are less clear, though it appears to have been a thriving trade center in the 1200s. It was destroyed by an attack from Java in 1377, and it would not rise to its former prosperity and stability for nearly five hundred years. Melaka meanwhile adopted Islam, probably in about 1400, and its rulers adapted many trappings of Islamic culture, including titles such as shah and sultan.

Trade fueled the spread of Islam: because the Muslims were successful merchants, many local businessmen considered it prudent to accept the new faith. Even the Turks established their influence in the region, and there are reports of gifts such as banners and cannons sent by the Ottoman sultan to Melaka and other far-off lands.

Australia and the Pacific

Australia, New Zealand, and the Pacific islands beyond them did not possess true civilizations during the Middle Ages—that is, their people did not build cities or possess a written language—and therefore information about these regions is scarce. Nonetheless, it is clear that life there was far from uneventful.

The native peoples of Australia, called Aborigines (ab-uh-RIJ-uh-neez), first migrated to that continent about 50,000 years ago, but the many islands of Polynesia were inhabited much later. For many centuries, shipbuilders from Indonesia had been constructing canoes big enough to cross wide stretches of ocean, so that by about 650, all Polynesian lands except New Zealand had been settled. A century later, people finally began arriving on New Zealand's North Island.

In about 1000, the inhabitants of Easter Island, a lonely spot several thousand miles off the west coast of South America, began carving the large, mysterious heads for which that place—so named because it was first discovered by Europeans on Easter Sunday 1722—is most famous.

Another "mystery" of the South Seas, however, would not remain a mystery. While visiting the East Indies (modern Indonesia) in the 1290s, Marco Polo heard about a faraway southern continent, which he assumed to be mythical like Atlantis. By the 1400s, however, Indonesian merchants began regularly traveling to this all-too-real place, but it would be another two centuries before Spanish voyagers "discovered" Australia.

Then in 1511 Portugal, by then the leading power of the high seas along with Spain, conquered Melaka and closed it off to trade with the Muslim world. Nonetheless, the spread of Islam continued, reaching Brunei (BROO-ny) on the northern coast of Borneo, as well as the southern Philippines.

For More Information

Books

Brittan, Dolly. *The People of Cambodia*. New York: PowerKids Press, 1997.

Brittan, Dolly. *The People of Thailand*. New York: PowerKids Press, 1997.

Brittan, Dolly. *The People of Vietnam*. New York: PowerKids Press, 1997.

Evans, Charlotte, consulting editor. *The Kingfisher Illustrated History of the World: 40,000 B.C. to Present Day*. New York: Kingfisher Books, 1993.

Schafer, Edward H. *Ancient China*. New York: Time-Life Books, 1967.

Web Sites

"Buddhist Empires." [Online] Available http://www.geocities.com/Tokyo/Flats/

3795/hindu.htm (last accessed July 28, 2000).

Mulaqah. [Online] Available http://www. mulaqah.com (last accessed July 28, 2000).

China

China has had an organized political system since the founding of the Shang dynasty in 1766 B.C. The nation was first unified, and the empire established, under the Ch'in dynasty in 221 B.C. Over the course of the centuries, China developed one of the world's most brilliant civilizations, even as nomadic peoples—ancestors of the Huns, Turks, and Mongols—threatened its borders. Not surprisingly, the Chinese came to think of themselves as the only civilized people in a world of barbarians. They also viewed history as a series of three- or four-century cycles marked by upheaval, renewal, and eventual decline. Medieval dynasties such as the T'ang (618–907) and Sung (960–1279) would bear out this expectation with eery precision.

New religions, new ideas

In A.D. 220, around the time the Western Roman Empire first began declining, China entered a three-century period of turmoil. This happened largely because the country lacked a strong government, but as time went on, many be-

Words to Know: China

Abacus: The earliest form of calculator, which used movable beads strung along parallel wires within a frame.

Block printing: An early printing process in which a negative, or reverse, image was carved out of wood.

Bureaucracy: A network of officials who run a government.

Calligraphy: The art of lettering, or in China, the art of writing Chinese characters.

Concubine: A woman whose role toward her husband is like that of a wife, but without the social and legal status of a wife.

Famine: A food shortage caused by crop failures.

Grid: A network of evenly spaced lines that intersect one another at right angles.

Mandate: Authority or permission.

Movable-type printing: An advanced printing process using pre-cast pieces of metal type.

Novel: An extended, usually book-length, work of fiction.

Prose: Written narrative, as opposed to poetry.

Sect: A small group within a larger religion.

Shaman: A holy man who enters a state of trance in which (in the view of believers) he contacts the supernatural world.

came concerned about the destructive effect a new religion was having. Just as Romans feared Christianity's challenge to their ancient religion, the Chinese believed that Buddhism was undermining the old-fashioned Confucian belief system.

Based on the teachings of the philosopher Confucius (551–479 B.C.), perhaps the most important figure in all of Chinese history, Confucianism emphasized basic virtues such as loyalty to family, respect for elders, hard work and study, and obedience to rulers. By contrast, Buddhism, which began to take hold in the 300s, urged

followers to concentrate on inner peace and enlightenment rather than social concerns. In fact Buddhism was no more nontraditional than Taoism (DOW-izm), a mystical Chinese belief system founded on the ideas of Lao-tzu (low-DZÜ; c. 500s B.C.). Though Taoism emerged from within China rather than outside, it too had once been perceived as a threat by Confucianists.

Taoism had gained acceptance in the mid-second century, and now gradually the Chinese began to accept Buddhism—particularly a variety called Mahayana (mah-huh-YAH-nuh) or "Great Vehicle." Mahayana held

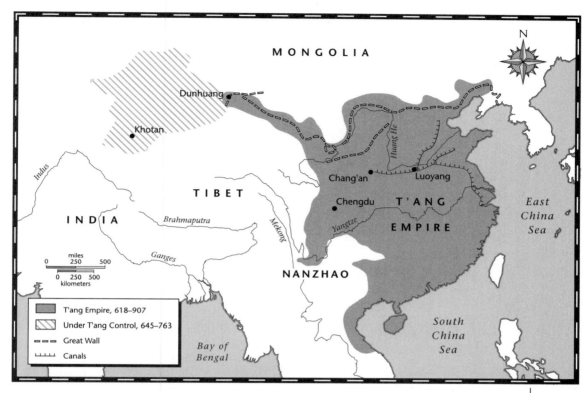

A map of China showing areas controlled by the T'ang dynasty, which ruled from 618 to 907.
Illustration by XNR Productions. Reproduced by permission of the Gale Group.

that by achieving enlightenment, a person could become a Buddha, meaning that there was not just one Buddha but many. Meanwhile, another sect, Chan—better known by its Japanese name, Zen—merged Buddhism with a Taoist-like mysticism.

As it turned out, this period between dynasties was a time of great intellectual as well as spiritual development in China. The era saw progress in the study of medicine, the first use of coal for heat, the first appearance of kites, and the writing of the first encyclopedias. No wonder writers of the later T'ang dynasty would look back with longing to this period, which they immortalized in a novel called *The Romance of the Three Kingdoms*.

The Sui dynasty (589–618)

The Sui dynasty (SWEE) would in many ways resemble the Ch'in, which first unified China and built its Great Wall. Both were shortlived, but extremely important; both saw great public works projects; and both were ruled by fierce tyrants. The Sui founder was Wen Ti (DEE; also known by his

The teachings of the philosopher Confucius formed the basis of Confucianism, which valued such principles as loyalty, respect, hard work, and obedience to authority figures.
Reproduced by permission of Archive Photos, Inc.

based on Confucian principles, which would remain in use up to the twentieth century. Furthermore, he introduced a new law code and moved aggressively against Mongol and Turkic nomads in northern China.

Remembered as one of China's greatest rulers, Wen Ti may have been assassinated by his son, Yang Ti (ruled 604–618). Yang Ti built a huge network of canals, most notably the Grand Canal, a thousand-mile waterway that connected the Yangtze (YAHNG-zay) River with the Yellow River to the north. But Yang Ti was ruthless, and his military campaigns proved costly. Though he enjoyed a measure of success in Vietnam and Central Asia, an expedition into Korea (612–14) failed. Yang Ti was assassinated, and thus the Sui dynasty ended, like the Ch'in, after the reign of just two emperors.

The T'ang dynasty (618–907)

The founders of the T'ang dynasty (TAHNG) were a father-son team, Li Yüan (ruled 618–26) and Li Shih-min (ZHUR-min; ruled 626–49). The son instigated a revolt and placed his father on the throne. Chinese emperors usually became known by a "reign title," assigned at the time of their death: thus these two became Kao Tsu (gow-DZÜ) and T'ai Tsung (dy-DZAWNG) respectively. Father and son allied China with a Turkic people called the Uighurs (WEE-gurz) against other Turks, extending T'ang

birth name, Yang Chien; ruled 589–604), who seized the throne in one of the many small states that controlled China during the period of upheaval. After eight years spent consolidating his power, he took the imperial throne.

It was Wen Ti's aim to build a strong central government, so he abolished inheritance of office, a corrupt practice that had spread among civil servants. To make sure government workers were qualified, he instituted a civil-service examination system,

The ideas of Lao-Tzu, who lived around the 500s B.C., led to the development of Taoism, a mystical Chinese belief system. *Reproduced by permission of the Granger Collection Ltd.*

rule deep into Central Asia and even Tibet, one of the world's most isolated lands (see box, "Tibet").

Both rulers issued a series of reforms, and in particular those of T'ai Tsung—considered by many historians the greatest of China's imperial rulers—were particularly sweeping. He put into place a complex but efficient bureaucracy (byoo-RAHK-ruh-see) divided into three branches for making,

Tibet

Situated atop a vast plateau in the Himalayas (him-ah-LAY-uz), the world's tallest mountain range, Tibet is one of the most isolated lands on Earth. Even the name of Tibet's first known king, Srong-brt-san-sgam-po (srawng-burt-SAHNG-SKAHM-poh; ruled 629–50), illustrates how unfamiliar its language and culture are to Westerners. Srong (to simplify his name) ordered the creation of a Tibetan written language and extended his rule into neighboring Nepal (neh-PAHL), as well as parts of India and China.

But the Tibetans would turn out to be a nation of priests, not warriors: Srong also introduced Buddhism and built huge temples and monasteries in and around his capital at Lhasa (LAHS-uh). Though influenced by the Mahayana school, Tibetan Buddhism incorporated elements of a much older native belief system, a religion of gods and demons that included elements of spirit worship and shamanism (SHAH-mun-izm). The religion spread to neighboring mountain lands, reaching as far away as Siberia.

Other distant converts included the Mongols, who in the 1200s succeeded where the Chinese had often failed, bringing Tibet under their political influence. The Tibetans remained linked with the

The Dalai Lama, political leader of Tibet.
Reproduced by permission of the Corbis Corporation.

Mongols long after the decline of Mongol power, and only in the 1700s did China succeed in taking at least a measure of control over the area.

In the mid-twentieth century, China's Communist government annexed the country following a brutal campaign against the peaceful Buddhist monks of Tibet. During the 1990s, the Dalai Lama (DAHL-ee LAH-muh), political leader of Tibet, emerged as a celebrity in the West, where Tibetan political freedom became a popular cause.

reviewing, and implementing policy. The review board was allowed to criticize the emperor's decisions, and the policy-making branch exercised fur-

ther checks on imperial authority by making suggestions as well. In a land where strong emperors enjoyed near-absolute power, it was highly unusual to see a regime exercise such a great degree of openness.

In the area of policy implementation, or carrying out the work of the government, the T'ang system had few rivals. Along the highways and waterways of the empire, the government placed monitoring stations to oversee taxation, review local grievances, police commercial activities, and even provide accommodations for travelers. Overseeing this smooth-running machine was one of the most talented and highly trained groups of civil servants China had ever seen. Even after T'ang power receded, its administrative system would prevail for several centuries.

A thriving economy

T'ai Tsung also instituted badly needed land reforms, redistributing property to reflect changes in the size of peasant families. Though taxes on farmers were high, peasants now felt a sense of ownership over their lands, which could no longer be snapped up by feudal lords. The T'ang government also greatly extended the canal network put in place by the Sui, thus aiding the transport of goods from north to south in a land where most major rivers flowed eastward.

As the economy of T'ang China thrived, new goods such as tea from Southeast Asia made their appearance. China in turn exported a variety of items, including silk and printed materials. The latter was an outgrowth of two outstanding Chinese innovations: paper, first developed around A.D. 100, and block printing, a process whereby a printer would carve out a piece of wood and, using ink, press the block onto paper, leaving behind an image of the carving. Ink came from the black substance secreted by burning wood and oil in lamps. Later, when this innovation passed to the West, it would be incorrectly called "India ink."

A vibrant cultural life

The T'ang capital was Ch'ang-an, today known as Xian (shee-AHN). Located deep in the heart of China, it would serve as capital for a total of eleven dynasties, but under T'ang rule it reached the peak of its splendor. Laid out on a grid, it covered some thirty square miles. With its two million residents, it may well have been the largest city of its time.

The golden age of the T'ang, which lasted until 751, saw great advancements in the arts and sciences. Aside from block printing, which increased the spread of new ideas, two other notable Chinese inventions, fireworks and the abacus (AB-uh-kus), made their appearance during this era. An early form of calculator, the abacus had existed in one form or another since ancient times and was known to the Romans; but the Chinese abacus, still used in parts of the Far East today, became the most well known version.

The T'ang Chinese were eager to import knowledge of astronomy and mathematics from India, and their own cultural advances spread to Korea and Japan, which modeled their leading cities on the plan of Ch'ang-an. An openness to non-Chinese ways of life characterized the T'ang and distinguished them from most dynasties of the past. Not only did they allow Buddhism to spread, the T'ang emperors tolerated faiths of even more distant origin: Islam, Zoroastrianism, Manichaeism, Nestorian Christianity, and even Judaism.

In such an environment, it is not surprising that the arts flourished. T'ang sculpture became widely noted for its beauty, and the expansion into Central Asia added new musical styles and dances. The era also produced some of China's greatest writers, including the poets Li Po (lee-BOH; 701–762) and Tu Fu (doo-FOO; 712–770). Even after T'ang China had passed its prime, an outstanding intellectual figure made his appearance: the writer and philosopher Han Yü (hahn-YOOEE; 768–824). Han Yü helped revive Confucianism as a living system of thought and established a new, naturalistic, and free-spirited prose style.

An imperial soap opera

T'ai Tsung's son Kao Tsung (gow-DZÜNG; ruled 649–83) found himself almost constantly at war, particularly against the Turks and Tibetans. In 668 he subdued the Koreans, but he did not prove as forceful a ruler as his father. During his later years, the empire was dominated by his concubine, Wu Ze-tian (zeh-CHEE-en; 625–705). By skillful manipulation and a ruthless approach to those who stood in her way, she made herself Kao Tsung's empress in 655, and after his death in 683 became the only female ruler in all of Chinese history. An able administrator and military leader, she proved herself the equal of any male sovereign.

Her grandson Hsüan Tsung (shwee-AHND-zoong; ruled 712–56), who ruled the T'ang dynasty at the height of its power, was also dominated by his concubine, Yang Kuei-fei (gway-FAY). A fascinating character, Yang was one of the only obese women in Chinese history also considered a great beauty. She started out as concubine of Hsüan Tsung's son before the emperor decided he wanted her for himself—along with her two sisters. The soap opera did not end there: later she took the general An Lu-shan (703–757) under her wing as her student, adopted son, and (according to palace rumors) lover.

Decline of the T'ang

Of Iranian descent, An Lu-shan rose rapidly at court and became a favorite of Hsüan Tsung. After Arab forces defeated Chinese troops at Talas in Central Asia (751), however, it became clear that the T'ang had reached the limits of their power. In 755 An launched a rebellion against the emperor. Soon afterward, palace guards killed Yang for her part in the rebellion, and in 757 An was murdered on the orders of his own son. The revolt continued until 763, however, further weakening T'ang power.

The dynasty would maintain control for another almost 150 years, but its glory days were over, and the spirit of tolerance that had marked T'ang rule soon faded as emperors persecuted Buddhists and other adherents of "foreign" religions. Famine ravaged northern China, and in 881 the rebel leader Huang Ch'ao (hwahng CHOW) sacked Ch'ang-an, forcing the government to Luoyang (lwoh-YAHNG), an ancient capital. In its last three decades, competing forces at court further sapped the dynasty's strength.

The Sung dynasty (960–1279)

After the fall of the T'ang, China entered a period of anarchy known to historians as "Five Dynasties and Ten Kingdoms." Then in 960, troops loyal to Chao K'uang-yin (ZHOW gwahng-YIN; ruled 960–76) declared him emperor, thus establishing the Sung (SOONG) dynasty.

Like the T'ang before them, the Sung reformed the government to create a stronger, more efficient bureaucracy, but they were not expansionists. Instead, the first two Sung emperors consolidated the empire's holdings, allowing Tibet, Mongolia, Vietnam, and other areas to break away. They tried to defeat the only remaining dynasty from the "Five Dynasties" period, the Liao (LYOW) of Mongolia, but in 1005 gave up and agreed to pay them tribute.

The cost of this tribute, along with other problems, affected the economy, so the powerful minister Wang An-shih (1021–1086) put in place economic reforms. These freed the peasantry from many burdens, but also gave the government huge power over the economy. The Sung system, an elaborate Confucian bureaucracy in which advancement was based on merit rather than social standing, proved to be one of the most efficient governments the world has ever known.

Northern and Southern Sung

Sung diplomats formed an alliance with the Juchen (zhur-SHIN), a dynasty of nomadic tribesmen in Manchuria to the northeast, against the Liao. The Juchen eliminated the Liao threat, but then turned against the Sung. Sweeping southward, in 1127 they destroyed the capital at Kaifeng (gy-FUNG) in central China, forcing the Sung to move south.

Often dynasties of the past had withstood invasion by moving their capitals; thus historians would refer to the Western and Eastern periods of a dynasty, or in the case of the Sung, the Northern and Southern. For the Sung, however, the latter phase was not a time of weakness: instead, they became stronger and more wealthy than before.

During the Southern Sung era, the population of lands under Chinese control reached 100 million, and their new capital at Hangchow (hahng-SHOH) became a mighty city of 1.5 million. Cities spread throughout Sung China, and Chinese culture flourished.

Artistic and technological advances

It was a time of great painters, noted for subtle landscapes influenced by Zen Buddhism. Among these was the emperor Hui Tsung (hwee-DZÜNG; ruled 1100–25), who formed the alliance with the Juchen; certainly he was a better artist than an administrator. This era also witnessed advances in distinctively Chinese arts such as porcelain-making and calligraphy (kuh-LIG-ruh-fee), the art of lettering.

Sung China produced several notable writers as well, among them the philosopher Chu Hsi (jü-SHEE; 1130–1200), who like Han Yü helped to reinvigorate Confucian teachings. He became a leader in the movement called Neo-Confucianism (*neo* means "new"), and Chu Hsi's philosophical writings became required reading for generations of civil service applicants.

Also during the Sung era, the historian Ssu-ma Kuang (sü-mah-GWAHNG, 1019–1086) wrote the *Comprehensive Mirror for Aid in Chinese Government,* which is one of the most important works of Chinese historical scholarship. Writers of the Sung dynasty also included a woman, the poetess Li Ch'ing-chao (1081–c. 1141). Thus the Sung era produced one of premodern China's few notable women other than imperial wives and concubines; but the Sung also introduced a practice that became a symbol of male domination (see box, "Women and Foot-Binding").

An explosion in scientific knowledge accompanied an economic boom. On the high seas, the development of the magnetic compass made navigation at sea much easier, and along with improvements in shipbuilding, enabled the Sung to send ships called junks on merchant voyages. The larger Sung junks could hold up to six hundred sailors, along with cargo.

Tea and cotton emerged as major exports, and a newly developed rice strain, along with advanced agricultural techniques, enhanced the yield from China's farming lands. China also sold a variety of manufactured goods, including books and porcelain, while steel production and mining grew dramatically.

In this vibrant economy, banks and paper money—one of Sung China's most notable contributions—made their appearance, and the development of movable-type printing aided the spread of information. Instead of carving out a whole block of wood, a printer assembled pre-cast pieces of clay type (later they used wood), each of which stood for a character in the Chinese language. Ultimately, however, the peculiarities of Chinese would encourage the use of block printing over movable type. It is easy enough to store and use pieces of type when a language has a twenty-six-letter alphabet, as English does; but Chinese has some 30,000 characters or symbols, meaning that printing by movable type was extremely slow.

End of the Sung

Great strides in science and technology continued right up to the end of the Sung dynasty, making its destruction all the more tragic. The Sung created pumps for lifting water, and experimented with water power as a means of operating silk looms and cotton mills. A scientist in 919, between the T'ang and Sung eras, had developed one of history's most significant inventions: gunpowder. The Sung expanded on this knowledge, and even experimented with rocketry.

Rockets made their first appearance in about 1240, in a war against the Mongols, who had been on the move against China since Genghis Khan first attacked in 1211. Yet the Chinese were thrilled when, in 1234, the Mongols defeated the Juchen and took northern China. The Sung probably thought they would let the barbarians destroy each other, then reoccupy their country; but instead the Mongols kept going southward, and by 1279 Kublai Khan's armies had overthrown the Sung.

Yüan dynasty (1279–1368)

When he established his capital at Khanbalik, Kublai Khan named his imperial house Yüan, meaning "beginning." Under the forceful Kublai, lands from Korea to Central Asia to Vietnam bowed to the military power of the Yüan. Kublai did not annex all these countries, but made many of them vassals, regions that relied on Kublai for military protection. The unity of the Mongol realm facilitated travel through areas formerly

Women and Foot-Binding

Men in premodern China believed that small feet on a woman were beautiful, and during the Sung dynasty years they developed a means to ensure that women's feet would remain small. In childhood, a Chinese girl would have her feet bound with strips of cloth, which constricted their growth. By the time she became a woman, she would have abnormally small feet, so much so that walking became difficult.

Of course foot-binding only applied to women of the upper classes; peasant girls had to work in the fields, and tiny feet would only slow them down. Nor did the practice attract many admirers outside of China: though Chinese men swooned at the sight of tiny feet, Westerners thought them grotesque. In the modern era, foot-binding became a symbol of the hard-line conservatism that prevailed during imperial times, and the end of the monarchy in 1912 also saw the end of foot-binding.

dominated by bandits and competing warlords. Thus Marco Polo was able to make his celebrated journey to Kublai's court, from which he would bring back to Europe all sorts of innovations: gunpowder, paper money, the compass, kites, even playing cards.

The Yüan were the first foreign ruling house in China's three-thousand-year history, and the Chinese resented them deeply. This had an unintended result. Rather than serve the "barbarians," many talented Chinese opted to become artists and educators rather than civil servants, and this led to a flowering in the arts.

Yet the Yüan depended on the Chinese to run the country for them and did not return their neighbors' contempt toward them. Whereas the Chinese were accustomed to looking down on outsiders, the Mongols were some of the most open-minded people of the Middle Ages. Precisely because they lacked a sophisticated culture, they admired those of the peoples they ruled, and they admired no culture as much as that of China. Thus they were eager to absorb the refined ways of the Chinese, and this produced yet another unintended effect: in becoming more sophisticated, the Mongols lost the brutal toughness that had aided them in their conquests and so become vulnerable to overthrow.

A series of failed invasions, both against Japan and Java, hastened the decline of Mongol power. Furthermore, the Mongols lacked the sheer numbers to truly dominate China: not only were the Chinese older and wiser, in terms of their civilization, they were also more numerous. As with their distant cousins the Huns before them, the Mongols soon faded into the larger population.

The last years of Mongol rule were marked by famines and other natural disasters, which the Chinese took as a sign that their rulers had lost what they called the "Mandate of Heaven"—

in other words, the favor of the gods. This is a consistent theme in Chinese history, and such calamities often attended the change of dynasties.

Glory days of the Ming dynasty (1368–c. 1500)

The founder of China's last native-ruled dynasty, the Ming (1368–1644), was Chu Yüan-chang (ruled 1368–98), who led a rebel group that seized control of Khanbalik in 1368. He created a network of secret police and soon consolidated his power throughout the country. Leadership passed to Chu's grandson, but in 1399 Yung-lo (ruled 1403–24), Chu's son, led a revolt against his nephew.

Yung-lo became one of the most fascinating emperors of Chinese history. He sent a series of naval expeditions, under the command of Admiral Cheng Ho (jung-HOH), to westward lands, including India, Ceylon, Yemen, and even Africa. Though the Ming ruled a wide array of tribute-paying states from Japan to Tibet, and from Central Asia to the Philippines, the purpose of these expeditions was not conquest or even trade, but simply to display the superiority of Ming China. These ships brought with them such luxuries as silks and porcelains, and returned bearing exotic animals, spices, and varieties of tropical wood. Centuries later, when archaeologists unearthed the ruins of Zimbabwe in Africa, they found broken pieces of Ming porcelain.

The naval expeditions were costly, and this helped bring them to

Tiananmen Square in Beijing, China, with the Forbidden City in the background. The Forbidden City, a palace five miles in circumference, was built to demonstrate the wealth and power of the Ming dynasty. *Photograph by Susan D. Rock. Reproduced by permission of Susan D. Rock.*

an end; also expensive was the establishment of a vast palace complex. In 1421, Yung-lo moved the capital from Nanjing (nahn-ZHEENG) in the interior to Beijing, where he built a palace five miles in circumference. Containing some two thousand rooms where more than ten thousand servants attended the imperial family, it was not so much a palace as a city: hence its name, "Forbidden City," meaning that only the emperor and the people directly around him were allowed to enter. Built to illustrate the boundless extent of Ming

power, the Forbidden City became— aside from the Great Wall—the best-known symbol of China in the eyes of the world.

These ventures, along with the restoration of the Grand Canal (which had fallen into disrepair under the Mongols), placed heavy burdens on the treasury and weakened the power of the Ming. So too did attacks by Chinese, Korean, and Japanese pirates on their merchant vessels, not to mention the appearance of European traders who were often pirates themselves. The Ming dynasty would continue for several centuries, but long before it fell to Manchurian invaders in 1644, it appeared to have lost the "Mandate of Heaven."

For More Information

Books

Gross, Susan Hill, and Marjorie Wall Bingham. *Women in Traditional China: Ancient Times to Modern Reform.* St. Paul, MN: The Upper Midwest Women's History Center, 1983.

Levy, Elizabeth. *Marco Polo: The Historic Adventure Based on the Television Spectacular.* New York: Random House, 1982.

Schafer, Edward H. *Ancient China.* New York: Time-Life Books, 1967.

Spencer, Cornelia. *The Yangtze: China's River Highway.* Illustrations by Kurt Wiese. London: Muller, 1966.

Web Sites

"Chinese History: The Main Dynasties." *The Chinese Odyssey.* [Online] Available http://library.thinkquest.org/10622/normal_dynasty.htm (last accessed July 28, 2000).

"History of China." [Online] Available http://www-chaos.umd.edu/history/toc.html (last accessed July 28, 2000).

Internet East Asian History Sourcebook. [Online] Available http://www.fordham.edu/halsall/eastasia/eastasiasbook.html (last accessed July 28, 2000).

Japan | 16

Though Japan had been inhabited for thousands of years, its history did not truly begin until the adoption of writing in the A.D. 400s. Yet the origins of the Japanese remain a mystery. Linguists are divided as to whether their language is related to those of Central Asia or to no other tongues on Earth. Certainly the Japanese language is not related to Chinese, though China would be Japan's greatest cultural influence in its early years.

From the Kofun to the Nara period (250–794)

Japan first emerged as a nation in the Kofun period (250–552), named for the impressive burial mounds built by the Yamato (yuh-MAH-toh; "imperial") clan, which united the nation. Given the suddenness with which the Japanese state appeared, it is possible that Japan may have been influenced by visitors from China, whose historical writings of the time

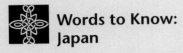

Words to Know: Japan

Animism: The belief that everything has a spirit.

Anthology: A collection of shorter writings, or excerpts from longer writings.

Census: A count of the people living in a country.

Commoner: Someone who is not a member of a royal or noble class.

Constitution: A set of written laws governing a nation.

Figurehead: A ruler who holds power in name only.

Regent: Someone who governs a country when the monarch is too young, too old, or too sick to lead.

Shogun: A military dictator in premodern Japan.

Typhoon: The equivalent of a hurricane, occurring along the Asian coast of the Pacific Ocean.

refer to it as the "Land of Wa," a realm of over a hundred separate "countries."

During the 300s, the Japanese welcomed a steady influx of Chinese and Korean immigrants, whose skills helped them rise quickly to positions of power. In 405, the Japanese adopted the Chinese written language, which they would use for half a millennium, until they developed a version more suited to Japanese.

The Asuka period (552–645)

A collection of scriptures, sent as a gift from the Paekche kingdom in Korea, helped introduce Buddhism to Japan during the Asuka period. Japan's native religion, Shinto ("way of the gods"), was animistic, meaning adherents believed that everything—living or inanimate, physical or mental—has a spirit. Shinto contrasts sharply with Buddhism: whereas Shinto exalts nature and its reproductive forces, and looks upon death as unclean, Buddhism's focus on enlightenment means that death simply breaks the cycle of eternal suffering.

At first Buddhism sparked a heated debate among Japan's ruling elite, but eventually the two religions became complementary elements in the Japanese way of life. Leading the movement for the acceptance of Buddhism was the Soga clan, whose most powerful member was Prince Shotoku (573–621). In 604, Shotoku issued his "Seventeen-Article Constitution." The constitution gave the central government exclusive authority to tax its citizens and instructed the ruling classes in Confucian ethics, more evidence of the Chinese influence. Shotoku was truly "the father of his country," giving it the name Nippon or Nihon; later the Chinese would use a name meaning "origins of the sun," and it was this version—*Jihpen*—that Marco Polo would take back to Europe with him.

The Hakuh period (645–710)

Soga power weakened after the death of Shotoku in 622, and in 645

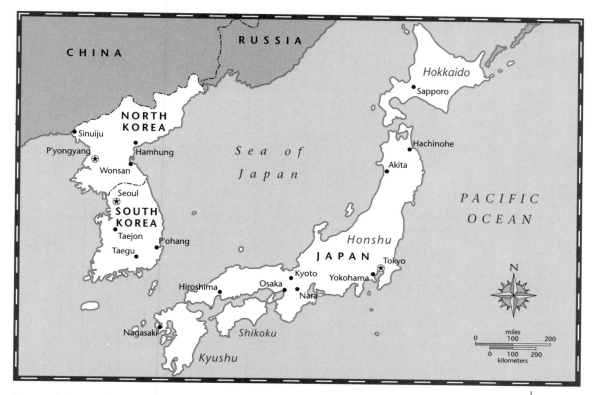

A map of the modern-day nations of Japan and North and South Korea. *Illustration by XNR Productions. Reproduced by permission of the Gale Group.*

two men conspired to murder the ruler. These two were Crown Prince Nakano Oe (OH-ee; 626–671) and Nakatomi Kamatari (614–669), but after they gained power, they both took on new names. The prince became Emperor Tenchi, and Kamatari's family became known as Fujiwara, a clan that would later dominate the imperial family.

A particularly strong Chinese influence characterized the Hakuh period, and this was evident in the new idea of the Tenno, or emperor, as a god who descended directly from the Shinto sun-goddess. Unlike their Chinese counterparts, however, most Japanese emperors were figureheads, rulers who held power in name only while others exerted the real influence. In this regard, Tenchi was something of an exception, though even he had to rule alongside the Fujiwara clan. Other measures adopted by Tenchi from the Chinese included the Chinese calendar, a bureaucracy modeled on the Confucian system, and a land-redistribution effort based on the reforms of the early T'ang dynasty.

Rooted in Confucian principles of equality, the Taika land re-

A Shinto temple in Nikko, Japan. The native religion of Japan, Shinto exalts nature, believing that everything has a spirit. *Reproduced by permission of the Corbis Corporation.*

forms abolished hereditary ownership of lands, created a taxation system, and established a census to provide the government with a means of monitoring taxpayers. This did little to end inequalities, however: the aristocracy found ways to use the reforms to their advantage, and within a century much of the land was back in their hands.

The Nara period (710–794)

Tenchi's successors continued his reforms, which were formalized in 702 with the Taiho law codes. To sym-

bolize the "new" Japan, its rulers began work on a new capital city at Heijo, now known as Nara. The city's designers started out trying to replicate the grid system of Ch'ang-an, China's magnificent capital, but as it took shape, Nara assumed a considerably more Japanese character.

The Nara period also saw a much more wide-ranging adoption of the Buddhist religion—including Buddhist temples and art forms, which the Japanese adapted for their own culture. Like Roman Catholicism, Buddhism has a monastic tradi-

Korea

The history of Korea is actually longer than that of Japan. In ancient times, a powerful state called Choson (choh-SAHN) emerged on the Korean Peninsula, but was destroyed by a Chinese invasion in 108 B.C. China maintained control until A.D. 220, when Korea split into three kingdoms: Paekche (pahk-CHAY) in the southwest, Silla in the southeast, and Koguryo (koh-GOOR-yoh) in the north.

Chinese rulers persisted in trying to control the country, and in 668 formed an alliance with Silla against the other two kingdoms. United under the rule of Silla, Korea adopted Buddhism, and a golden age ensued; but after two centuries the land was once again divided into the three old kingdoms. Then in 936, a new powerful state called Koryo united the country. Its new capital at Kaesong near Seoul was based on the grid plan of the Chinese capital at Ch'ang-an.

Korea withstood invasion by the Liao and Juchen dynasties, which also plagued Sung China, but it fell to the Mongols in 1270. For many years thereafter, the Korean aristocracy was split between pro-Mongol and pro-Chinese factions. Then in 1388, a general named Yi Song-ye seized power. In 1392, Yi established Korea's longest-lived dynasty, which held the throne until the Japanese invasion in 1910.

The Yi dynasty, with its capital at Seoul, adopted Confucianism at the expense of Buddhism. Despite the heavy Chinese influence in this era, during this time Korea adopted its own phonetic alphabet, which replaced Chinese characters.

Japan invaded in 1592, but with the aid of China, Korea resisted the attack. Part of Korea's strength came from its impressive navy, whose "turtle ships" may have been the world's first armored warships. The Japanese threat, along with the eclipse of Ming Chinese power by the Manchus, led the Koreans to increasingly shut themselves off from the world. For many centuries, Korea would be known as the "hermit kingdom."

tion, and the emperor Shomu (ruled 715–749) embarked on an ambitious program of building temples and convents.

Eventually Buddhist clerics became too influential at court for their own good: as it turned out, the nobles and people were not prepared to support Shomu's building program, and it ended soon after his death. His daughter (and successor) Koken came so heavily under the influence of the monk Dokyo that it provoked hostility from the ruling classes. Dokyo tried to make himself Koken's successor, but after Koken's death he was banished from court.

A Japanese samurai on horseback. Like the knights of medieval Western Europe, the samurai were warriors who were governed by their own code of honor in the defense of their feudal lords. *Reproduced by permission of the Corbis Corporation.*

his power. Also during the Nara period, Japan's first poetic anthology, containing some 4,500 poems, appeared as *Collection of a Myriad of Leaves.* The book exhibits a distinctly Japanese style, and includes poems by members of various social classes.

The Heian period (794–1185)

Wishing to sever all ties with the strong Buddhist influence at the Nara court, the emperor Kammu in 794 moved to a new capital at Heian (hay-YAHN; now Kyoto), a city also based on the plan of Ch'ang-an. This move set the tone for the Heian period, in which the Japanese aristocracy sought to cut off all ties with China.

As time went on, in fact, the nobility began to scorn not only foreigners, but even Japanese who lived outside Heian. This contempt for rural Japan had several consequences, among them the rise of the Fujiwara clan. Yoshifusa Fujiwara (804–872) married into the royal family, and in 858 became the first commoner to rule the country, serving as regent for his underage son. This became more common, and eventually it was typical for an emperor to retire early so that his son could "rule"—with one of the Fujiwaras as regent.

Feudalism and the samurai

Heian rulers ignored the countryside, so that by the 900s the provinces had become almost com-

The Nara period, a time of great cultural flowering, saw the writing of the two oldest Japanese books now in existence. Translated as the *Records of Ancient Times* (712) and *Chronicles of Japan* (720), these "histories" rely heavily on myth, though the second book is more reliable. Both books mention the emperor's descent from the sun-goddess, an idea that probably appeared at the time of Tenchi's reforms as a way of justifying

pletely separated from the capital. At the same time, changes in the Taika and Taiho laws made it possible for feudal lords to build large country estates, and these factors helped give rise to feudalism in Japan.

Without a central government, provinces became like tiny nations, settling their disputes with the aid of small fighting bands. This led to the rise of a new warrior class called the samurai—Japan's knights. Like knights, samurai were not soldiers, but individual warriors sworn to defend their feudal lord. They also wore armor, though it was made of bamboo and not metal, and they placed a somewhat greater emphasis on the sword than European knights did. In Europe, lances and crossbows made it possible to fight at a greater remove, but combat in Japan was face-to-face, and swords were so sharp they could slice a man's body in half with a single stroke.

In the Heian and the later Kamakura period, the samurai developed their own code of honor, called *bushido* ("way of the warrior"), but this was quite different from chivalry. For all its flaws, chivalry was based in Christian notions of gentleness and compassion, and as such helped curb knights' penchant for brutality; bushido, on the other hand, defined a samurai's virtue in terms of his ability to strike quickly and decisively against an enemy. Nor was there any European equivalent for ritual suicide, a central aspect of life not only among the samurai, but the Japanese upper classes as a whole (see box, "Ritual Suicide").

An age of courtly refinement

As in Europe, an emphasis on courtly refinement attended the rise of knighthood in Japan. Despite the official ban on Chinese influences, members of the court read Chinese books, enjoyed Chinese music and dance, and studied Chinese etiquette in order to carry themselves with greater elegance. But they were not mere cultural slaves of the Chinese: the era produced a distinctly Japanese style of painting called *yamatoe,* noted for its simple and delicate lines, which often appeared on screens and sliding doors. Japanese poetry also became markedly distinct from that of China.

New developments in writing spurred the creation of Japanese written characters, called *kana,* to replace Chinese characters, which had proven cumbersome for writing in Japanese. Kana in turn brought on a literary explosion. Europeans would later claim credit for developing the novel as a literary form, but in fact the world's first novel appeared in Japan—and its author was a woman. *The Tale of Genji* by Murasaki Shikibu (c. 978–1026) tells the story of a character named Prince Genji, his life and loves, with astounding subtlety and complexity of plot.

The Kamakura and Muromachi periods (1185–1573)

In the countryside, two clans had long battled for power. The victory of one family, the Minamoto, marked

Ritual Suicide

Though Americans use the terms *hara-kiri* (HAH-duh KEE-dee) and the less well known *seppuku* interchangeably, in fact they are different. *Seppuku* refers to the practice of ritual suicide, whereas *hara-kiri*, an indelicate term seldom used by the Japanese themselves, identifies the method—literally, "belly-cutting."

Any number of occasions would require a samurai to slice open his stomach, using a knife that he carried for that purpose. Dishonor or the need to prevent dishonor was a principal motivation: a samurai would kill himself rather than surrender in battle, and a condemned nobleman had the right to do himself in rather than confront the disgrace of an executioner. On

the one hand, a samurai whose master died might commit seppuku so that he could protect his lord in the afterlife; on the other hand, a warrior offended by something his lord had done might slice himself open at the master's gates as a means of protest.

Women and members of the lower classes were denied the "honor" of seppuku; on the other hand, noble ladies could, as a form of protest, commit *jigaki*, suicide by piercing the throat. As part of her training, a woman of the aristocracy learned how to slice her throat properly and—before she did the deed—to bind her legs together so that her body would not be found in an immodest position.

the beginning of the Kamakura period (1185–1333), named after the new capital city. There a shogun, or military dictator, named Yoritomo Minamoto (ruled 1192–99) established his power, but his sons did not prove successful in holding on to it. In their place came the Hojo family, relatives of Yoritomo's widow, who took power in 1219.

Government by the shogunate was exceedingly complex, with the Hojo family ruling lesser shoguns—the equivalent of feudal lords—who in turn controlled a series of figurehead emperors. This, plus the maintenance of two capitals at Kamakura and Kyoto, created a confused situation. Anarchy

continually threatened, but the adoption of the fully developed bushido code helped give a measure of stability.

Bushido demanded that both men and women adhere to its high standards of loyalty and discipline. It is interesting to note that unlike feudal societies in Europe, the shogunate permitted women—at least, women of the upper classes—a great degree of freedom, allowing them to own land and hold positions of esteem.

Invasion and overthrow

Some Koreans who feared Japanese power convinced Mongol

leader Kublai Khan that Japan contained great wealth. In 1274, Kublai Khan launched an unsuccessful naval invasion of Japan. When he tried again in 1281, he sent a fleet of some 3,500 ships containing an estimated 100,000 men; but nature was on the side of the Japanese. A huge wind, probably a typhoon, rose up and smashed the Mongols' vessels to shreds. The grateful Japanese dubbed this a "divine wind," or *kamikaze*, a title adopted centuries later by Japanese suicide bombers in World War II (1939–45).

Though it withstood the Mongols, the Hojo Shogunate weakened over the years that followed, and by 1333 it was ripe for overthrow by a faction that placed Emperor Daigo II (1287–1339) in power. The men driving the Temmu Restoration, as it was called, were Ashikaga Takauji (tah-kah-OO-jee; 1305–1358) and Kusunoki Masashige (mah-sah-SHEE-gay; 1294–1336). Both were military leaders, but their motivations could not have been more different. Kusunoki acted out of loyalty to his emperor, whereas Ashikaga, after selling out his allies in the Hojo family, turned against Daigo in 1336 and made himself shogun. Daigo went on to rule a rival government outside Kyoto, while Ashikaga established himself as leader of a new regime in the city of Muromachi.

The Muromachi period

The Ashikaga Shogunate dominated Japan during much of the Muromachi period (1333–1573), but it had to share power with a new class of warlords called *daimyo* (dy-EEM-yoh). This created an unstable situation, but the shogun Yoshimitsu (ruled 1368–94) managed to successfully balance the shoguns and the daimyo. With the death of his grandson in 1428, however, the uneasy peace came to an end, and the shogunate began to weaken. Clan disputes led to all-out conflict in 1467.

The Onin War raged for ten years, destroying the power of the Ashikagas and devastating Kyoto. Warlords controlled the land until 1568, during which time the balance of power on the battlefield shifted from samurai to mass foot-soldiers. The arrival of Portuguese traders in 1543 created an external threat that aided the daimyo in consolidating their power, and the Europeans' introduction of firearms gave them a particularly effective means for doing so. The Portuguese gradually gained a degree of acceptance, and introduced castles to Japan, where they appeared in military towns around the country.

Despite the unrest of the times, a number of vital social changes took place. The feudal system actually gave more power to the people, because the daimyo were closer to the populace than the faraway imperial court had been. Zen Buddhism, which emphasized meditation and discipline, took hold in Japan during this period, as did a number of distinctly Japanese arts such as flower arranging, gardening, landscape painting, Nō theatre, and the tea ceremony. At the same time, new forces were at work in the upper levels of the Japanese military, and these would end the era of unrest with the unification of the country in 1573.

For More Information

Books

Dijkstra, Henk, editor. *History of the Ancient and Medieval World,* Volume 11: *Empires of the Ancient World.* New York: Marshall Cavendish, 1996, pp. 1519–30.

Farley, Carol. *Korea, A Land Divided.* Minneapolis: Dillon Press, 1983.

Pilbeam, Mavis. *Japan: 5000 B.C.–Today.* New York: Franklin Watts, 1988.

Wolfe, Bob. *Lessons from the Samurai: Ancient Self-Defense Strategies and Techniques.* Photographs by Bob Wolfe. Minneapolis: Lerner Publications, 1987.

Web Sites

Castles of Japan. [Online] Available http://www.magi.com/~ttoyooka/oshiro/ (last accessed July 28, 2000).

Internet East Asian History Sourcebook. [Online] Available http://www.fordham.edu/halsall/eastasia/eastasiasbook.html (last accessed July 28, 2000).

"Japan." *World Art Treasures.* [Online] Available http://sgwww.epfl.ch/wat1/japon.pl (last accessed July 28, 2000).

The Americas

The most notable civilizations in the New World during ancient times were the Olmec and other groups in Mesoamerica, or Central America, as well as the Chavín culture of the Andes Mountains in South America. Both began developing in about 3500 B.C., and in time a number of other civilizations developed around them. In Mesoamerica, these included the Maya and the people of the Teotihuacán city-state. The Maya would continue to flourish through medieval times, and the Mesoamerican and Andean cultural centers provided a foundation for the brilliant Aztec and Inca civilizations that appeared later.

The Maya

The Maya first emerged in the jungle lowlands of what is now northern Guatemala in about 2500 B.C. By 800 B.C., they had settled the area around them, and in the years that followed, Mayan cities sprang up in what is now southern Mexico, Belize, Guatemala, El Salvador, and Honduras. No doubt they came under the influence of southern Mexico's Olmec,

Words to Know: The Americas

Aqueduct: A long pipe, usually mounted on a high stone wall that slopes gently, used to carry water from the mountains to the lowlands.

Archaeology: The scientific study of past civilizations.

Causeway: A raised highway over water.

Conquistador: A leader in the Spanish conquest of the Americas during the 1500s.

Conscription: Compulsory, or required, enrollment of persons in public service, particularly the military.

Divination: The study of physical material—for example, tea leaves or a person's palms—in order to discover what the future holds.

Extended family: A household comprising not just immediate family (parents and siblings), but also grandparents, aunts and uncles, cousins, and other relatives.

Hieroglyphics: A system of written symbols, often consisting of pictograms, which look like the things they represent, and phonograms, which represent a specific syllable.

Jade: A greenish gemstone that acquires a high shine when polished.

Maize: Corn.

New World: The Americas, or the Western Hemisphere.

Observatory: A building set aside for the purpose of studying natural phenomena such as the movement of bodies in the heavens.

Plaza: A large open area or public square, usually but not always in the center of a town.

Staple: A commodity with widespread or constant appeal.

who flourished between 1200 and 100 B.C. The Olmec were noted for their sophisticated 365-day calendar, their system of mathematical notation, and the creation of some sixteen giant stone heads, weighing as much as 30,000 pounds, which archaeologists in the 1800s began finding throughout the jungles of Central America.

Both the Olmec and the people of Teotihuacán (tay-oh-tee-hwah-KAHN) in Mexico built enormous stone pyramids, the most well known of which was the Pyramid of the Sun in Teotihuacán. These structures are particularly impressive in light of the fact that no premodern American culture had use of the wheel or—with the exception of the Incas' llamas—domesticated beasts of burden. Teotihuacán, which flourished from A.D. 100 to 750, was at one point the sixth-largest city in the world.

A map of the Americas showing the three major Mesoamerican civilizations of the Middle Ages: the Maya, the Aztecs, and the Incas. *Illustration by XNR Productions. Reproduced by permission of the Gale Group.*

Agriculture and cities

Like the Olmec before them, the early Maya practiced the slash-and-burn method of clearing land, cutting down larger vegetation with stone tools and burning away underbrush. They grew a variety of crops: maize (corn), beans, squash, avocados, tomatoes, and chili peppers.

Agriculture made possible the creation of urban areas, which originated as ceremonial centers—that is, places for worship—but also became home to large populations. The oldest

Mayan city dates back to about 2000 B.C., and later became the site of Mérida (MAY-ree-thah), established by the Spanish in 1542.

One of the most notable Mayan cities was Tikal (tee-KAHL) in northern Guatemala. Probably founded in the third century A.D., Tikal thrived from 600 to 900, and became home to some 50,000 people—huge by the standards of premodern America. The city included a school where scholars studied astronomy and other disciplines. Among the structures of interest found at Tikal were agricultural earthworks and canals, fortifications against invasion, and—sixteen miles to the northwest—an impressive pyramid with four staircases.

The city of Uxmal (üz-MAHL) near Mérida, which flourished at the same time as Tikal, may have been a center for priestesses who led the people in fertility rites associated with the rain god Chac. Palenque (pah-LING-kay), where archaeologists in 1952 found the tomb of a Mayan ruler from the 600s, was said to be the most beautiful of Mayan ceremonial centers, as well as a center of scientific study that included a seven-story tower for astronomical observations.

The Mayan religion

Perhaps the greatest of the Mayan cities was Chichén Itzá (chee-CHEN eet-SAH), built around a number of *cenotes* (si-NO-tees), or deep natural water holes. Chichén Itzá had impressive pyramids, an advanced observatory, a school for the training of male and female priests, and a 545-foot long ceremonial ball court—the largest in the Americas. Each of these structures served a religious purpose.

The pyramids, huge flat-topped structures, were in many cases as impressive as their counterparts in ancient Egypt, and in some regards even more remarkable. Archaeologists have discovered that Mayan pyramids were designed so as to transmit voices perfectly from the summit to the plaza below. Atop other types of temple structures, Mayan builders attached roof combs, which made the building seem to touch the sky. These were perforated in such a way as to catch the wind, making eery sounds that the Maya equated with the voices of the gods. Typically a pyramid included long series of steps on each side, and on the days of religious festivals—with some 160 gods, there were plenty of these—priests would ascend the stairs in view of the populace below.

What the spectators witnessed was not always pretty: the Maya practiced human sacrifice, and often presented captured enemy warriors to appease the gods. The victim would be held down on an altar, and a priest would slit his chest under the rib cage and tear out the heart. The Maya also practiced ritual torture, and sometimes drowned victims in cenotes to plead with the rain god for water.

The Maya also used a ball game, which they called *pok-a-tok,* as a form of worship. Sharing aspects with the modern games of tennis, volleyball, and even basketball, the ball game had taken different forms and names at various places and times in Mesoamerica's history. In its Mayan incarnation, it involved a set of rings through which the ball had to pass. These rings were said to represent the movement of the planets through the heavens. Just as sports were inseparable from religion, so was astronomy—hence the religious significance of the observatory.

Science and mathematics

The Maya became extraordinary astronomers, carefully observing the movements of the Sun, Moon, and stars, and predicting eclipses and the orbit of Venus. Like many other premodern peoples, they treated astrology with just as much seriousness as astronomy and performed detailed calculations regarding the birth date of a young man and young woman when it came time for matchmaking.

Along with their multitude of gods, the Maya appear to have worshiped time itself. They adapted the ancient calendar of the Olmec and another group, the Zapotec, who used both the 365-day cycle and a 260-day religious calendar. Once every fifty-two years, the first days of both would match up, and that was a day of celebration for the renewal of the Earth.

The Maya used mathematical notation and systems created by the Olmec, who used the number 20 as a base rather than 10 as in the decimal system. Independent of the mathematicians of India, they developed the number zero, and used it centuries before Europeans became aware of the concept.

The arts, writing, and fashion

Like science, art served a religious—not to mention a patriotic—purpose. Most examples of Mayan artwork can be found in the carvings that appeared in their temples. These showed scenes of leaders torturing and defeating their enemies, and priests and priestesses preparing for sacrificial bloodletting. Alongside these were hieroglyphic writings explaining the events depicted.

 Mayan Ideas of Beauty

The Maya had ideas about beauty that modern people would consider perplexing. Because they considered an elongated skull highly attractive, they practiced ritual skull deformation, binding the heads of infants between two boards. People who wanted to look truly spectacular, in the Mayan view, would file their teeth down to sharp points and inlay them with jade.

On the other hand, modern people who practice body-piercing might be surprised to learn that the idea is nothing new: the Maya pierced various parts of their bodies and attached ornaments to them. Also, priests sometimes bled themselves or pierced specific parts of the body—the penis included—in order to achieve higher spiritual consciousness.

The Maya and other Mesoamerican civilizations were exceptional among New World peoples, few of whom possessed a written language. By contrast, the Maya even produced books, though most of these were later destroyed by Spanish priests intent on removing all record of the Mayan religion. Made of fig-tree bark, the books contained astronomical tables, calendars of planting days, and information about religious ceremonies and other aspects of Mayan life. There are also a few surviving works of history (laced with a great deal of myth) and even a play.

The end of the Maya

Mayan culture flourished during the era called the Classic period (c. 300–925), which saw the majority of their building projects; then the Maya went into rapid decline. Most likely an attack by the Toltecs in 950 was more a symptom than a cause of this decline. Other possibilities include an epidemic of some kind, or even discontent with the government. One of the most plausible suggestions is that slash-and-burn agriculture, which is highly detrimental to the soil, simply depleted the land.

Whatever the reasons, the Maya began to abandon their old homeland in the 900s and move northward into Mexico's Yucatán Peninsula. Invasion and subsequent domination by the Toltecs in about 1000 further sapped their strength, but by about 1200, the Maya had absorbed the less numerous Toltecs. Despite the fact that many of their splendid cities had disappeared into the jungle, not to be found until the 1700s, the Maya continued to survive as a civilization throughout the Post-Classic period (c. 1000–1540). They endured the onslaught of the Spanish conquerors, and today some 4 million Maya live in Mexico and surrounding areas.

The Aztecs

The Aztecs replaced the Maya as the dominant power in the region, but the warlike Toltecs, who began coming down from what is now northern Mexico in the period from about 600 to 800, helped bridge the gap. The Toltecs worshiped the god Quetzalcóatl (kwet-zuhl-KWAH-tuhl), a feathered serpent-god that would later be adopted by the Aztecs. From the destruction of Teotihuacán in about 900, the Toltecs controlled central Mexico, but after they moved into Mayan lands, their departure opened the way for other groups.

Among the new arrivals were the Aztecs, who came from a place they called Aztlan (AHZ't-lahn) to the northwest. They reached central Mexico in about 1250, and established the city that would become their capital, Tenochtitlán (tay-nawch-teet-LAHN), around 1325. According to legend, the gods had told them to settle in a place where they saw a cactus growing from a rock, and an eagle perched on the cactus eating a snake. The Aztec priests claimed to have seen just such a sight on a tiny island along the marshy western edge of Lake Texcoco (tays-KOH-koh).

Today it is easy to find both the place they picked and an image of the strange scene. The area around Tenochtitlán became Mexico City, Mexico's capital, and the scene itself appears on the Mexican flag. Even the name "Mexico" is an inheritance from the Aztecs, who also called themselves *Mexica*.

Tenochtitlán

The industrious Aztecs set about turning the marshes into a city so gorgeous that later Spanish conquerors would dub Tenochtitlán "the Venice of the New World." Like its Ital-

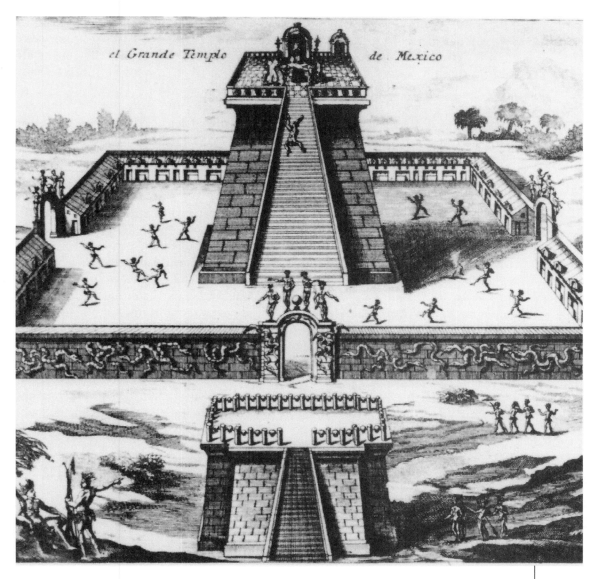

el Grande Templo de Mexico

The temple at the Aztec capital city, Tenochtitlán. The Aztecs offered human sacrifices to their gods, sometimes eating the flesh of the sacrificed victim afterward. *Reproduced by permission of the New York Public Library Picture Collection.*

ian counterpart, Tenochtitlán was built on a number of islands, though in this case the islands—"floating gardens," or *chinampas*—were artificial. To create the chinampas, the Aztecs piled lake-bottom soil onto floating rafts made of interlaced twigs, then planted trees and bushes in the soil. Eventually, as the roots of the plants kept growing deeper, they anchored the rafts in place, and what had been the surface of the lake became a meadow laced with canals.

Aside from their beauty, the canals served a purely practical purpose, aiding the transport of goods and people. The Aztecs also built causeways and bridges to connect the city to the mainland, and constructed aqueducts for bringing in fresh water. The city, designed to conform to precise astronomical principles, was well planned, with wide plazas and streets, as well as some twenty-five large, flat-topped pyramids regularly spaced throughout. The growth of the empire in later times made the Aztecs' capital an extraordinarily wealthy city, with tribute pouring in from subject territories in the form of gold, copper, rubber, chocolate, gemstones, jaguar skins, and jade.

Aztec religion and society

Chief among the Aztec gods was Huitzilopochtli (hwit-zil-oh-POHCH-t'lee), though they also worshiped a number of others, including Quetzalcóatl. In fact, the world's largest monument is a temple to Quetzalcóatl (see box, "The Quetzalcóatl Pyramid"). All of these deities required human sacrifice, which the Aztecs practiced with more frequency —and more cruelty—than any other Mesoamerican peoples.

Of course the accusation of cruelty would have meant nothing to the Aztecs; theirs was not a society that put a premium on mercy or kindness to the weak. It was common for

an Aztec priest to cut the heart out of a living person. Nor were victims only drawn from enemy armies: Aztec warriors considered it an honor to be chosen as a sacrifice to the gods, and in one year alone, more than 20,000 people met their end on the altars of Huitzilopochtli. The Aztecs often ate the flesh of the sacrificed victim, and sometimes priests would flay (skin) a body and dance in the skin.

A prominent feature of Tenochtitlán was its skull racks, on which the priests displayed the skulls of sacrificed victims as a sign of the peoples' devotion to the gods. Like the Maya, the Aztecs used two calendars, and the first day of the fifty-third year, when the two came into alignment, required a special sacrifice called the New Fire Ceremony. After cutting out the victim's heart, the priest would build a fire in the open chest cavity to symbolize the continuance of life for the Aztec people.

The Aztec Empire

When they first arrived in the Valley of Mexico, the Aztecs came under the dominance of Azcapotzalco (as-kuh-puht-SAL-koh), the leading city-state in the area. Eventually, however, they gathered support from other tribes and conquered the great city. Then in 1431 they formed a triple alliance with two other city-states, Texcoco and Tlatelóco (t'laht-eh-LOH-koh), and soon the three controlled the Valley of Mexico.

Quickly it became clear that the triple alliance was not a gathering of equals: the other two were mere city-

The Quetzalcóatl Pyramid

The world's largest pyramid is located not in Egypt, but some sixty-three miles southeast of Mexico City. Though the Great Pyramid of Egypt is three times as tall as the 177-foot Quetzalcóatl Pyramid, the latter is much larger. The pyramid's base covers nearly forty-five acres—that is, more than one-sixth of a square mile—making it the largest monument (as opposed to a functional structure such as an office building) in the world. Its total volume has been estimated at 4.3 million cubic yards, equivalent to a 200-story building as long and wide as a football field.

A close-up view of sculptures on the Quetzalcóatl Pyramid. *Reproduced by permission of the Corbis Corporation.*

states, whereas the Aztecs were empire-builders. Using the other two cities' help, they established dominance over the region, and the Aztec Empire eventually covered an area from central Mexico to the Guatemalan border.

Perhaps not surprisingly, given their religious practices, the Aztecs proved to be cruel rulers. Fear and resentment by the conquered peoples around them would later aid the Spaniards in rallying local support against the Aztecs.

The Aztecs' downfall

In 1507, the Aztecs celebrated a New Fire Ceremony, and afterward the emperor Montezuma II (ruled 1502–1520) began hearing strange omens from his priests. By 1519, when he had come to believe that Quetzalcóatl would soon return to Earth, he began hearing rumors of a strange, godlike figure roaming the jungles. This creature had strangely white skin and a beard, something hardly ever seen among the Aztecs. He carried amazing deadly weapons, including a stick that shot fire, and he rode a fantastic four-legged monster.

With his horse—a creature unknown before the arrival of the Europeans—and his gun, the Spanish

Montezuma and Hernán Cortés greet each other. Montezuma initially thought Cortés was a savior for the Aztecs, but in fact he was there to conquer and destroy them. *Reproduced by permission of the Corbis Corporation.*

conquistador Hernán Cortés (1485–1547) probably did seem like a creature from another world. Meanwhile Montezuma, believing Cortés must surely be the hoped-for savior, sent representatives bearing gold and other treasures, gifts that only excited the conquistador's greed for more. Their superior military technology and tactics—not to mention the surrounding peoples' resentment of the Aztecs—gave the Spaniards an enormous advantage. They conquered and destroyed the Aztecs in 1521.

The Incas

The term *Inca*, though used to describe an entire people, was actually the name for a line of fourteen rulers who controlled the vast Inca Empire before the arrival of the Spanish in 1533. Their native language was Quechua (KECH-oo-ah), still spoken by thousands of people in the Andean highlands of Peru, where the Inca had their origins.

Influenced by the ancient Chavín (shah-VEEN) culture, as well as that of the Huari (HWAH-ree), who flourished between 300 and 750, the Incas emerged as a civilization in about 1100. Around that time, they moved into a nearby valley and established a capital named Cuzco (KOOZ-koh), meaning "navel of the world." Today Cuzco is the oldest continually inhabited city in the Americas.

Building an empire

Over the next three centuries the Incas, like the Aztecs, began to dominate and receive tribute from surrounding villages. But unlike the Aztecs, they were slow to build an empire—and when they did, it became much bigger than that of the Aztecs. Only in the mid-1400s, during the reign of Viracocha (veer-ah-KOH-kah), did they begin to expand, and then only to an area about twenty-five miles around Cuzco. Viracocha, named after the Incas' principal deity, had a son named Pachacutec (pah-cha-KOO-tek; ruled 1438–71), who lived up to the meaning of his own name: "he who transforms the Earth." Pachacutec and his son Topa built an empire that reached its peak during the reign of Topa's son Huayna Capac (WY-nuh KAH-pahk; ruled 1493–1525).

By then the Incas controlled an area equal to the U.S. Eastern Seaboard (the coastal states from Maine to Florida), and called their realm "Land of the Four Quarters"—in other words, the four directional points of the compass. Its population became as large as 16 million, an extraordinary statistic at a time when England had only about 5 million people. Controlling it all was one of the most efficient, well-organized governments anywhere in the world during medieval times. For this, Pachacutec—considered one of the greatest rulers of all time by some historians—deserves much of the credit.

Roads and other structures

Under the reign of this extraordinary empire-builder, the Incas constructed some 2,500 miles of stone roads, many of them across high mountain passes. These included way stations placed at intervals equal to a day's travel, so that the traveler could rest and obtain supplies. Trained runners, the Pony Express of their day, traversed the road system, keeping the emperor abreast of events throughout his empire. Like the roads built by the Romans, those of the Incas (along with many of their other structures) proved more enduring than those built by later peoples—in this case, the Spanish.

The stones on Inca roads and buildings were cut to fit together so precisely that mortar was not necessary. Inca cities were marvels of urban planning, with broad avenues intersected by smaller streets, all converging on an open central square. At Cuzco this center was occupied by the Temple of the Sun, and later archaeologists discovered an impressive fort near the city. Other feats of Inca engineering include the construction of aqueducts and irrigation canals, as well as rope suspension bridges. The latter, many of them more than 300 feet

An aerial view of Machu Picchu, the mysterious Inca city built high in the Andes. *Photograph by John M. Barth. Reproduced by permission of John M. Barth.*

long, spanned cliffs high above turbulent rivers; and many are still in use.

Machu Picchu (MAH-choo PEEK-choo), tucked high in the Andes, shows much about the Incas' skills as builders. Yet it raises far more questions than it answers. Accessible only by means of a dangerous climb up a 2,000-foot cliff, it had never been seen by a white man until the American explorer Hiram Bingham found it with the aid on a Peruvian guide in 1911. Given the difficulty in even reaching it, archaeologists are unsure how the Incas built Machu Picchu's massive stone structures. Even more perplexing is the purpose behind this isolated city in the clouds.

A sophisticated bureaucratic state

A central mystery of the Incas is their administrative system, which they managed to maintain in the face of extraordinary limitations. Not only did they, like other American peoples, lack the use of the wheel and iron tools, but unlike the Maya and Aztecs, they lacked even a system of writing.

It boggles the mind to imagine how they created a sophisticated bureaucratic state—a place where civil servants kept detailed records of population, food stores, supplies, and other information—under such limitations.

Yet they managed to do so, using the abacus for counting and the *quipu,* knotted strings of varying lengths and colors, for recording numerical information and keeping track of inventories. They also possessed something unknown to the peoples of Mesoamerica: a domesticated beast of burden in the form of the llama (YAH-muh), a relative of the camel that lives in the high Andes.

The rulers demanded a tribute of grain from each village. A portion of this they set aside in case of famine, at which time they would distribute it to the hungry. They also taxed the women for a certain amount of woven cloth, and the men for a certain amount of labor over a given period of time. This form of conscription, similar in concept to the military draft, permitted them to build roads and other structures throughout their empire.

The life of the Incas

Using foot plows, Inca farmers cultivated land and grew a number of crops, most notably potatoes and corn. (Just as the people of the New World had never seen horses, the Europeans had never tasted these foods and many others that were destined to become staple crops in Europe, Asia, and Africa.) In addition to the llama, which was too small to support the weight of adults but could carry lighter loads, they domesticated the alpaca, another relative of the camel that is prized for its wool. Other domesticated animals included dogs, guinea pigs, and ducks.

To identify themselves as members of the Inca Empire, the people sported bowler hats of a type still worn by the Indians of Peru and Bolivia. They lived in extended families, as indeed most people outside the West do today: instead of just a husband, wife, and children, households included aunts and uncles, cousins, grandparents, and other relatives. Nobles could have more than one wife, and beautiful and intelligent women were chosen from villages around the empire to go to Cuzco and become concubines for the nobility. Emperors might have concubines, but the empress was usually the emperor's sister, and their firstborn son became his successor.

Religion and science

The Incas worshiped a variety of gods, though Viracocha was supreme as creator and ruler of all living things. The Incas also practiced human sacrifice, though they were not nearly so enthusiastic about it as the Aztecs, and abandoned the method of tearing out a living heart.

Many things were regarded as sacred, or *huaca,* including mummies, temples and historical places, springs, certain stones, and mountain peaks. (Inca shrines and ceremonial sites have been found at elevations as high as 22,000 feet—more than four miles

Francisco Pizarro journeyed from Spain to the Inca lands, and in 1533, he led a force that toppled the Inca ruler and destroyed the empire. *Reproduced by permission of the Corbis Corporation.*

in the sky.) The priests practiced divination (DIV-i-nay-shun) to learn the will of the gods, but some of their efforts at curing peoples' ailments verged on genuine science and medicine.

In addition to dispensing herbal remedies, priests actually performed a type of surgery on people who suffered chronic headaches, cutting away part of the skull to relieve pressure on the brain. Sometimes, however, the purpose was less scientific in nature—in other words, releasing evil spirits believed to be the source of the headache. Perhaps most remarkable was the work of priestly "dentists," who replaced broken or decayed teeth with metal crowns similar to the ones used by modern dentists.

Fall of the empire

Though the Incas were much kinder rulers of subject peoples than the Aztecs, their end was much the same. Like Montezuma, the emperor Atahualpa (ah-tuh-HWAHL-puh; c. 1502–1533) believed that the conquering Spaniards were gods; and like Cortés, Francisco Pizarro (c. 1475–1541) came not to save them, but to rob them. Pizarro imprisoned Atahualpa and allowed him to rule his empire from prison for eight months, but this was only in order to gain ransom from the Incas.

Atahualpa ordered his people to fill a room of almost 375 square feet with treasures, whose value has been estimated at $25 million in today's money. Assembled by July 1533, the treasure included precious art objects, most of which were melted down and made into gold coins. Instead of keeping his word, however, Pizarro had Atahualpa killed, then marched on Cuzco and destroyed the empire.

As with the Maya, however, Inca culture survives today, carried on by millions of Indians in the Andean highlands. Peruvian schoolchildren are still taught to recite the names of the fourteen Inca rulers, and the memory of this great American empire remains alive.

For More Information

Books

Defrates, Joanna. *What Do We Know about the Aztecs?* New York: P. Bedrick Books, 1993.

Dijkstra, Henk, editor. *History of the Ancient and Medieval World,* Volume 11: *Empires of the Ancient World.* New York: Marshall Cavendish, 1996, pp. 1447–88.

Leonard, Jonathan Norton. *Ancient America.* Alexandria, VA: Time-Life Books, 1967.

Newman, Shirlee Petkin. *The Incas.* New York: Franklin Watts, 1992.

Web Sites

The Aztec. [Online] Available http://north-coast.com/~spdtom/aztec.html (last accessed July 28, 2000).

The Empire of the Incas. [Online] Available http://www.sscf.ucsb.edu/~ogburn/inca/inca.htm (last accessed July 28, 2000).

The Maya Ruins Page. [Online] Available http://mayaruins.com/ (last accessed July 28, 2000).

"Rollout Photography: The Maya Vase Database." [Online] Available http://www.famsi.org/rollout_photography.htm (last accessed July 28, 2000).

Africa | 18

The African continent is divided by one of the most impenetrable natural boundaries in the world: the Sahara Desert. Covering an area larger than the continental United States, this greatest of all deserts ensured that northern Africa—Egypt and the Mediterranean coast—would develop along dramatically different lines than the southern part. Aside from Egypt itself, the two principal African civilizations of ancient times formed on the Red Sea coast, below Egypt and east of the Sahara. Southward lay various lands controlled by the Bantu peoples, tribal groups who would later develop a number of civilizations.

Ethiopia

The name "Ethiopia" comes from a Greek expression meaning "burned skin" and suggesting a dark complexion. Ancient peoples used the term to describe the entire region south of Egypt, but in fact these were two distinct civilizations there: Kush, or Nubia, and Aksum. Founded along the southern Nile River, where the nation of Sudan is today, Kush

Words to Know: Africa

Arid: Dry.

Inflation: An economic situation in which an oversupply of money causes a drop in the value of currency.

Lingua franca: A common language.

Matrilineal: Through the mother's line rather than the father's.

Patron: A supporter, particularly of arts, education, or sciences. The term is often used to refer to a ruler or wealthy person who provides economic as well as personal support.

Racism: The belief that race is the primary factor determining peoples' abilities, and that one race is superior to another.

controlled Egypt for a time (712–667 B.C.) and developed its own form of writing. To the east was Aksum, based in the Red Sea port of Adulis (ah-DOO-lis), in modern-day Eritrea.

Aksum began evolving into a larger Ethiopian state when its King Ezana (AY-zah-nah; ruled A.D. 325–360) subdued Kush in 325. Around this time, a young Syrian missionary converted Ezana to Christianity, which became the religion of Ethiopia from that time forward. Meanwhile, across the Red Sea in an area known as the "incense states," a lush region known for its spices, the Himyarite kingdom of Yemen had made Judaism its religion.

Eager to gain control of the "incense states," Ethiopia formed an alliance with Byzantium against the Sassanid Persians and their allies in Yemen. Between the 300s and 500s, Ethiopia gradually assumed control over the "incense states," though much of the area later fell under Persian authority.

Isolated by Islam

In the 600s, the spread of Islam wiped the Sassanids off the map, but this was no cause for rejoicing in Ethiopia. The Muslims dealt a severe blow to Ethiopia's Byzantine allies when they took control over most of the Middle East. Many Greek manuscripts were destroyed during this time, and some only survived through Ethiopian translations. Meanwhile, Muslim power ended Ethiopians' dominance over Red Sea trade and cut Ethiopia off from the rest of the Christian world.

Gradually the nation's focus shifted away from the Red Sea and toward the Nubian interior. In the centuries that followed, large Muslim populations formed along the Red Sea coast and in southern Ethiopia, and Jewish communities appeared in other areas of the country. Yet Christianity remained dominant, and a line of kings who claimed descent from the biblical King Solomon and Queen of Sheba maintained control. Christians in southern Muslim lands such as Egypt looked to Ethiopia for leadership, and this in turn may have influenced Europeans' association of the country with the Prester John legend (see box, "Prester John").

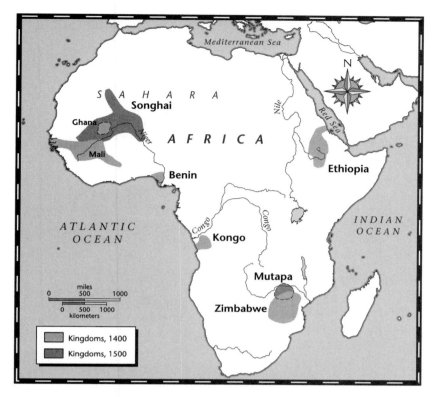

A map of Africa showing the locations of the African kingdoms in 1400 and in 1500. *Illustration by XNR Productions. Reproduced by permission of the Gale Group.*

Contacts with Europe

During the latter part of the Crusades, leaders in Ethiopia and Europe entertained the idea of an alliance against the Muslims. In 1317, a Dominican monk called for a joint crusade, with Ethiopia blocking the Red Sea while the Europeans attacked the Holy Land. Though the Muslim world feared such a two-pronged attack, nothing ever came of it.

European interest in Ethiopia remained strong during the 1400s, as the Portuguese tried to establish trade links and gain an edge over Venice in the spice trade. This period also saw exchanges of missionaries between Europe and Ethiopia, and in fact Ethiopian monks attended the Council of Florence in 1441. As an outgrowth of this visit, the papacy set up a house for Ethiopian pilgrims behind St. Peter's. Later Ethiopian visitors to Rome helped increase Europeans' interest in, and knowledge of, their exotic Christian homeland.

The Sudan

Though in modern times there is a nation called Sudan, geographers

Prester John

During the Middle Ages, people all over Europe came to believe in the existence of Prester John, or John the Priest, a Christian king in a faraway land who they believed would come to their aid against the Muslims. This legend first took form in the writings of Otto of Freising (FRY-sing; c. 1111–1158), a German bishop and historian, who claimed that Prester John was a descendant of the Magi (MAY-zhy), the wise men who had attended the birth of Jesus. According to Otto, Prester John's armies had conquered the Persians and forced the Muslims to submit to Christianity.

In 1165, a letter supposedly written by Prester John to several European monarchs turned up in Europe. His land, the letter-writer claimed, was a perfect society in which everyone was wealthy, a place where peace and contentment prevailed. Some Europeans believed that this land must be Ethiopia, known to have a Christian king; therefore in 1177, Pope Alexander III sent a letter to Ethiopia's king, asking for his aid against Muslim enemies. The messenger never returned.

Europeans also identified the homeland of Prester John with India, and the king himself with the Mongols. The myth persisted into the 1500s and 1600s, spurring on the voyages of European explorers eager to find the mythical Christian kingdom.

use the term "the Sudan" to describe a region of some two million square miles south of the Sahara. About the size of the United States west of the Mississippi River, the Sudan runs from the Atlantic coast in the west almost to the Red Sea coast in the east. Its climate is arid, or dry, and farming is difficult, but during the Middle Ages the region became home to a number of wealthy empires.

Ghana

The first of these was Ghana (GAH-nuh), a kingdom that came into existence during the 400s in what is now southern Mauritania. Despite the climate, its people were originally farmers, but over time Ghana's wealth came from a number of sources. One of these was conquest: by the 1000s Ghana had an army of some 200,000 men. A principal source of Ghana's wealth was gold, so plentiful that the king's advisors carried swords made of it. His horses bore blankets of spun gold, and even the royal dogs had gold collars. The king, whose people considered him divine, held absolute control over the gold supply, and further increased his wealth by taxing trade caravans that passed through the area.

Ghana's capital was Kumbi-Saleh, formed from two towns about six miles apart. One town became a local center for Islam, which merchants brought with them from across the desert, and eventually it had twelve mosques. This created an unusual religious situation: officially the king still consulted the wisdom of his traditional priests, but in private he held council with Muslim lawyers and theologians.

The other town remained a stronghold of the native religion, and there Islamic practices were not permitted in public because they might challenge the spiritual authority of the king. Perhaps the influence of Islam helped make Ghana vulnerable to attack by the Almoravids from Morocco, who arrived in 1080. The people of Ghana did not unite to resist the conquerors, and their kingdom came to an end.

Mali

Many nations created in the nineteenth and twentieth centuries share names with regions from premodern times, but in many cases the borders are not the same. Such is the case with Mali (MAH-lee), a kingdom that included nations to the southwest of modern-day Mali, along with a corner of the present nation.

Mali formed as an Islamic kingdom in the 1000s, but took shape as an empire under the leadership of Sundiata Keita (sun-JAH-tah; died 1255), who established his power through a series of conquests that began in about 1235. He greatly broadened the realm controlled by Mali and established a new capital at Niana. By the 1300s, his dynasty ruled some 40 million people—a population two-fifths the size of Europe at the time—in a region from the upper Niger River (NY-jur) to the Atlantic Ocean.

Mansa Musa (ruled 1307–c. 1332) reigned at the height of Mali's power, and became the first African ruler to become widely known throughout Europe and the Middle East. His fame resulted in part from a pilgrimage to Mecca, on which he was attended by thousands of advisors and servants dressed in splendid garments, riding animals adorned with gold ornaments. Along the way, he gave his hosts generous gifts, and in Egypt spent so much gold that he caused massive inflation in the country's economy.

But Mansa Musa was far more than just a showman: an effective administrator who ruled a highly organized state, he was also a patron of the arts and education. He brought Muslim scholars and architects to Mali, where they built mosques, promoted learning, and assisted his advisors in ruling the vast realm.

As with many other great rulers, however, Mansa Musa's power resided mostly in his strong personality and talents; therefore his successors found the vast empire difficult to govern. They were plagued by the breakdown of administrative systems and by the competition of rising states on their borders. One of these was Song-

The Glory of Timbuktu

Today the name of "Timbuktu" is a synonym for a faraway, almost mythical place, and in modern times the city of some 30,000 inhabitants—now known as Tombouctou (tohn-buk-TOO) in Mali—is certainly well off the beaten path. But under the Mali and Songhai empires, it was one of the most extraordinary cultural centers of premodern Africa, and indeed of the world.

Starting in the 1400s, Europeans became fascinated by tales of a great city on the edge of the desert, which housed both wealthy merchants and scholars wealthy in knowledge. In 1470, an Italian journeyer became one of the first Europeans to visit, and more information surfaced with the publication of a book called *Description of Africa* in 1550.

Written by Leo Africanus (c. 1485–c.1554), an Arab captured and brought to Rome, the book remained for many centuries Europeans' principal source of knowledge regarding the Sudan. Leo reported that, of the many products sold in the rich markets of Timbuktu, none was more prized and profitable than books—a fact that says a great deal about the rich intellectual life there.

Unfortunately, a series of wars and invasions by neighboring peoples during the early modern era robbed Timbuktu of its glory. In 1828, a French explorer went to find the legendary Timbuktu, and in its place he found a "mass of ill-looking houses built of earth."

hai (SAWNG-hy), which Mansa Musa had conquered; in the mid-1400s, as his dynasty fell into decline, Songhai won its independence.

Songhai

Established by Muslims in about 1000 on the bend of the Niger, at a spot in the center of present-day Mali, Songhai would eventually extend along much of the river's length and far inland. For a long time it had existed under the shadow of Mali, but it came into its own under Sonni Ali (SAW-nee; ruled c. 1464–92), a brilliant military strategist and empire-builder who in 1468 captured the city of Timbuktu. One of Mali's greatest cultural centers, Timbuktu was destined to reach its peak under Songhai rule (see box, "The Glory of Timbuktu").

Sonni Ali conquered many more cities, ending Mali dominance and replacing it with his military dictatorship. His successor, Mohammed I Askia (as-KEE-uh; ruled 1493–1528), set about reorganizing the entire empire, creating a central administration controlled from the capital in Gao (GOW). He developed a professional army and even a navy of sorts—a fleet of canoes that regularly patrolled the Niger.

Mohammed also reformed the tax system, established a set of weights and measures, and reformed judicial procedures. Over the course of his reign, he made the Songhai Empire one of the most respected nations in the Islamic world. In 1528, however, his son Musa overthrew him and exiled him to an island. Nine years later, another son brought him back to Gao, where he died in 1538. His tomb is one of the most revered mosques in West Africa.

As with Mali, the death of a strong ruler brought on disorder; and as with Ghana, the conquerors came from Morocco. They arrived in 1590, and this time they had firearms, giving them an overwhelming advantage. Songhai fell in 1591.

Kanem-Bornu and the Hausa city-states

Far to the east of the area where Ghana, Mali, and Songhai had thrived was an area called Bornu, a vast plain in what is now northeastern Nigeria. With the downfall of the earlier states, trade routes—dependent as they were on strong kingdoms to provide them protection—began shifting toward the central Sudan, which was dominated by two centers of power. To the east was Kanem-Bornu (kah-NEM), a state that first developed in about 800, and to the west a group of city-states controlled by the Hausa (HOW-suh) people.

Both Kanem-Bornu and the Hausa lands had a matrilineal (mat-ri-LIN-ee-ul) system, meaning that inheritance was passed down through the mother's line rather than the father's. This gave women an exceptionally high social status, and they were even allowed to hold positions in regional and national government. The adoption of Islam in the 1000s and afterward ended this arrangement.

The Hausa states never formed a unified political entity, which made them vulnerable to attack by neighboring states and ultimately led to their downfall. Kanem-Bornu, on the other hand, did form an empire, which reached the height of its power in the late 1500s. By then, however, the Sudan was not the only location of trade routes across the African continent: the interest of European and Arab traders had shifted to the southwest and the south.

Bantu kingdoms and cities

Starting in about 1200 B.C., the Bantu peoples began migrating from the region of modern-day Nigeria, spreading westward and southward. The Bantu constituted a loose collection of tribes and nations united by language. In each of the Bantu tongues, of which there were eventually sixteen, the word for "people" is the same: *bantu*.

Though Westerners are accustomed to speaking of "Africa" as though it were one country, in fact modern Africa consists of more than

The Great Enclosure in the modern nation of Zimbabwe; these ruins were originally the royal palace. *Reproduced by permission of the Corbis Corporation.*

fifty official nations—and hundreds upon hundreds of national groups with their own language and way of life. In such an ethnically splintered environment, the average African language has only a half-million speakers. By contrast, Swahili (swah-HEEL-ee), the most well known of the Bantu languages, is today spoken by 49 million people in Kenya, Tanzania, the Congo, and Uganda.

Swahili is the lingua franca of southern Africa, a common language much as Arabic became in the Middle East and as Latin was among educated Europeans of the Middle Ages. No doubt Swahili's broad base has its roots in medieval times, specifically in a group of east African city-states with trade contacts as far away as China.

Coastal city-states

The east African coast had been a center of trade since ancient times, and during the 1100s a wave of Arab and Persian merchants arrived. Over the period from 1200 to 1500, when trade there was at its height, the native peoples and the Muslims together established some thirty-seven city-states in what is now Kenya, Tanzania, and Mozambique. Most notable among these were Malindi, Mombasa, Kilwa, and later, Zanzibar.

Typically, city-states lay on islands just off the coast, a situation that protected them from land invasion. Indeed, the mainland represented a different world: in the interior were tribal peoples with little exposure to the outside, whereas the offshore islands became thriving centers of international trade. Kilwa was the major port for gold, which went through Egypt to Europe, and iron ore from Malindi supplied the furnaces of India.

The coastal city-states also served as ports of call for Admiral Cheng Ho's expeditions from China. A Ming dynasty scroll commemorates a most unusual event: the arrival of a giraffe from Malindi at the Chinese emperor's court in 1415. After about 1500, however, merchant activity in East Africa began to die out, primarily because of the Europeans' rising dominance of sea trade.

Zimbabwe and Mutapa

In the early 1500s the Portuguese began penetrating East Africa's interior, laying the foundations of the colony called Mozambique (moh-zum-BEEK), which they would retain until 1975. In so doing, they established control over a kingdom called Mutapa, which ruled the entire southern half of Mozambique between the Zambezi (zam-BEE-zee) and Limpopo rivers. As it turned out, the eastern kingdom of Mutapa was

The Zanj

Though Europeans and their descendants in America are most identified with the slave trade, in fact slavery existed in Africa for centuries before the first Europeans arrived in the 1400s. Not only did Africans buy and sell members of other tribes, but Arab and Persian merchants were enthusiastic slave-traders.

The first Mideastern reference to sub-Saharan Africans, whom the Muslims called Zanj (ZAHNJ), occurred in about 680. These writings prove that racism is nothing new: frequently Islamic writers described the Zanj as their social inferiors, a lazy and dishonest people, and they often commented negatively on the black skin of the Zanj. Yet the Muslims also believed that the Zanj possessed magical powers.

Because the Africans on the continent's east coast admired the Arabs, this made them easy targets for capture. Many of the Zanj were brought to serve as slaves in the Abbasid caliphate, and in 868 a revolt broke out among them. For nearly fifteen years, the rebels controlled much of southern Iraq, but by 883 the Muslim government had suppressed the revolt.

an extension of an even older realm controlled from Zimbabwe (zim-BAHB-way).

The latter reached its peak between 1250 and 1450, when it thrived on a flourishing gold trade. Its ruins

Kinshasa, in the Democratic Republic of the Congo, became a battleground in the late twentieth century as civil war gripped the nation. *Reproduced by permission of AP/Wide World Photos.*

lie in the southeastern corner of the modern nation called Zimbabwe, though in fact there are two sets of ruins: Great Zimbabwe, older and larger, and Little Zimbabwe some eight miles distant. The most impressive set of stone buildings in premodern southern Africa, Great Zimbabwe extended over more than sixty acres, and included a palace capable of housing a thousand servants. Its circular temple complex, modeled on a tribal chief's enclosure, had walls ten feet thick and twenty feet high, comprising some 15,000 tons of cut stone—all laid without use of mortar.

Though the people of Zimbabwe left behind no written records and the city had long been abandoned when the Portuguese arrived, the royal court of Mutapa in the east provided visitors with an idea of Zimbabwe's glory. The king was attended by a royal pharmacist, a head musician, young pages who had been sent as hostages from subject peoples, and many other aides—including a council of ministers composed primarily of women. Apparently at some earlier stage in Mutapa, women had been in control. There was even a female military contingent, which played a decisive role in the choosing of kings.

Kongo

Far to the northwest of Zimbabwe, along the mouth of the Congo River near the Atlantic coast, was the kingdom of Kongo. The area is today part of Angola, which like Mozambique became a Portuguese colony that only received its independence in 1975. Today, to the north and east, in areas also controlled by Kongo at different times, are the Republic of the Congo and the Democratic Republic of the Congo (formerly Zaire).

Established in the 1300s by a prince from the north, Kongo spread over a large area in the years that followed. By the time the Portuguese arrived in the 1400s, the nation had developed an extensive bureaucracy. Its economy depended on trade between the coast and the interior, and copper and cloth served as its currency. Perhaps its greatest king was Afonso I (ruled c. 1506–c. 1550), who in 1512 signed a treaty with the king of Portugal. Kongo continued to flourish into the 1600s.

Benin and the Yoruba

As with many another African nation, the modern state of Benin (bay-NEEN) shares a name with an empire of medieval times, but it is not the same country. What is today southern Nigeria was once Benin, which established one of the most highly organized states of West Africa in the two centuries preceding the arrival of the Portuguese in 1485. As with most other African kingdoms, Benin built its wealth on trade, in this case between the Atlantic coast and the Sudan.

The people of Benin were not the only ones who profited from the trade routes between the ocean and the desert. To the west, in what is now Burkina Faso, the Mossi and Yoruba peoples (who later formed a state called Oyo) settled along the upper headwaters of the Volta River. This placed them in close proximity with Mali and Songhai, but the peoples of the Volta were worlds apart from their neighbors to the north. In contrast to the Muslim kingdoms of the Sudan, which maintained strong links with the outside world, the peoples of the coast retained their traditional African religion and way of life.

For More Information

Books

Davidson, Basil. *African Kingdoms*. Alexandria, VA: Time-Life Books, 1978.

Dijkstra, Henk, editor. *History of the Ancient and Medieval World*, Volume 11: *Empires of the Ancient World*. New York: Marshall Cavendish, 1996, pp. 1543–54.

McKissack, Pat. *The Royal Kingdoms of Ghana, Mali, and Songhay: Life in Medieval Africa*. New York: Henry Holt, 1994.

Web Sites

"African Empires Timeline." [Online] Available http://www.cocc.edu/cagatucci/classes/hum211/timelines/htimeline2.htm (last accessed July 28, 2000).

Internet African History Sourcebook. [Online] Available http://www.fordham.edu/halsall/africa/africasbook.html (last accessed July 28, 2000).

Medieval Africa. [Online] Available http://historymedren.about.com/education/history/historymedren/msubafr.htm (last accessed July 28, 2000).

The Late Middle Ages | 19

The period known as the Late Middle Ages (1300–1500) can also be considered the beginning of the Renaissance, which had its roots in the changes that began to gather speed during those two centuries. Yet there was plenty about this time that was truly medieval, and whereas some events pointed to the future, other occurrences signaled the end of an era. Among these were the upheaval created by the Black Death and Hundred Years' War, and the decline of the two institutions that had long dominated European life: feudalism and the papacy.

Pestilence and war

In 1300, Europe had about 100 million people; then a series of calamities struck. First Germany and other northern countries experienced crop failures from 1315 to 1317, and these resulted in widespread starvation and death. Then, in 1347, Europe was hit by one of the worst disasters in human history, an epidemic called the Black Death. Sometimes called simply "the Plague," the Black Death killed between twenty-

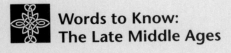

Words to Know: The Late Middle Ages

Dauphin: The crown prince in prerevolutionary France.

Flagellants: Religious enthusiasts of the Middle Ages who beat themselves with lashes as a way of doing penance.

Joust: Personal combat, particularly on horseback and involving a lance.

Mercenary: A professional soldier who will fight for anyone who pays him.

Nationalism: A sense of loyalty and devotion to one's nation.

Perspective: An artistic technique of representing faraway objects so that they appear smaller than objects close by.

Pogrom: An organized massacre of unarmed people, in particular groups of Jews.

Tournament: A contest in which knights fought, usually with blunted lances, for a prize or a favor given by a lady.

five and forty-five percent of the European population.

The Black Death (1347–51)

The outbreak began in Asia. Thanks to the Mongols' conquests, which had made travel between East and West safer and easier than ever before, it quickly made its way to the Black Sea shore, where it erupted in September 1346. Likewise the opening of trade that had followed the Crusades aided its spread, as Italian merchants unknowingly brought the disease home in their ships. The first outbreak in Western Europe occurred in October 1347, in the city of Messina at the northeastern corner of Sicily. From there it was an easy jump to the Italian mainland, and by the following April all of Italy was infected. Meanwhile, it had reached Paris in January 1348, and within a year, 800 people a day were dying in that city alone. Quickly it penetrated the entire European continent and beyond, from Palestine to Greenland.

The only merciful thing about the Black Death was its quickness. Victims typically died within four days—a hundred hours of agony. If they caught a strain of bubonic (byoo-BAHN-ik) plague, their lymph glands swelled; or if it was pneumonic (nyoo-MAHN-ik) plague, the lungs succumbed first. Either way, as the end approached, the victim turned purplish-black from respiratory failure; hence the name. The ironic thing was that the force at the center of all this devastation was too small to see with the naked eye: a bacteria that lived on fleas, who in turn fed on rats.

The people of the time had no idea of this scientific explanation for the Plague and instead looked for spiritual causes and cures. Some believed that the world was coming to an end, and some joined sects such as the flagellants (FLAJ-uh-luntz), religious enthusiasts who wandered the countryside, beating themselves with whips as a way of doing penance.

The flagellants were closely tied with a rising anti-Semitic trend. Searching for someone to blame, Europeans found a convenient scapegoat in the Jews, who they claimed had started the Plague by poisoning the wells of Europe. This absurd explanation provided justification for many a pogrom (poh-GRAHM), or organized massacre.

Peasant uprisings of the late 1300s

By the end of 1351, the Plague had run its course, but it left behind a population change equivalent to that which would occur in the modern United States if everyone in the six most populous states—California, New York, Texas, Florida, Pennsylvania, and Illinois—died over a four-year period. Not until 1500, about 150 years after the Black Death, would the European population return to the levels of 1300. All over the continent, farms were empty and villages abandoned, leading to scarcity and higher prices— conditions that sparked a number of peasant revolts.

First came the French Jacquerie (zhah-keh-RHEE) in the spring of 1358. The latter took its name from Jacques Bonhomme (ZHAHK bun-AWM), a traditional nickname for a peasant meaning "John the Good Man," and the rebels collectively called themselves Jacques. In the space of a few weeks, the Jacques gathered support from a range of discontented persons, including even minor royal officials. Their targets were the wealthy

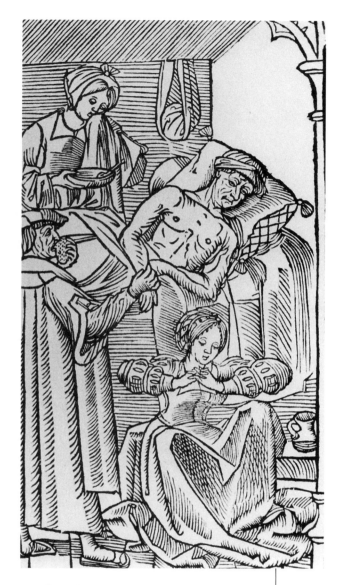

People gather around the bed of a victim dying from the Black Death. The Plague, which struck in the mid-1300s, reduced the population of Europe by at least one quarter. *Reproduced by permission of the Library of Congress.*

Wat Tyler, leader of a peasants' revolt in England in 1381, is dragged to his death. *Reproduced by permission of the Corbis Corporation.*

and powerful, and in their furious onslaught, which consumed much of the region around Paris, they did not spare even the children of their enemies. Then, just as suddenly as it began, the Jacquerie was brutally suppressed by the French royalty and nobility, who ordered wholesale executions of peasants—many of whom had not even participated in the revolt.

Across the English Channel in 1381, revolts against royal taxation broke out in several English counties, including Essex, Kent, and several others. The most well known of the rebel

leaders was Wat Tyler from Kent, who captured the sheriff there and destroyed property records. The Essex force did much the same, then joined the faction from Kent and marched on London to meet with fourteen-year-old Richard II (ruled 1377–99).

Though Richard agreed to meet with the rebels against his advisors' counsel, the government's failure to keep the promises he made them only further enraged the peasants. The rebels destroyed a home belonging to John of Gaunt (1340–1399), Richard's uncle, and killed several of John's advisors. The violence associated with the English revolt, however, did not equal that of the Jacquerie.

One hundred fifty years of war (1337–1485)

The Black Death and peasant uprisings occurred against the backdrop of the Hundred Years' War (1337–1453), which actually lasted 116 years, making it by far the longest armed conflict in history. Fought between France and England, the "war" was really a series of wars broken by long periods of truce, and the combined duration of all major battles was less than a month. The real devastation of the war came from the long sieges against towns, as well as periodic raids during times of official ceasefire. In both cases, it was France that sustained the injury.

The first phase of the war saw a series of English victories, most notably at Poitiers (pwah-tee-AY) in 1356. The hero of the latter was Edward the Black Prince (1330–1376) of England, whose military leadership gave England power over northern France. Discontent over Poitiers in turn spawned the Jacquerie, but by 1360 the war had entered a second phase, when little happened except for occasional French raids against the English.

Then after more than fifty years, the English returned to the offensive under Henry V (ruled 1413–22), who led them to victory at Agincourt (AH-zhin-kohr) in 1415. Henry, whose deeds would later be cel-ebrated in several plays by William Shakespeare (1564–1616), solidified his power by marrying Catherine of Valois (val-WAH), daughter of the French king, in 1420.

English victory appeared certain, yet the French were about to unleash a secret weapon. This was a teenaged girl named Joan, just three years old at the time of Agincourt, who at the age of twelve believed she had heard the voice of God telling her to follow the path of holiness. When she was sixteen, this voice commanded her to come to the aid of the crown prince or *dauphin* (doh-FAN), Charles VII (ruled 1422–61), and so Joan of Arc (1412–1431) embarked on one of history's shortest and most brilliant careers. Once she had the dauphin's attention, she laid out a plan to force an English withdrawal from the French city of Orléans (ohr-lay-AWn). Clad in the armor of a boy, she and the tiny army Charles gave her broke the English siege on May 8, 1429, turning the tide of the war.

A year later, in May 1430, Joan was captured by a force from Burgundy, which had temporarily sided with England, and was sold to the English six months later. The English did not simply execute her, but sought to destroy French morale by trying her for heresy. A highly biased court composed of pro-English French priests found her guilty of witchcraft and burned her at the stake. Yet the French initiative in the war did not die with Joan, and France enjoyed victory under Charles. By 1453, the English had lost all their gains in France, and they returned to England in dejection.

More war awaited them in England as the houses of York and Lancaster launched the Wars of the Roses (1455–85), so named because of the flowers that symbolized the competing dynasties. The Lancaster line emerged victorious when Henry VII assumed the throne. Henry's son Henry VIII (ruled 1509–1547) would become one of England's greatest kings, and would father its greatest queen, Elizabeth I (ruled 1558–1603).

Wars and warlords in Italy

The Black Death hit Italy particularly hard, and much of the country remained in a state of anarchy through the 1400s. This led to the rise of mercenary military commanders, warlords, and a new class of ruthless local leadership. In Rome, Cola di Rienzo (RYENT-soh; 1313–1354) led a revolt in 1347, whereby he attempted to restore the glories of ancient Rome; but instead he simply provoked the Roman people and the papacy to anger with his reckless policies.

Much more successful were the Medici (MED-uh-chee), a family of bankers who controlled Florence from 1421 to 1737. The most famous member of the family was Lorenzo di Medici (1449–1492), sometimes known as "Lorenzo the Magnificent." As a ruler he could be a tyrant, but he also became a highly influential patron of the arts who assisted greatly in ushering in the Renaissance.

Whatever Lorenzo's sins, they paled in comparison to those of the Borgia (BOR-zhuh) family, who had their origins in Spain but came to power in Rome. Two of them became popes, Calixtus III and Alexander VI (ruled 1492–1503), and the latter fathered a number of children, the most notorious being the cruel Cesare (CHAY-zur-ay, c. 1476–1507) and his lustful sister Lucrezia (loo-KREET-zee-uh; 1480–1519).

The destruction of Byzantium

One of the most significant events in the history of Eastern Europe was the Battle of Kosovo Field, on June 28, 1389. Byzantium, well on its way to final ruin, had long before recognized Serbia as an independent nation, and at Kosovo the Serbs led a failed effort to protect Orthodox lands from invasion by the Ottoman Turks. As a result, Serbia and Bulgaria fell to the Turks, leaving a permanent Muslim influence on the Balkan Peninsula.

Half a century later, in 1448, Turkish forces defeated a Hungarian army under János Hunyadi (YAH-nos HOON-yahd-ee; c. 1407–1456), again at Kosovo Field. By the early 1500s, the Ottomans had gained control over much of Hungary, and like the Mongols before them, threatened Austria.

By then, the Turks had absorbed what remained of the Byzantine Empire. On the last night of Byzantium's history, May 28–29, 1453—just before troops under Mehmed the Conqueror entered Constantinople—Orthodox priests held the last Christian services in the Hagia Sophia. Four days later, the church reopened, but now it was a mosque, as it is today.

The Iberian Peninsula

Following the Islamic conquest of Spain in 711, the history of the Iberian Peninsula followed a course separate from that of Europe as a whole. At that point there was no such thing as "Spain," except as a geographical designation: there were the Moorish emirates in the south and the Christian region of Asturias in the north.

Gradually a number of power centers evolved in Asturias, and over time these developed into separate kingdoms. Portugal had been calling itself a separate country in the 800s, and under the reign of Afonso I (ruled 1128–85), this became a reality. Christian Spain remained a collection of various principalities, but as the leaders of various states began reconquering lands from the Muslims, a distinctive Spanish Catholic culture began to unite the country.

The destruction of Muslim power in Spain was called the Reconquista (ray-kawn-KEES-tah), and its most famous leader was the warrior Rodrigo Díaz de Vivar (c. 1043–1099), better known as El Cid. As the Reconquista gained force, two kingdoms emerged to dominate the rest of Spain: Aragon and Castile (kas-TEEL), so named because of its many castles. In 1469, by which time the Christians had conquered all of Spain except for Granada in the southeast, Ferdinand II of Aragon married Isabella I of Castile, thus uniting the country.

Spain's few remaining Muslims, along with Jews, became early victims of the Spanish Inquisition. The latter, launched in 1478, was Spain's separate—and much more cruel—version of the Catholic Inquisition. Many people were imprisoned, tortured, or killed under the Spanish Inquisition, which officially ended only in 1834.

In 1492, the same year they conquered Granada, Ferdinand and Isabella expelled all Jews from Spain. Of course the most famous event of 1492 was the discovery of the New World by Christopher Columbus, sent by Ferdinand and Isabella to find a westward sea route to China. Meanwhile Portuguese sailors had greatly extended the influence of their own kingdom, and over the next century, exploration and conquest would make Spain and Portugal world powers.

Greece soon became part of the Ottoman Empire, and would not win its independence until the early 1800s. Meanwhile a new nation was born, one that proclaimed itself the "Third Rome"—in other words, the third Roman Empire after Rome itself and Byzantium. That new nation was Russia. The imperial transformation of Muscovy began when Ivan III (the Great; 1440–1505) began conquering city-states, starting with Novgorod in

1471 to 1478. In 1472, he married Sophia, or Zoë, niece of the last Byzantine emperor, thus establishing his claims as preserver of Orthodox Christianity. At that time, he also added the two-headed eagle, long a symbol of Byzantium, to Muscovy's coat of arms.

In 1480, Ivan established Russian independence by cutting off all tribute to the Tatar-Mongol overlords, who had never recovered from Tamerlane's attacks almost a century before. His grandson Ivan IV (1530–1584), better known as Ivan the Terrible, in 1547 took the old Slavic form of "caesar," and was crowned czar. As his name suggests, Ivan was a cruel emperor, establishing a pattern for most Russian rulers through the twentieth century.

The people and the powers

The Crusades and the Mongol conquests had greatly increased contact between Europe and the rest of the world, and in about 1300, the continent began to experience a sudden explosion of curiosity and creativity. This in turn would spawn the Renaissance in the arts and literature; the Reformation in religion; and the Age of Discovery in exploration and science.

Symbolic of old and new, respectively, were the Scholastic philosophers John Duns Scotus (c. 1266–1308) and William of Ockham (AH-kum; c. 1285–c. 1349). The latter is most famous for "Ockham's razor," which holds that "entities must not be unnecessarily multiplied"—in other words, one should always seek the most simple, logical, and straightforward explanation for something, avoiding conclusions not warranted by the known facts. Ockham's razor was a hallmark of the emerging revolution in science and thought, and it represented the complete opposite of medieval beliefs.

Ockham also supported the German emperor in a struggle with the pope. By contrast, Duns Scotus and his followers, the Scotists, held firmly to the old ways, including belief in the church and all its teachings. In the 1300s, aspects of the Scotists' ideas seemed forward-looking; but as the Renaissance gained momentum and they resisted all new ways of thought, the term *duns* or *dunce* became a hallmark of ignorance.

New ways of seeing the world

The transition from medieval to Renaissance could be seen in a variety of arts. Giotto (JAHT-oh; 1276–1337), the last great pre-Renaissance painter, showed the stirrings of new ideas in his use of highly expressive gestures, which turned a painting into a sort of story. Filippo Brunelleschi (fu-LIP-oh broo-nuh-LES-kee; 1337–1446) applied science to architecture, establishing the concept of perspective, whereby faraway objects appear smaller than objects close by.

Perspective greatly increased the sense of depth in the paintings of Masaccio (muh-ZAHT-choh; 1401–1428), who also took a scientific approach to lighting. No longer were all figures equally lit, as in medieval art; in Masaccio's paintings, it was clear that light came from a definite source such as the Sun or a candle.

Donatello (c. 1386–1466), a student of Brunelleschi, helped usher in Renaissance sculpture by turning from purely biblical subjects—the only subjects permitted for medieval artists—to scenes from ancient Greece and Rome. In Flanders, the painter Jan van Eyck (YAHN vahn IKE; c. 1395–1441) made equally important strides, becoming the first major artist to depict ordinary, if wealthy, people—merchants who had paid for portraits of themselves and their families.

A change in the language

A number of Italian writers, most notably the poet Dante Alighieri (DAHN-tay al-ig-YEER-ee; 1265–1321), helped bridge the medieval and Renaissance periods. In his masterpiece, the *Divine Comedy* (1308–21), Dante described an allegorical journey through Hell (the Inferno), Purgatory, and Paradise. The book, a "comedy," in the ancient sense, meaning that it ends on a happy note, is a veritable encyclopedia of the Middle Ages. Practically every important person from premodern Europe is mentioned somewhere on its pages.

Like the troubadours before him, Dante wrote in the vernacular, the language of everyday people—in this case Italian instead of Latin. Petrarch (PEE-trark; 1304–1374) also wrote in Italian, but gained his greatest recogni-

tion during his lifetime for his work in Latin. Petrarch's purpose in using Latin, however, was very un-medieval. He was one of the first writers to take note of the growing Renaissance movement, and he used ancient Rome's language as a way of harkening back to the last great flowering of civilization.

Medieval events and trends influenced the writings of Giovanni Boccaccio (boh-KAHT-choh; 1313–1375) and Geoffrey Chaucer (c. 1342–1400), yet their work was far from medieval in character. In Boccaccio's *Decameron* (dee-KAM-uh-rahn; 1353), a group of young men and women escape the Plague by going to the countryside, and there they amuse themselves by telling tales. What sets the *Decameron* apart from most earlier literature is its natural, everyday tone, which influenced Chaucer in writing *The Canterbury Tales*. The latter is a collection of stories—some moral and uplifting, some bawdy and off-color—told by a group of pilgrims on their way to Canterbury.

A change of systems

The changes in the life of the mind at the end of the Middle Ages reflected larger economic and social changes as feudalism declined and the middle class gained power. It is ironic, then, that the style of armor most commonly associated with the medieval period only appeared during this era (see box, "Plate Armor"), when a number of factors combined to render medieval knighthood and its trappings irrelevant.

Most important among these factors was the development of gunpowder and cannons, which together with the pike, or spear, and the longbow (a weapon six to eight feet in length used for shooting arrows rapidly) completely changed the face of battle. As in Japan around the same time, massed formations became more important than individual warriors. By the time Miguel de Cervantes (sur-VAHN-tays; 1547–1616) wrote his hilarious novel *Don Quixote* (1605–15), knighthood had become something of a joke. Thus Don Quixote (kee-YOH-tay) rides around the Spanish countryside in a tattered suit of armor, fighting battles with windmills.

As knighthood and feudalism became a thing of the past, a new middle class was on the rise. From the time of the Crusades, Europe's economy had been on the upsurge, and changing views on usury and money-lending helped spur an economic explosion. No longer did the charging of interest—essential if an economy is going to grow—seem ungodly. The latter change was in turn tied with a revolution sweeping the world of religion, a revolution that would forever change the way Christians approached God.

The decline of the papacy

Due to the inability of Pope Boniface VIII to control the French king, the papal court had been moved to Avignon in 1309, signaling the beginning of the end of the powerful medieval papacy. Petrarch called the Avignon papacy the "Babylonian Captivity," referring to the period in the Old Testament when the people of Israel were carried off to slavery in Babylon. Worse was to follow, however, as the church became embroiled in the Great Schism (SKIZ-um; 1378–1417).

In 1378, just before he died, Gregory XI (the first non-French pope in years), moved the papacy back to Rome. Upon his death, the cardinals chose Urban VI (ruled 1378–89), but Urban became so unpopular that they elected Clement VII (ruled 1378–94) in his place. When Urban refused to give up his throne, Clement fled to Avignon and there set up a rival papacy. France, Scotland, Sicily, and parts of Spain supported the Avignon popes, while England and most of Western Europe continued to back Rome.

In 1409, the Council of Pisa attempted to rectify the situation by removing both popes and replacing them with a new one. Not surprisingly, the Avignon and Rome popes refused to step down, so now there were *three* popes, including the new one at Pisa. Only in 1417 did the Council of Constance end the Schism by removing all three popes and choosing Martin V (ruled 1417–31) to lead the church. All non-Roman popes of the Great Schism were declared antipopes. The Council of Constance also declared that the decisions of an ecumenical council had more authority than those of an individual pope, which further signaled the decline of the papacy.

Winds of reformation

The downfall of the papacy had come not because of external ene-

Plate Armor

The type of armor most often associated with the medieval period is plate, or full-body armor; but ironically, it did not make its appearance until the Middle Ages were almost over. Improvements in the crossbow in the early 1300s made it necessary to develop a more protective style of armor, though in fact the concept behind the "new" armor was old: the barbarians who helped bring down the Roman Empire had worn plates of armor held together with animal skins.

With the advent of plate armor, helmets became more protective, and usually covered the entire face, with eye slits in the metal. Knights typically wore a particularly heavy piece of armor on their left shoulder, since most men were right-hand-ed and they were therefore most likely to take blows on the left side.

Yet as armor changed in these ways, even more significant changes—particularly the development of firearms—were occurring on the field of battle. Therefore armor began disappearing from the battlefield.

Knights still wore armor for tournaments, however: in the joust, in which two knights rode at one another and each tried to unhorse the other with his lance, armor made for valuable protection. It could also be worn for purely decorative purposes, as was the case through the 1600s. This ceremonial armor typically included detailed decorations, and gleaming, polished metal plates.

mies, but because of problems within the church itself—particularly its efforts to control politics. From the church's viewpoint, this could not have come at a worse time, because Rome now faced a threat more formidable than all the armies of Islam: a new group of religious leaders who questioned the authority of the church to stand between God and Christians. These leaders led a movement that came to be known as the Reformation. It arose from attempts to change Roman Catholicism and resulted in the founding of Protestantism. First among the movement's leaders was John Wycliffe (WIK-lif; 1330–1384), who rose to prominence in England just as the Great Schism was beginning.

Wycliffe challenged virtually every doctrine of medieval Christianity, and in fact questioned the idea that the Catholic Church was *the* Church. He declared that the church of Rome was not the "real church," which he said existed wherever two or more believers in Jesus Christ were gathered together. Transubstantiation (see box, page 101), he said, was an empty be-

Jan Hus was a religious reformer who was burned at the stake for heresy. *Reproduced by permission of the Hulton-Getty Picture Library.*

lief, since there is nothing in the Bible to support it; and he condemned the monastic way of life because its idea of separation from the world went against the Bible as well.

These were the kind of teachings that could get a man killed, but Wycliffe survived in large part because he had powerful friends. Less fortunate was Jan Hus (HOOS; 1373–1415), a Bohemian reformer. Influenced by Wycliffe, Hus challenged a practice whereby the church peddled forgiveness by granting indulgences in exchange for monetary contributions. Ordered to appear before the Council of Constance in 1414, he was tried for heresy, and on July 6, 1415, was burned at the stake.

New nations

Hus was a hero not only of the Reformation, but of Bohemian or Czech nationalism because he supported greater Czech authority over the German-dominated University of Prague, Bohemia's capital. Later, when the Reformation reached its height, German nationalism would in turn be tied with the movement led by Martin Luther (1483–1546). Similarly, Henry

VIII's establishment of the Church of England (known as the Anglican, or in the United States, Episcopal Church) strengthened the formation of a distinctly English identity.

As the Middle Ages ended, medieval lands became incorporated in larger nations. Such was the fate of Burgundy, which briefly created a court noted as a center of music in the 1400s. By 1477 it had ceased to exist, divided among a number of growing nations, most notably France. To the south, Spain and Portugal (see box, "The Iberian Peninsula") had emerged as nations, as did Holland and a number of other countries to the north.

New horizons

Spain's unification coincided with the opening stages of the Age of Discovery. Already Portugal had become a powerful force on the high seas, primarily through the efforts of Prince Henry the Navigator (1394–1460), who made no voyages himself but directed a number of expeditions around the coast of Africa. While the rest of Europe was embroiled in political struggles, tiny Portugal began building a colonial empire many times larger than Portugal itself. Spain asserted itself as a nation by sending three ships under the command of Christopher Columbus (1451–1506) to find a sea route to China.

What Columbus found was not China, of course; but that is another story, since by Columbus's time the Middle Ages were clearly over. Yet Columbus did not bring on the end of the Middle Ages, nor did Ockham or Dante or Hus or any number of other great figures. The man who deserves credit, perhaps more than any other person, for launching the modern era was a German printer by the name of Johannes Gutenberg (yoh-HAH-nes; c. 1395–1468). Improving on ideas pioneered by the Chinese several centuries before, Gutenberg developed a process of movable-type printing that would change the world as no one had ever done.

A fast and economical process of printing meant that books could be widely distributed, and this in turn led to an explosive growth in literacy. It also strengthened vernacular tongues. Newly literate merchants and others did not want to read dry old documents in Latin; they wanted to read the latest novel or a report on explorations in the East Indies in their native language, whether that be German, Italian, or English. This of course meant that the church would no longer be able to maintain the wall it had set up between believers and their God. In fact the first book Gutenberg printed in 1455 was a book constantly mentioned in the Middle Ages, yet rarely seen and almost never read: the Bible.

For More Information

Books

Dijkstra, Henk, editor. *History of the Ancient and Medieval World,* Volume 10: *Medieval Politics and Life.* New York: Marshall Cavendish, 1996, pp. 1345–68, 1375–1422.

Severy, Merle, editor. *The Age of Chivalry.* Washington, D.C.: National Geographic Society, 1969, pp. 299–368.

Web Sites

"The Black Death." *Discovery Online.* [Online] Available http://www.discovery.com/stories/history/blackdeath/blackdeath.html (last accessed July 28, 2000).

"Avignon Papacy: Historical Summary." [Online] Available http://www.humnet.ucla.edu/humnet/cmrs/faculty/geary/instr/students/history.htm (last accessed July 28, 2000).

"The Hundred Years' War." [Online] Available http://www.bnf.fr/enluminures/texte/atx2_02.htm (last accessed July 28, 2000).

Where to Learn More

The following list focuses on works written for readers of middle school or high school age. Books aimed at adult readers have been included when they are especially important in providing information or analysis that would otherwise be unavailable, or because they have become classics.

Books

Asimov, Isaac. *The Dark Ages.* Boston: Houghton Mifflin, 1968.

Davidson, Basil. *African Kingdoms.* Alexandria, VA: Time-Life Books, 1978.

Dijkstra, Henk, editor. *History of the Ancient and Medieval World,* Volume 8: *Christianity and Islam.* New York: Marshall Cavendish, 1996.

Dijkstra, Henk, editor. *History of the Ancient and Medieval World,* Volume 9: *The Middle Ages.* New York: Marshall Cavendish, 1996.

Dijkstra, Henk, editor. *History of the Ancient and Medieval World,* Volume 10: *Medieval Politics and Life.* New York: Marshall Cavendish, 1996.

Dijkstra, Henk, editor. *History of the Ancient and Medieval World,* Volume 11: *Empires of the Ancient World.* New York: Marshall Cavendish, 1996.

Durant, Will. *The Age of Faith.* New York: Simon and Schuster, 1950.

Durant, Will. *Our Oriental Heritage.* New York: Simon and Schuster, 1954.

Encyclopedia of World Biography, second edition. Detroit: Gale, 1998.

Hale, John R. *Age of Exploration.* New York: Time-Life Books, 1974.

Hanawalt, Barbara A. *The Middle Ages: An Illustrated History.* New York: Oxford University Press, 1998.

Historic World Leaders. Detroit: Gale, 1994.

Jones, Terry, and Alan Ereira. *Crusades.* New York: Facts on File, 1995.

Jordan, William Chester, editor in chief. *The Middle Ages: An Encyclopedia for Students.* New York: Macmillan Library Reference, 1996.

Langley, Andrew. *Medieval Life.* New York: Knopf, 1996.

Leonard, Jonathan Norton. *Ancient America.* Alexandria, VA: Time-Life Books, 1967.

Roberts, J. M. *The Illustrated History of the World,* Volume 4: *The Age of Diverging Traditions.* New York: Oxford, 1998.

Schafer, Edward H. *Ancient China.* New York: Time-Life Books, 1967.

Schulberg, Lucille. *Historic India.* New York: Time-Life Books, 1968.

Severy, Merle, editor. *The Age of Chivalry.* Washington, D.C.: National Geographic Society, 1969.

Stewart, Desmond, and The Editors of Time-Life Books. *Early Islam.* New York: Time-Life Books, 1967.

Web Sites

The Catholic Encyclopedia. [Online] Available http://www. newadvent.org/cathen/ (last accessed August 14, 2000).

Catholic Online Saints and Angels. [Online] Available http:// www.catholic.org/saints/ index.shtml (last accessed August 14, 2000).

Imperium. [Online] Available http:// www.ghgcorp.com/shetler/ oldimp/ (last accessed August 14, 2000).

Internet Medieval Sourcebook. [Online] Available http://www. fordham.edu/halsall/sbook. html (last accessed August 14, 2000).

Lives of the Saints. [Online] Available http://www.pitt.edu/ ~eflst4/saint_bios.html (last accessed August 14, 2000).

Medieval History. [Online] Available http://historymedren. about.com/education/history medren/mbody.htm (last accessed August 14, 2000).

ORB: The Online Reference Book for Medieval Studies. [Online] Available http://orb.rhodes. edu/ (last accessed August 14, 2000).

World Civilizations. [Online] Available http://www.wsu.edu: 8080/~dee/TITLE.HTM (last accessed August 14, 2000).

The WorldRoots Royal Pages. [Online] Available http://www. worldroots.com (last accessed August 14, 2000).

Index

Note: Illustrations are marked by (ill).

Bajazed 83, 138
Balban 148
Baldwin of Boulogne 103
Bali 155
Balkan Peninsula 218
Baltic Sea 41
Bantu 201, 207–11
Barbarians 6, 9, 10, 13, 17, 28, 33, 48, 90, 134, 146, 161, 171, 172, 223
"Base-10" system 146
Basil II 50, 53, 58, 59
Batu 135
Bavaria 34, 96
Bayeux Tapestry 95
Becket, Thomas à 114, 116
Bedouins 64
Beijing 134, 173
Belasitsa 59
Belgium 126
Belgrade 104
Belisarius 48, 52
Belize 185
Benedict 25–27
Benedictine monks 27, 45
Benin 211
Bernard of Clairvaux 109, 110
Bible 24, 27–29, 73, 85, 87, 102, 113, 130, 224, 225
Bingham, Hiram 196
Bishops 10, 12, 100, 101, 123, 132
Black Death 91, 213–15, 217, 218, 226
Black Sea 57, 58, 78, 79, 139, 214
Boccaccio, Giovanni 221
Bohemia 56, 99, 224
Bohemond 102, 103, 106
Bolivia 197
Boniface VIII (pope) 132, 222
Book of Kells 28
Borneo 155, 158
Borobudur 155
Bosnia 83
Bosporus 104
Britain 19, 21, 22, 39, 42, 92, 119. *See also* England
British Isles 13, 28, 36, 39
Britons 21, 22, 118
Brunelleschi, Filippo 220
Buddha. *See* Siddhartha Gautama
Buddhism 66, 68, 141–45, 155, 162, 163, 166, 168, 170, 176, 178, 179, 183

Bulgaria 48, 50, 55, 59, 78, 82, 83, 104, 218
Bulgars 50, 54, 55, 58, 78
Burgundians 21, 30
Burgundy 96, 217, 225
Burkina Faso 211
Burma 137, 152–54
Bursa 82
Bushido 181, 182
Buwayhids 79
Byzantine Empire 3, 5, 12, 13, 14, 18, 47–60, 72, 74, 78, 83, 96, 98, 99, 104, 123, 127, 130, 139, 202, 218–20
Byzantines 23, 42, 48–50, 52–54, 59, 64, 80, 96, 98, 99, 104, 110, 122
Byzantium. *See* Byzantine Empire

C

Cabala 86, 90
Cairo 72, 75, 82
Caliph 37, 62, 68, 88, 89, 136
Caliphate 49, 62, 68–71, 75, 78, 79, 102, 139, 145, 209
Calixtus III (pope) 218
Calligraphy 162, 170
Cambodia 152, 154, 155, 158, 159
Camelot 118
Canonization 20, 24, 114
Canossa 101
Canterbury 107, 114, 221
Canterbury Tales 221
Canute 42, 44, 95
Capetians 94
Cardinals 94, 100, 222
Carolingian Age 33–46, 90
Carolingian Renaissance 35–36
Caspian Sea 68, 139
Castile 219
Castles 4–6, 110, 111, 117, 120, 183, 184, 219
Cathars 123
Cathedrals 112–14
Catholic Church 1, 2, 8, 10, 19, 20, 51, 91, 94, 132, 141, 178, 223
Caucasus 83, 139
Cavalry 8, 14, 37, 50
Celts 7, 13, 21

F

Famine 162, 169, 197
Fa Ngum 154
Far East 6, 25, 127, 152, 167
Farsi 74
Fatima 65, 68, 69
Fatimids 75, 81, 88
Ferdinand 219
Feudalism 2, 3, 20, 31, 37–39, 50, 114, 124, 129, 180, 181, 213, 221, 222
Finns 57, 99
First Amendment 115
First Crusade 91, 102–04, 106, 107, 109
"Five Dynasties and Ten Kingdoms" 169
Flagellants 214, 215
Florence 126, 203, 218
Foot-binding 170, 171
Forbidden City 173
Fourth Council of Constantinople 100
Fourth Crusade 121
Fourth Lateran Council 101
Frame story 71
France 4, 13, 19, 21, 23, 30, 31, 34, 37, 41, 45, 65, 89, 91–96, 100, 102, 103, 108, 109, 111, 113–17, 119, 121, 123, 124, 126, 129, 132, 156, 214, 217, 222, 225
Franciscans 123
Francis of Assisi 123
Franks 21, 23, 29, 30, 32, 38, 104
Frederick I Barbarossa 113, 114
Frederick II 124, 126
Friars 123
Frisians 31
Fujiwara 177, 180
Fujiwara Yoshifusa 180
Funan 152

G

Gaiseric 17
Gallipoli 82
Ganges 141, 142, 146
Garden of Paradise 81
Gao 206, 207
Gaul 17, 21

Gauls 7, 13, 16
Gautama, Siddhartha. *See* Siddhartha Gautama
Gautier Sans Avoir 103
Gemara 89
Genghis Khan 133–36, 138, 140, 171
Genoa 115, 126
Geography 127, 142, 155
Geometry 34, 36, 72
George (St.) 24
Georgia 138, 139
Germanic 16, 19, 21, 23, 28, 31, 33, 34, 98
Germans 22, 47, 114, 118
Germany 19, 22, 23, 30, 34, 37, 96, 101, 109, 118, 124, 128, 131, 213
Ghana 204–05, 207, 211
Ghaznavids 79, 146, 147
Ghibellines 114, 115
Ghurids 146, 147
Giotto 220
God 10, 12, 15, 16, 24, 25, 45, 48, 52, 61–63, 65, 66, 68, 85–87, 91, 99, 102, 103, 108, 109, 113, 116, 127, 136, 142, 144, 177, 188, 190, 193, 217, 222, 223, 225
Godfrey of Bouillon 103, 106
Golden Horde 135, 137, 138
Goliath Spring 136
Gothic architecture 4, 36, 111, 112, 156
Goths 13, 14
Granada 219
Grand Canal 164, 173
Great Khan 137
Great Pyramid of Egypt 193
Great Schism 222, 223
Great Wall 13, 14, 22, 163, 173
Great Zimbabwe 210
Greece 1, 2, 5, 6, 12, 13, 18, 28, 47, 48, 59, 72, 77, 108, 119, 122, 127, 130, 201, 202, 219, 221
Greenland 40, 214
Gregorian chants 27
Gregory I (pope; Gregory the Great) 27
Gregory VII (pope) 100
Gregory IX (pope) 124
Gregory XI (pope) 222

Guatemala 6, 185, 187
Guelph-Ghibelline conflict 124
Guelphs 114, 115
Guilds 128, 129
Guinea 155, 197
Guiscard, Robert. *See* Robert Guiscard
Gulf of Finland 58
Gupta Empire 141, 142, 146
Gutenberg, Johannes 225

H

Hadrian's Wall 22
Hagia Sophia 54, 55, 218
Hagiography 48, 56
Hajj 62, 67
Hajjaj 145
Hakuh period 176, 177
Hanseatic League 128
Han Yü 168, 170
Hapsburg dynasty 132
Hara-kiri 182
Harsha 142
Harun al-Rashid 37, 71
Hasan-e Sabbah 81
Hastings (Battle of) 95
Hausa 207
Heaven 20, 29, 45, 68, 172, 174
Hebrew 74, 86–88, 90, 118
Hegira 66
Heian period 180–81
Heijo 178
Hell 29, 68, 221
Héloïse 109
Henry I (of England) 108
Henry II (of England) 114, 116, 119
Henry IV (Holy Roman Emperor) 101, 102
Henry V (of England) 217
Henry VII (of England) 218
Henry VIII (of England) 218
Henry the Lion 114
Henry the Navigator 225
Heraclius 49
Heraldry 108, 111
Heresy 8, 12, 16, 25, 100, 123, 124, 217, 224
Herzegovina 83
Hieroglyphics 186

High Middle Ages 24, 25, 119, 130
Himalayas 166
Hinduism 66, 141, 142, 144, 145, 148, 152, 155
Hippo 15
Hippodrome 52
Hisdai ibn Shaprut 88
Hittin 115
Hohenstaufen dynasty 109, 132
Hojo family 182, 183
Holland 31, 37, 126, 225
Holy Grail 27, 118
Holy Land 80, 86, 90, 102, 104, 110, 124–26, 203
Holy Roman Empire 35, 96, 126
Holy Sepulchre 117
Honduras 185
Horde 134, 135, 137, 138
Hsiung-Nu. *See* Huns
Hsüan-tsang (journeyer) 143
Hsüan Tsung (emperor) 168
Huaca 197
Huang Ch'ao 169
Huari 194
Huayna Capac 195
Hugh Capet 94
Hui Tsung 170
Huitzilopochtli 192
Hulagu 136, 137
Hundred Years' War 213, 217, 226
Hungary 17, 42, 45, 56, 83, 104, 124, 131, 135, 218
Huns 13, 14, 16, 17, 37, 54, 57, 133, 142, 145, 161, 172
Hunyadi, János 218
Hus, Jan 224
Husayn 69

I

Iberian Peninsula 92, 124, 126, 219, 225
Iceland 40
Iconoclasm 52–54
Iconophiles 53
Il-Khan 136, 137
Illumination (manuscript) 4, 20
Iltutmish 148
Imam 62
Inca Empire 1, 186, 187, 194–98

N

Z